Mobilizing Memory

Mobilizing Memory

The Great War and the Language of Politics in Colonial Algeria, 1918–39

DÓNAL HASSETT

OXFORD
UNIVERSITY PRESS

OXFORD
UNIVERSITY PRESS

Great Clarendon Street, Oxford, OX2 6DP,
United Kingdom

Oxford University Press is a department of the University of Oxford.
It furthers the University's objective of excellence in research, scholarship,
and education by publishing worldwide. Oxford is a registered trade mark of
Oxford University Press in the UK and in certain other countries

First Edition published in 2019

Impression: 1

Published in the United States of America by Oxford University Press
198 Madison Avenue, New York, NY 10016, United States of America

British Library Cataloguing in Publication Data
Data available

Library of Congress Control Number: 2019934013

ISBN 978–0–19–883168–6

Printed and bound by
CPI Group (UK) Ltd, Croydon, CR0 4YY

To Mam and Dad, thanks for everything

Acknowledgements

When I first started out on the long road to the completion of this project, I believed it would be a largely solitary journey. Thankfully, this could not have been further from the truth. Throughout the lengthy research and writing processes, I have benefitted from the support and advice of friends and colleagues, new and old.

I owe a significant debt of gratitude to my doctoral supervisor, Ann Thomson. Her guidance, dedication, and belief in my project were essential to its successful conclusion. For this and for her friendship, I will be forever grateful.

The European University Institute (EUI) was the ideal environment in which develop this project and I would like to thank the academic, library, and administrative staff who made my time in Florence such a positive experience. While at the EUI, I had the pleasure to study alongside many very talented scholars working across a range of disciplines and their contributions have greatly enriched this work. I will spare the blushes of all those who frequented the hallowed halls of Bar Fiasco with me. They know who they are and they know I will always be grateful for their friendship.

Throughout this project, I benefitted from the generosity of scholars of the Great War. John Horne was a constant source of advice and encouragement. Tomás Irish read various parts of the manuscript and provided me with extremely useful feedback. Researchers affiliated with Trinity College Dublin's Centre for War Studies and the Historial de Péronne's 2016 Summer School always made this historian of empire feel welcome in First World War studies.

Colonial historians, and particularly my fellow Algerianists, have played a fundamental role in shaping this project. I am grateful to Sylvie Thénault for facilitating my integration into the world of historians of Algeria in Paris. For their insightful comments and questions, and indeed, for their friendship, I would especially like to thank Arthur Asseraf, Claire Fredj, Muriam Haleh Davis, Thomas Serres, Chris Rominger, Samuel André-Bercovici, Michelle Mann, Claire Eldridge, Natalya Vince, and Sarah Frank.

I would also like to express my gratitude to the staff at all the archives and libraries I visited on both sides of the Mediterranean. The assistance of

Robert Parks and Karim Ouras of the Centre d'Etudes Maghrébines en Algérie proved essential in securing a visa and access to the archives for my trip to Algeria. I am grateful to the staff at Les Glycines in Algiers and at the Centre Pierre Claverie in Oran who graciously hosted me. Finally, I must especially thank the Algerian soldier who lent me his spare jeans to wear over my shorts so I could enter the National Archives in Algiers, thus providing me with the archive mishap story that is obligatory for every true historian.

In my two years working at the University of Bristol, I benefited from the support and wisdom of colleagues not just in the French Department but across the School of Modern Languages and the Faculty of Arts. I am grateful to colleagues in the History Department and the scholars of colonial history, conflict studies, and post-colonial studies scattered throughout the faculty who kindly shared their insights with me. I would particularly like to thank Martin Hurcombe, Ruth Bush, James Hawkey, Will Pooley, Su Lin Lewis, Kaya Davies Hayon, and Damien Mooney for shepherding me through the book-writing process with kind words and generous servings of wine.

My new home in the French Department at University College Cork has been the perfect environment in which to put the finishing touches to this project. I am very grateful to my colleagues for supporting me through the final submission phase. I especially wish to thank Patrick Crowley for reading elements of the final draft and offering feedback that was insightful and reassuring in equal measure.

The team at Oxford University Press have shown remarkable patience and professionalism throughout the publication process and for this I am very grateful.

As always, my biggest debts lie closer to home. My grandmother, who passed away before this book was finished, was a constant source of encouragement and love. My sisters, Liz and Nóirín, offered support and light relief whenever needed. They also provided me with some very welcome distractions during the research and writing processes: my two nephews, Liam and Aidan, and my nieces, Niamh and Bronagh.

Finally, I would like to thank my parents. From my earliest years, my mother fostered in me a passion for travelling and for languages that stays with me to this day. Her willingness to visit me at the drop of a hat and to share a good laugh over a bottle of wine made this process a lot less stressful. My father inculcated in me a love of history that we continue to share. All my academic learning is no match for his wisdom. Without them, this book would not have been possible.

Contents

List of Figures

Note on Terminology

The question of what terminology to use when describing the various populations of colonial Algeria is always complex. Leading French scholars have increasingly rejected the use of the term '*indigène*', quite rightly refusing to replicate the racialized language of colonial taxonomy.[1] However, their proposed alternative terminology, which favours the term '*Algérien*' for indigenous Algerians and '*Europeén*' for the settler population is ill suited to the interwar period when in contemporary parlance, at least in the 1920s, the term '*algérien*' often referred to the settlers and not the indigenous. In this book, I use the term indigenous. I contend that this term does not carry the negative connotations associated with '*indigène*' in French, which is best translated as 'native' in English colonial terminology. For the non-indigenous population, I use the term 'European'. This terminology remains problematic. For example, the Jews, the majority of whom had lived in Algeria prior to the French invasion, fall under the umbrella 'European' due to their status as citizens. Nevertheless, I will stick to these categories as far as possible.

Throughout the book, I will use colonial-era place names with the modern name provided in brackets.

[1] Emmanuel Blanchard and Sylvie Thénault, 'Quel "monde du contact"? Pour une histoire sociale de l'Algérie pendant la période coloniale', *Le Mouvement Social* 236, No. 3 (2011): 3–7, 4.

Introduction

On 14 July 2014 a small group of soldiers from the Algerian National Popular Army marched through the Place de la Concorde in Paris prior to the traditional Bastille Day military parade. The presence of Algerian troops was envisaged as an act of commemoration for the centenary of the Great War, a tribute to the thousands of Algerian troops who had died on the battlefields of northern France and south-eastern Europe. The participation of the official heirs of the anti-colonial *Front de Libération Nationale* (FLN) in a French military parade was a controversial gesture. In France, the extreme-right *Front National* denounced 'this shameful military presence', given that the Algerian Army was 'born of the FLN, a terrorist organisation'.[1] Across the Mediterranean in Algeria, François Hollande's initial invitation to participate in the event met with hostility from a leading figure of President Abdelaziz Bouteflika's regime. Saïd Abadou, president of the *Organisation Nationale des Moudjahidine*, the official association of veterans of the War of Independence, declared that Algerian participation would be impossible until 'the former colonial power apologises for the crimes committed in Algeria'.[2] However, shortly afterwards, President Bouteflika announced his intention to send Algerian troops to participate in the commemoration. The Francophone newspaper *El Watan* condemned this decision in an editorial entitled 'We Are Murdering Fanon', denouncing French selective memory and the 'politics of sound-bites' that had facilitated Algerian participation.[3] For nationalist Algeria and the French extreme right, the participation of Algerian troops was a historical betrayal both of those who had died in the conflict of 1914–18 and their descendants who had fallen for either France or Algeria in the bloody war of 1954–62.

Yet, for both governments the joint commemoration was the logical conclusion of a rapprochement between the countries. The Algerian president

[1] Abel Mestre, '14-Juillet: l'extrême droite vent debout contre la présence d'Algériens', *Le Monde*, 12 July, 2014. All translations in this book are my own.

[2] Olivier Hanquier, 'A Alger, un 14-Juillet qui passe mal', *Le Monde*, 12 July 2014.

[3] Adlène Meddi, 'C'est Fanon qu'on assassine', *El Watan*, 4 July 2014.

presented his country's participation as an act of both historical justice and good diplomacy. His speech drew a direct comparison between the role Algerian troops played in defending France in the Great War and that played by the heroes of the War of Independence who secured Algeria's freedom, tying together the national narratives that underpin the French and Algerian states:

> By deciding to pay homage to the thousands of Algerian victims of the First World War, in the 14 July celebrations, you have recognised the sacrifices of the Algerian people their attachment to the ideal of liberty that allowed them to recover, at great cost, their independence and sovereignty and to participate in the recovery of the liberty of the French people.[4]

In Paris, officials insisted that Algerian participation underlined François Hollande's commitment to promoting 'a shared and measured memory', a policy that has much more to do with the post-colonial legacies of immigration than any desire to deepen understanding of a complex past.[5] Political leaders on both sides of the Mediterranean sought to mobilize the common experience of the Great War to build a shared project, economic and diplomatic, for the future.

In these controversial debates around the centenary, the multi-layered memory of Algeria's Great War has been twisted to fit wider political agendas that seem to have a limited interest in actually commemorating the former colony's contribution to the war. Whether the agenda is narrow French nationalism or a post-colonial 'pluralist' republicanism, revolutionary Algerian nationalism or diplomatic realpolitik, the memory of Algeria's Great War continues to be instrumentalized by political elites on both sides of the Mediterranean.[6] The mobilization of the memory of Algeria's Great War by contemporary politicians is, this book will argue, firmly rooted in the continuity of political attitudes towards the one-time colony's wartime contribution. Political actors of all ideological and ethnic backgrounds in the Algeria of the interwar period evoked their own narratives of the colony's experience of the war in defence of their political projects. Likewise,

[4] 'Bouteflika salue la présence de l'Algérie aux cérémonies du 14-Juillet', *Le Monde*, 14 July 2014.

[5] Farid Alliat, 'Cérémonie du 14 Juillet en France: les Algériens sur les Champs, polémique au tournant', *Jeune Afrique*, 10 July 2014.

[6] For a detailed account of the controversy over the centenary see Dónal Hassett, 'Contested Commemoration: The Great War, Memory and Politics in Contemporary Algeria', *International Journal of Francophone Studies* 21, Nos 3–4 (October 2018): 209–31.

civil society organizations and individuals outside the traditional sphere of politics attempted to secure financial, social, and/or political advantage by mobilizing their own memories of the war. Just as in the centenary period, where the Great War has been evoked to legitimize competing visions of the relationship between Algeria and France, in interwar Algeria the Great War was a potent source of legitimation common to but contested between a range of rival historical actors.

In this book, I bridge the gap between the separate fields of colonial history and the history of the Great War by analysing the impact of this global conflict on the language and practice of politics in Algeria, the 'centrepiece of the French Empire'.[7] I contend throughout that, in a colonial society where activity in the public sphere was shaped by the reality of a legally instituted racial hierarchy, the Great War provided a transcendent form of political language seized upon by rival political actors, regardless of their position in the power structure of the colony. From the illiterate indigenous war widow to the governor general himself, the evocation of the Great War became omnipresent in public discourse in interwar Algeria.

Toward an Imperial History of the Great War

Algeria's participation in the Great War was just one element in a much wider story of the mobilization of global empires in what was truly a world war. The colonial contribution to the war efforts of the various imperial powers and its long-term effects on politics in the colonies have, until recently, been marginal in wider debates about the Great War. Historians of the First World War often did not engage with the extensive scholarship on the involvement of British, French, and, more recently, German colonies in the conflict.[8] The wide range of works focusing on one specific territory or ethnic group, its military contribution to the war effort, and the role this played in fostering a sense of national, even anti-colonial, identity, was rarely incorporated into overarching narratives of the war.[9] Even those works that took

[7] Gilbert Meynier, *L'Algérie Révélé: La guerre de 1914–1918 et le premier quart du XXe siècle* (Geneva: Librairie Droz, 1981), 1.

[8] Andrew Tait Jarboe and Richard S. Fogarty, 'Introduction: An Imperial Turn in First World War Studies', in *Empires in World War I: Shifting Frontiers and Imperial Dynamics in a Global Conflict*, eds. Andrew Tait Jarboe and Richard S. Fogarty (London: I.B. Tauris, 2014): 1–22, 4–8.

[9] For the French Empire see Mohammed Bekraoui, *Les Marocains dans la Grande Guerre* (Rabat: Publications de la Commission Marocaine d'Histoire Militaire, 2009), Mireille Le Van

an empire-wide or a continent-specific approach to the colonial aspects of the war have been slow to impact on the overall understanding of the conflict.[10] The recent rise of global history has facilitated a shift in wider narratives of the Great War toward a greater focus on the colonial aspects of the conflict. The 'imperial turn in First World War Studies'[11] is evident in a whole range of recently published collected works that bring together scholars of different colonial territories, across imperial boundaries, to consider the contrasts and commonalities that marked colonial participation in the war.[12] As a result, the colonial contribution to the Great War is no longer simply a 'sideshow' of the European conflict but now stands as an essential element of the historical narrative of the war.[13]

This embrace of the colonial history of the Great War has, however, stopped short of engaging with the long-term implications of colonial participation. The legacies of the war are not completely absent from the emergent literature. Three of the principal collected volumes on the empire and war dedicate their final sections to the exploration of issues of 'memory',[14]

Ho, *Des Vietnamiens dans la Grande Guerre: 50,000 recrues dans les usines françaises* (Paris: Vendémiaire, 2014), Meynier, *L'Algérie Révélé*, and Chantal Valensky, *Le Soldat occulté: Les Malgaches de l'Armée française, 1884–1920* (Paris: L'Harmattan, 2000). For the British Empire Keith Jeffrey, *Ireland and the Great War* (Cambridge: Cambridge University Press, 2000), Bill Nasson, *Springboks on the Somme: South Africa in the Great War, 1914–1918* (Johannesburg: Penguin, 2007), David Omissi, ed., *Indian Voices of the Great War, 1914–1918* (Basingstoke: Macmillan, 1994), and Richard Smith, *Jamaican Volunteers in the First World War: Race, Masculinity and the Development of National Consciousness* (Manchester: Manchester University Press, 2004). For Germany see Michelle R. Moyd, *Violent Intermediaries: Africans Soldiers, Conquest and Everyday Colonialism in German East Africa* (Athens, OH: Ohio University Press, 2014).

[10] Richard S. Fogarty, *Race and War in France: Colonial Subjects in the French Army, 1914–1918* (Baltimore, MD: Johns Hopkins University Press, 2008), Jacques Frémeaux, *Les Colonies dans la Grande Guerre: Combats et Epreuves des Peuples d'Outre-Mer* (Paris: SOTECA, 14–18 Editions, 2006), Marc Michel, *Les Africains et la Grande Guerre: l'appel à l'Afrique (1914–1918)* (Paris: Karthala, 2003), John H. Morrow, *The Great War: An Imperial History* (Oxford: Routledge, 2004), and Hew Strachan, *The First World War in Africa* (Oxford: Oxford University Press, 2004).

[11] Jarboe and Fogarty, 'Introduction', 1–22.

[12] See for example Robert Gerwarth and Erez Manela, eds, *Empires at War, 1911–1923* (Oxford: Oxford University Press, 2014), Jarboe and Fogarty, *Empires in World War I*, Santanu Das, ed., *Race, Empire and First World War Writing* (Cambridge: Cambridge University Press, 2011), Gearóid Barry, Enrico Dal Lago, and Róisín Healy, eds, *Small Nations and Colonial Peripheries in World War I* (Leiden: Brill, 2016), and Heike Liebau, Katrin Bromber, Katharina Lange, Dyala Hamzah, and Ravi Ahuja, eds, *The World in World Wars: Experiences and Perspectives from Africa and Asia* (Boston, MA: Brill, 2010).

[13] Das, 'Introduction', in *Race, Empire and First World War Writing*, 2.

[14] Das, *Race, Empire and First World War Writing*, 211–300.

'social and political transformations',[15] or the 'afterlives of war and Empire'.[16] Robert Gerwarth and Erez Manela's *Empires at War, 1911–1923* takes the concept of 'Long First World War', first developed to describe the conflict's extended duration in Eastern Europe,[17] and applies it to the colonial world, as a first step to tracing the most immediate consequences of the war in the empires.[18] These admirable attempts to engage with the legacies of the conflict in the colonies have greatly enriched our understanding of the war's global impact. Nevertheless, the resulting analysis is undermined by two key weaknesses. On the one hand, the focus on the immediate post-war period, what Erez Manela has called the 'Wilsonian moment',[19] has distorted the political legacies of the war by stressing anti-colonial nationalism over other forms of claims-making. This book will show that, at least in Algeria, the war became the central reference point for those seeking to reimagine empire, not bring an end to it. On the other hand, the preoccupation with abstract questions of 'memory' has obscured the concrete political use made of wartime participation by actors across the colonial world.[20] This book argues that what matters most is not how the war is 'remembered' in the colonial world, but to what end its memory is mobilized. Thus, while an imperial history of the Great War is slowly emerging, a colonial history of its long-term consequences remains to be written. By studying the evocation of the Great War in colonial Algeria, this book lays one of the foundation blocks for the construction of such a history.

(Re)Writing the History of Interwar Algeria

If the role of the First World War as a turning point in European history is widely acknowledged, it has been largely overshadowed in popular narratives of colonial Algeria by the dominance of the War of Independence. In this book, I not only seek to bring Algeria into the global history of the Great War, but also to bring the Great War into the longer colonial history of

[15] Jarboe and Fogarty, *Empires in World War I*, 303–75.

[16] Liebau et al., *The World in World Wars*, 401–578.

[17] Jochen Böhler, Włodzimierz Borodziej, and Joachim von Puttkamer, 'Introduction', in *Legacies of Violence: Eastern Europe's First World War* (Munich: Oldenburg Verlag, 2014): 1–6, 2.

[18] Robert Gerwarth and Erez Manela, 'Introduction', in *Empires at War, 1911–1923*, 1–16, 10–13.

[19] Erez Manela, *The Wilsonian Moment: Self-Determination and the International Origins of Anticolonial Nationalism* (Oxford: Oxford University Press, 2007).

[20] Das, *Race, Empire and First World War Writing*, 211–300.

Algeria. The widely acknowledged 'hypertrophy of the War of Independence in historical production about Algeria'[21] has not meant that the Great War and the interwar period have gone completely unexamined.[22] In the latter years of French rule and the immediate post-independence period, French scholars often focused on the interwar years as a key moment in the colony's history. Their works are not an apologia for the crimes of colonialism but rather centre on 'the missed opportunities' when reactionary forces blocked the possibility of reforms, scuppering the prospect of constructing a multi-ethnic social democracy.[23] These historians, for all their criticism of the abuses of colonial rule, still believed in the possibility of change through the interaction between progressive Europeans and the indigenous reformists.[24] The space where this dialogue would take place was labelled the '*monde du contact*' or 'world of contact'.[25] With its stress on the possibility of open dialogue between actors of different racial and legal statuses, the concept of the 'world of contact' would prove problematic and controversial.

For the nationalist historians of the newly independent Algeria, the suggestion that the French colonial system could be reformed from within was anathema. Their works attacked the structures of colonialism in language that echoed the propaganda of the FLN and the writings of Fanon and Sartre.[26] The resulting narrative reinterpreted the complex history of colonial rule in Algeria, presenting the victory of the revolution as 'the triumphant climax of one long, unending struggle'.[27] Little room was left for the layers of ambiguity that defined political and cultural interaction under the colonial regime.

[21] Abderrahmane Bouchène, Jean-Pierre Peyroulou, Ouanassa Siari Tengour, and Sylvie Thénault, 'Pour une histoire partagée et critique de l'Algérie à la période coloniale', in *Histoire de l'Algérie à la période coloniale: 1830–1962* (Paris: La Découverte, 2012): 7–16, 9.

[22] See Claire Marynower, 'Être socialiste dans l'Algérie coloniale: Pratiques, cultures et identités d'un milieu partisan dans le département d'Oran, 1919–1939' (PhD diss., IEP Paris, 2013), 20.

[23] John Wansbrough, 'The Decolonization of North African History', *Journal of African History* 9, No. 4 (1968): 643–50, 648.

[24] See for example Charles Robert Ageron, *Histoire de l'Algérie Contemporaine Vol. 2 1871–1954: De l'insurrection de 1871 au déclenchement de la guerre de libération* (Paris: Presses Universitaires de France, 1979), Jacques Berque, *Le Maghreb entre deux guerres* (Paris: Éditions La Seuil, 1962), and Charles-André Julien, *L'Afrique du Nord en marche: Algérie, Tunisie, Maroc, 1880–1952* (Paris: Julliard, 1953).

[25] Emmanuel Blanchard and Sylvie Thénault, 'Quel "monde du contact"? Pour une histoire sociale de l'Algérie pendant la période coloniale'. *Le Mouvement Social* 236, No. 3 (2011): 3–7.

[26] Mohamed Sahli, *Décoloniser l'histoire: Introduction à l'histoire du Maghreb* (Paris: Maspero, 1965) and Mostefa Lacheraf, *L'Algérie: nation et société* (Paris: Maspero, 1965).

[27] James McDougall, 'Savage Wars? Codes of Violence in Algeria, 1830s–1990s', *Third World Quarterly* 26, No. 1 (2005): 117–31, 123.

In the years that followed, historical analysis moved away from these intensely political debates, focusing instead on the origins of Algeria's nationalist movement in the interwar period.[28] Benjamin Stora's work on the early years of nationalism exposed both the prevalence of dialogue between European-led political movements and the indigenous and the limits that constrained it.[29] However, the dominance of nationalists in these narratives betrayed a certain teleological focus that obscured the role played by other types of political movements and civil society organizations in shaping politics in the colony.

Recent years have seen an upsurge in scholarship offering a more plural and complex narrative of politics and society in interwar Algeria.[30] The picture that emerges from this new scholarship takes us far closer to the realities of the practice of politics in interwar Algeria. What has not emerged, however, is a clear theoretical or methodological basis for conceptualizing relationships between indigenous and Europeans in the political sphere.

Achieving the balance between the necessary acknowledgement of the harsh realities of a colonial regime predicated on exclusion and oppression and the reality of the multiple interactions between colonial subjects, colonial citizens, and the colonial authorities is a crucial but complicated task. As Edward Said put it: 'The problem, then, is to keep in mind two ideas that are in many ways antithetical—the fact of the imperial divide, on the one hand, and the notion of shared experiences, on the other—without diminishing the force of either'.[31] In this book, I argue that the study of forms of political language that transcended ethnic and ideological boundaries offers an ideal prism through which cooperation, contestation, and coercion in political life in the colonial space can be examined.

[28] Mahfoud Kaddache, *La vie politique à Alger de 1919 à 1939* (Algiers: SNED, 1970), Mahfoud Kaddache, ed., *L'Emir Khaled, Documents et témoignages pour servir à l'étude du nationalisme algérien* (Algiers: Office des Publications Universitaires, 1987), and Mahfoud Kaddache and Mohamed Guenaneche, eds, *L'Etoile nord-africaine 1926–1937. Documents et témoignages pour servir à l'étude du nationalisme algérien* (Algiers: Office des Publication Universitaires, 1984).

[29] Benjamin Stora, *Messali Hadj, 1898–1974* (Paris: Hachette Littératures, 2004; first published in 1986) and *Nationalistes algériens et révolutionnaires français au temps du Front Populaire* (Paris: L'Harmattan, 1987).

[30] This trend can be traced back to Carlier's *Entre Nation et Jihad: Histoire sociale des radicalismes algériens* (Paris: Presses de la Fondation Nationale des Sciences Politiques, 1995). Recent examples of this new thematic diversity include Samuel Kalman, *French Colonial Fascism: The Extreme Right in Algeria, 1919–1939* (New York: Palgrave MacMillan, 2013), James McDougall, *History and the Culture of Nationalism in Algeria* (Cambridge: Cambridge University Press, 2006), and Marynower, 'Être socialiste'.

[31] Edward Saïd, 'Always on Top', *London Review of Books* 25, No. 6 (March 2003): 3–6, 4.

Reimagining 'Contact' in the Colonial Space

Historians of colonial Algeria have been seeking to move beyond narrow understandings of 'contact' for some time. The French scholars Emmanuel Blanchard and Sylvie Thénault have led the way in advocating a nuanced understanding of 'contact' grounded in the realities of social relations in the colony.[32] 'Contact', they contend, is not limited to personal encounters and moments of interethnic political collaboration; it defines a whole range of interactions between the colonial authorities, colonial citizens, and colonial subjects.[33] The 'world of contact' was as much (if not more) a space of frustration, of discrimination, and of violence, as it was a space of possibility and opportunity. Their appeal for 'an attempt to analyse the consistency of social relations between actors assigned to different affiliations by the colonial situation' using the 'ordinary tools and concepts of social history' is commendable.[34] However, restricting the reorientation of the study of intercommunal relations in colonial Algeria to historians using a social history approach would be an error. Social relations in the context of a racially stratified colonial society did play a key role in shaping the conduct and the outcomes of political debate. Nevertheless, the range of rhetorical strategies available to and employed by political actors of different ethnic backgrounds and political ideologies were also crucial in shaping the way colonial power was negotiated in the interwar period. This book contends that a discourse analysis drawing on the methodologies of colonial and intellectual history would deepen our understanding of the possibilities and limits that shaped politics in interwar Algeria.

All political actors make strategic choices when framing their demands in a particular 'political language'. Yet, because language is a medium over which actors have limited control, these choices may have unintended consequences. In his seminal essay, 'Discourse on the Novel' (1935), the Russian theorist Mikhail Bakhtin rejected narrow understandings of language as a 'system of abstract grammatical categories', stressing its existence as a 'living, socio-ideological thing'.[35] While the dominant social group attempts to impose its worldview through an official and legitimate form of language, Bakhtin contended that this is constantly challenged and undermined by rival social

[32] Blanchard and Thénault, 'Quel "monde du contact"?'. [33] Ibid., 5. [34] Ibid.

[35] Mikhail Bakhtin, 'Discourse in the Novel', in *The Dialogic Imagination: Four Essays*, ed. Michael Holquist, trans. Caryl Emerson and Michael Holquist (Austin, TX: University of Texas Press, 2008): 259–421, 271 and 293.

and ideological groups.[36] This results in a linguistic sphere characterized by 'a multitude of verbal-ideological and social belief systems'.[37] In a world defined by a plurality of languages, or 'heteroglossia',[38] 'there are no "neutral" words and forms', rather all forms of expression are 'shot through with intentions and accents'.[39] The meaning of words is not static but rather is 'dialogic', constantly shifting and struggled over between rival political actors.[40] Actors themselves are conscious of this struggle and tailor their language to counter and anticipate rival meanings, seeking to 'break through the alien conceptual horizon of the listener'.[41] In the process, the object itself 'may simply be overshadowed', as what counts most is not the semantic meaning of a phrase but rather its socio-cultural and political meaning, fashioned in the give and take between speaker and listener.[42] However, words are not infinitely malleable weapons that can be employed in the defence of any cause or group interest; they must fit or be made to fit in the wider language of an actor.[43] This dynamic lies at the heart of this book. Drawing on Bakhtin's insights, it traces the attempts of various political groups and individual actors to adopt and adapt the evocation of the Great War as a crucial motif in the linguistic struggle for power, privilege, and patronage in interwar Algeria.

In a colonial society like Algeria, the official language of the administration had a particularly powerful monopoly on acceptable forms of political discourse. Yet, as this book argues, employing elements of the administration's discourse did not imply a wholesale endorsement of the system of colonial rule in Algeria. In the colonial context, where the language of the ruling class is not only different in socio-ideological terms but also in simple linguistic terms (French and not Arabic or Berber), indigenous activists who expressed their demands in French were both adopting the language of the colonial system and challenging the dominance of this same system. This dialectic permeated all forms of discourse in interwar Algeria. As political actors, indigenous and European, addressed their demands to the colonial authorities they employed a form of discourse that simultaneously embraced aspects of the administration's official rhetoric while fundamentally challenging others. In particular, I argue, the evocation of the Great War implied both a recognition of the existence of a 'mutual obligation' between the colonial state, its citizens, and its subjects and an attempt to constantly redefine what such an obligation meant in concrete terms.

[36] Ibid., 272–3. [37] Ibid., 288. [38] Ibid., 270. [39] Ibid., 293.
[40] Ibid., 276. [41] Ibid., 282. [42] Ibid. [43] Ibid., 294.

Bakhtin's theory emerged from the study of spaces, temporal and geographical, that differ radically from interwar Algeria. How then are we to apply an approach based on the analysis of languages of public discourse to a colonial context? Erez Manela's seminal work, *The Wilsonian Moment*,[44] with its specific focus on how colonial peoples claimed the concept of self-determination for themselves, shows the potential of an analysis of the language of politics in the interwar colonial world. Yet, his focus was broad in terms of its geographical scope, impressively covering vast swathes of the 'non-Western' world, and narrow in its conception of politics, centred almost solely on elite political claims-making, especially nationalism. This book pursues a rhetorical analysis of a broad range of claims-making in the narrow space of colonial Algeria. To achieve this, I draw heavily on the theory and methodology advanced by the African historian Fred Cooper and the cultural anthropologist Ann Laura Stoler.

In their influential book, *Tensions of Empire*, Cooper and Stoler argue that the notion of difference between colonizer and colonized underpinned the skewed power relations in the colonies. They recognize that the colonizer-colonized dichotomy was a construct of colonial rule, 'neither inherent nor static…it had to be defined and maintained'.[45] In a settler colony with an indigenous majority like Algeria, the triangular nature of the relationship between metropole, colonial subject, and colonial citizen made maintaining the boundaries of difference even more complicated. Cooper and Stoler present politics in the colonies as a kind of tug-of-war between the rulers and the ruled in which each side seeks to delineate difference: 'a grammar of difference was continuously and vigilantly crafted as people in the colonies refashioned and contested European claims to superiority'.[46] Thus, not only were the potential languages of politics constantly evolving and taking on new meanings but they were also reflecting and refracting the ever changing forms of rule in the colony.

Drawing on the theoretical insights of Bakhtin and Cooper and Stoler, I use the analysis of the evocation of the Great War to answer key questions about politics in colonial Algeria. Participation in the war fundamentally altered the social contract between state and citizen in the metropole, but what were its repercussions for the complex relationships between colonial

[44] Manela, *The Wilsonian Moment*.

[45] Frederick Cooper and Ann Laura Stoler, 'Between Metropole and Colony: Rethinking a Research Agenda', in *Tensions of Empire: Colonial Cultures in a Bourgeois World* (Berkeley, CA: University of California Press, 1997): 1–56, 7.

[46] Ibid., 3–4.

citizens, colonial subjects, and the colonial state? How did political actors in the colony seize the opportunity to reshape these relations and to what extent were their efforts framed in a language that evoked the Great War? How successful was this rhetorical strategy and what were its unintended consequences? In addressing these questions, I combine the recent reorientation of historiography in Algerian history with elements of the historiography of the Great War to present a much needed reassessment of the practice of politics in colonial Algeria.

By moving beyond narrow conceptions of 'contact', this book also contributes to our wider understanding of French colonial history. Its disavowal of a binary narrative in which there were only two possible outcomes to the colonial project, hard-fought national independence or complete assimilation to the French metropole, speaks to contemporary debates in the field. Many of the actors discussed in this book shared the alternative visions of a reconfigured empire advanced by the interwar pan-Africanists who Gary Wilder has studied and/or the defenders of federalism analysed by Fred Cooper.[47] Where the interwar proponents of *négritude* called for a reimagined 'Greater France' in the language of 'African humanism'[48] and the advocates of a Euro-African federation in the 1950s evoked notions of 'equality and difference',[49] many reformists in interwar Algeria framed their demand for a differentiated imperial citizenship in terms of their participation in the Great War. The variety of alternative paths to imperial reform that they sought to legitimize by mobilizing their contribution to the defence of the *Patrie* demonstrates that, despite the skewed power relations that defined the Empire, citizens and subjects across the colonies believed they could reshape the imperial polity in their own favour. This was never solely about gaining political rights. The interwar period saw a whole range of actors outside the world of high politics seek to redefine their individual and collective relationships with the colonial state. Thus, this book broadens our understanding of the colonial legacies of the First World War, showing that while this global conflict may have given rise to anti-colonial movements for self-determination across the world, it also led many inhabitants of the empire to envision a reformed political order firmly within the imperial framework.

[47] Gary Wilder, *The French Imperial Nation-State: Negritude and Colonial Humanism between the Two World Wars* (Chicago, IL: University of Chicago Press, 2005) and Frederick Cooper, *Citizenship between Empire and Nation: Remaking France and French Africa, 1945–1960* (Princeton, NJ: Princeton University Press, 2014).

[48] Wilder, *The French Imperial Nation-State*, 254.

[49] Cooper, *Citizenship between Empire and Nation*, 11.

Evoking the Great War in the Colonial Archive: A Note on Sources

Tracing the rhetorical strategies of political actors in a colony like Algeria means casting a wide net in the trawl through archival sources. This book relies on three types of primary source: official documents from the colonial archive, the Francophone press, and the correspondence of indigenous claimants with the military and pensions administration. Each of these sources poses specific problems for the historian.

The bias of the colonial archive is a challenge with which the colonial historian must always grapple. It is not simply a question of differentiating 'fact' from 'fiction'; the colonial historian must also ask why and how a certain 'fact' made its way into the colonial archive and what other 'facts' it obscured in the process.[50] The particular vision of the past contained in the colonial archive offers an insight into the structures and the mentalities that underpinned, as well as the spectres that haunted, the knowledge acquisition of colonial administrators. By reading 'along the archival grain' the colonial historian can go some way towards avoiding the pitfalls of the colonial archive and questioning the 'hierarchies of credibility' that inform the reports of colonial administrators.[51] Throughout this book, I temper my reliance on the bureaucracy and, particularly, the security apparatus of the colonial state with a critical reading that considers the exaggerations and omissions that have shaped the colonial archive.

The clear partisan allegiance of most newspapers in the colony make bias easier to identify and analyse in the press than in the colonial archive. The principal weakness of this source-base lies in the exclusion of the Arabic press. During the interwar period, the independent Arabic-language press grew in importance and diversity, becoming particularly associated with the emergent Islamic reform movement.[52] The supporters of the *Association des 'Ulama Algériens*, a religious reform movement founded in 1931, published a range of newspapers in Arabic alongside the francophone *La Défense*. While the latter maintained a relatively moderate tone and escaped official

[50] Ann Laura Stoler, 'Colonial Archives and the Arts of Governance', *Archival Science* 2, No. 1 (2002): 87–109, 91.

[51] Ann Laura Stoler, *Along the Archival Grain: Epistemic Anxieties and Colonial Common Sense* (Princeton, NJ: Princeton University Press, 2009): 180–234.

[52] Phillip Zessin, 'Presse et journalistes "indigènes" en Algérie coloniale (année 1890–années 1950)', *Le Mouvement Social* 236, No. 3 (2011): 35–46.

censorship, the Arabic titles were seen as hostile by colonial administrators, with one, *al-Sunna*, judged 'dangerous to public order' and banned in 1933.[53] Thus, it is possible that the absence of the Arabophone press, a product of my, as yet, too limited Arabic, obscures an element of the rhetoric and philosophy of certain political actors that was not reflected in their Francophone literary production. However, given my focus on the politics of the colonial public sphere, an overwhelmingly Francophone space where contact took place between indigenous subjects, colonial citizens, and colonial administrators, the reliance on French-language sources is less of a weak point than one might imagine. My central preoccupation with the efforts of political actors to use the Great War to assert their membership of a distinctly French imperial polity means that the kind of debates that lie at the heart of this book were almost always conducted in French. Furthermore, the book does draw heavily on the works of scholars such as Omar Carlier and James McDougall who have explored in depth the evolution of Arabic political discourse in Algeria over the course of the interwar period.[54]

Finally, the study of the correspondence of indigenous claimants with the military and pension authorities poses its own problems. Given the high rates of illiteracy among the indigenous population, most of these claims had to be mediated through the services of a public scribe. The implications of this mediation are discussed in depth in the relevant chapter of this book. Furthermore, the reliance on the incomplete and selective collections of pension files in the military and colonial archives means that the representativeness of the cases considered must be questioned when analysing these sources. Nevertheless, these files, which have heretofore gone unexploited by historians, are an invaluable source for the study of the system of post-war provision for indigenous veterans in the colony.

With this critical approach to the use of sources in mind, this book combines documents from five different archives on both sides of the Mediterranean with evidence drawn from over forty press titles to present a comprehensive analysis of the place of the Great War in the language of politics in colonial Algeria.

[53] Ali Merad, *Le réformisme musulman en Algérie de 1925 à 1940: Essai d'histoire religieuse et sociale* (The Hague: Mouton & Co., 1967), 149–50.

[54] Carlier, *Entre Nation et Jihad* and McDougall, *History and the Culture of Nationalism.*

Book Structure

The book is organized into six thematic chapters. The opening chapter, 'Fighting for the Empire', explores the history of military service in Algeria and across the colonial world before and during the Great War. It explains the legal categories that underpinned colonial rule in Algeria and considers how the rights and responsibilities they implied were connected to and altered by service in the army. It also introduces key concepts from the fields of colonial history and First World War studies that are crucial to understanding the political legacies of Algeria's involvement in the Great War.

Chapter 2, 'Remaking the Post-War Colonial Order', focuses on the question of colonial reform in interwar Algeria, asking how political actors sought to redefine their place within the imperial polity in the wake of the war. It explores how politicians and activists from across ethnic and ideological divides understood and framed the transformation of politics in Algeria as a result of the mass mobilization of the colony's inhabitants. It examines their rival visions of a new post-war colonial settlement and their attempts to impose these on the colonial authorities by constantly highlighting their wartime service.

The third chapter, 'Social Claims in the Shadow of the Fallen', examines the left's attempts to mobilize the wartime 'moral economy of sacrifice' in support of its vision of a just post-war order in the colony. Focusing on the immediate post-war moment, it examines how the campaigns of strike action and political protests led by socialists and trade unionists in the colony relied heavily on egalitarian notions grounded in the wartime experience. It also considers the response this provoked from conservative forces, which sought to counter the left's rhetoric by stressing the 'fraternity of arms'. Finally, it assesses the place of indigenous workers in these debates, asking how the left reconciled its use of an egalitarian language, drawn in part from the experience of the war, with its ambiguous attitude toward any erosion of European hegemony in the colony.

Chapter 4, 'Communal Contributions and Racial Hierarchies', analyses the place of the Great War in the rhetoric of the extreme-right movements that played an important role in the politics of interwar Algeria. It argues that the visions of the Great War that they promoted reflected an intrinsically racial understanding of Algeria's wartime contribution. This chapter examines the rhetoric developed around the participation of the Jewish, Muslim, and European communities, considering how it embodied these organisations' wider aspirations for the reshaping of colonial society in line with imagined racial hierarchies. The strategies employed by opponents of these ideas from all ethnic and ideological backgrounds underline the potency of the war as a contested source of legitimacy.

The fifth chapter, '"They Have Rights over Us": Algeria's Veteran Activists', turns away from partisan politics to analyse the development of the Algerian veterans' movement over the course of the interwar period. It considers organizations that drew members not only from different ethnic and social backgrounds but also from a pool of men with an unparalleled claim to legitimacy born of participation in the war. Here it is not so much the legitimacy itself that is contested but rather to what end it should be mobilized as the movement attempted to reconcile its supposedly non-racial notion of veteran primacy with the real primacy of the European community in the colonial state.

The sixth and final chapter, 'Pensions, Posts, and Petitions', shifts from the collective toward the individual, considering how indigenous veterans, war widows, and orphans evoked participation in the war to ensure access to state provision. It examines how actors often considered marginal in the colonial order set about claiming their entitlements. Using the correspondence between individual claimants and the colonial administration, this chapter explores the complexity of the daily negotiation between the colonized, their intermediaries, and the apparatus of the colonial state. It considers the extent to which the colonial state's conception of its duties to indigenous rights holders and its attempts to meet these duties overlapped and/or contrasted with claimants' understanding of their own rights.

In the wake of the centenary period of the Great War, when political recuperations of the war dead were once more the subject of fierce public debate, this book demonstrates how the evocation of the war simultaneously transcended, subverted, and reinforced the racial barriers of colonial rule in Algeria.

1
Fighting for the Empire

> France is under attack, I must go. My place is there, where we fight.
>
> Le Caïd, *Ahmed Ben Mostapha, goumier*[1]

In his semi-autobiographical novel, *Ahmed Ben Mostapha, goumier*, the Algerian veteran Mohamed Bencherif recounts the life of a volunteer soldier in the ranks of the French colonial army. This book, the first published in French by an indigenous Algerian writer (1920), offers a unique insight into the mind-set of a colonial subject whose elevated position in society is, in part, a result of his service in defence of the Empire.[2] Bencherif's membership of both the traditional Algerian nobility and the Francophone educated elite set him apart from the mass of colonial subjects who served in the French Army during the Great War. Furthermore, the constant declarations of loyalty to France and its colonial civilizing mission that mark both his public statements and the musings of his literary avatar are hardly representative of the range of opinions held by colonial soldiers participating in the defence of the empire. Nonetheless, the fictional story of Ahmed Ben Mostapha and the real-life career path of Bencherif point to a wider truth that encompasses most colonial soldiers who served in the Great War. Like Bencherif, many of those who fought in this global conflict would seek to mobilize their wartime service to secure some form of compensation in the post-war settlement. In the colonies, the evocation of wartime service would prove a particularly popular means of seeking advancement within the strict constraints imposed by the colonial regime. Few would reach the high position in the colonial apparatus that awaited Bencherif after the war,[3] and even fewer would manage to publish an

[1] Mohamed Bencherif, *Ahmed Ben Mostapha, goumier* (Paris: Edilivre, 2014; 1st Edition 1920), 216.

[2] Christian Koller, 'Representing Otherness: African, Indian and European Soldiers' Letters and Memoirs', in *Race, Empire and First World War Writing*, ed. Santanu Das (Cambridge: Cambridge University Press, 2011): 127–42, 135.

[3] Bencherif served as the head of his tribe.

account of their wartime experiences. Yet, colonial subjects across the French and other empires would mobilize the memory of their wartime service, with varying degrees of success, in an effort to expand their rights and, thus, reshape the imperial polity.

Before we consider the post-war campaigns to redefine empire, we must study the practice of colonial rule and the transformation it underwent as a result of the Great War. This chapter will examine the history of French colonial rule in Algeria, focusing on the important distinction between citizenship and subjecthood. It will also consider the role military service played in shaping the colonial system in Algeria and elsewhere in the colonial world. Finally, it will address the specifics of colonial participation in the Great War, asking how the experiences of colonial citizens and subjects in the trenches and on the Home Front altered understandings of the colonial relationship.

Citizenship and Subjecthood in Pre-War Colonial Algeria

Algerian history does not begin with the French invasion of 1830; the territory had a long and diverse history, playing host to a variety of ethno-religious groups organized in distinct polities. However, the arrival of the French and the brutal conquest that followed transformed the structure of Algerian society. The ferocity with which French forces crushed the resistance of indigenous Algerians, many of whom rallied to the banner of the charismatic Emir Abdelkader, has been well documented,[4] as has the long and brutal campaign of dispossession which paved the way for mass European settlement in Algeria.[5] French rule was sufficiently secure by 1848 for the Second Republic to officially integrate Algeria fully into the republic, with the three *départements* of Algiers, Constantine, and Oran considered the trans-Mediterranean extension of the metropole. The Second Empire would also leave an enduring legal legacy for the framework of governance in Algeria. Napoleon III's *Sénatus-Consulte* of 1865 clarified the legal position of indigenous Algerians (Jews and Muslims) as French nationals but not

[4] See William Gallois, *A History of Violence in the Early Algerian Colony* (Basingstoke: Palgrave Macmillan, 2013).

[5] See André Nouschi, 'La dépossession foncière et la paupérisation de la paysannerie algérienne', in *Histoire de l'Algérie à la période coloniale: 1830–1962*, eds. Abderrahmane Bouchène, Jean-Pierre Peyroulou, Quanassa Siari Tengour, and Sylvie Thénault (Paris, La Découverte, 2012): 189–94.

French citizens. It created a new legal category, the 'personal status', which meant that indigenous Algerians could resolve their private affairs in religious courts, a practice seen as irreconcilable with French citizenship. The criteria set out to govern the accession of indigenous Algerians to citizenship were so strict that, in practice, they rendered naturalization almost unattainable. Furthermore, the requirement to renounce the 'personal status' to secure citizenship made naturalization culturally repugnant to the vast majority of the indigenous Muslim population. Ironically, as James McDougall has highlighted, the personal status became simultaneously the 'site in which the colonial oppression of Algerian Muslims was organised and exercised' and 'a strictly sacred space whose limits for most Algerians marked the boundary between apostasy and belief'.[6] From this point on, the question of its compatibility with French citizenship would be a central point of contention in debates around reform in the colony.

The arrival of the Third Republic in 1870 radically transformed the status of one category of the population: the Jewish community. That year, the republican government's Crémieux Decree unilaterally naturalized the Jews of Algeria's three departments as full French citizens.[7] The early years of the republic also witnessed the defeat of the last of the major insurrections of indigenous Algerians before the outbreak of the War of Independence, solidifying French hegemony in the colony.[8] The advent of the republic saw the army yield positions of power to the emergent apparatus of the civilian-controlled republican state. For all the talk of Algeria as the trans-Mediterranean extension of France, administrative regimes in the colony differed widely from those in place in the metropole. Colony-specific institutions, such as the *Délégations Financières*, granted local French citizens a degree of limited autonomy and underlined the distinction between the rights and responsibilities of colonial citizenship and those attached to French citizenship in the metropole.[9] This period was marked by a dramatic increase in inward migration of Europeans, coming from the metropole but especially from poor agrarian societies in the Mediterranean.[10] The presence

[6] McDougall, *History and the Culture of Nationalism*, 91.

[7] Patrick Weil, *How to Be French: Nationality in the Making since 1789*, trans. Catherine Porter (London: Duke University Press, 2008; first published in French 2002), 209–11.

[8] See Charles-André Julien, *Histoire de l'Algérie Contemporaine: La Conquête et les débuts de la colonisation (1827–71)* (Paris: Presses Universitaires de France, 1964), 473–500.

[9] James McDougall, *A History of Algeria* (Cambridge: Cambridge University Press, 2017), 103–6.

[10] Hugo Vermeren, 'Les migrations françaises et européennes vers l'Algérie au début de la IIIe République', in *Histoire de l'Algérie à la période coloniale*, eds. Bouchène, Peyroulou, Siari Tengour, and Thénault: 194–200.

of a large non-naturalized European population gave rise to tensions in local political life, particularly manifest in the increase in violent anti-Semitism.[11] Moving to solidify European hegemony in Algeria (and to tighten control on immigrants in the metropole), the French government introduced the Nationality Code of 1889, which facilitated access to French citizenship for Europeans born on French soil, including Algeria.[12] The Jewish community and the European migrants now had a clear path to full equality as citizens of France.

No such path existed for the vast majority of the inhabitants in Algeria. The expansion of the authority of the colonial state had only served to multiply the discriminatory and repressive measures aimed at the indigenous. In 1881, the colonial authorities introduced a legal code known as the *Indigénat*, which established a broad range of crimes and a series of often arbitrary punishments that applied only to subjects in the colony.[13] Indigenous actors were excluded from the exercise of any real form of political power in a colonial system that rested, above all else, on the principle of European hegemony. By this time, violent resistance had become a marginal feature of life in the colony. Instead, the indigenous population developed a wide range of strategies to minimize the exercise of colonial oppression, from the avoidance of contact with the colonial authorities to negotiation with the agents of colonial power. While life among the indigenous was marked by a near constant effort to subvert, escape, and/or attenuate the coercive power of the colonial regime, attempts to transform the regime through political action were rare in the last decades of the nineteenth century.

Nevertheless, the limited access to the French education system granted to certain indigenous elites did eventually give rise to a contestatory form of indigenous political action within the institutions of the colonial state. In the early years of the twentieth century, a small number of intellectuals, inspired in part by the Young Turk movement in the Ottoman Empire, developed an elite-based critique of the system of French colonial rule that called for greater rights for indigenous Algerians.[14] Far from advocating an end to French rule in Algeria, they sought the integration of indigenous Algerians into the French national community. In the pages of the movement's

[11] Geneviève Dermenjian, *La Crise anti-juive oranaise (1895–1905), l'antisémitisme dans l'Algérie coloniale* (Paris: L'Harmattan, 1986).

[12] Weil, *How to Be French*, 211–4.

[13] McDougall, *A History of Algeria*, 123–8.

[14] See Julien Fromage, 'L'expérience des "Jeunes Algériens" et l'émergence du militantisme moderne en Algérie (1880–1919)', in *Histoire de l'Algérie à la période coloniale*, eds. Bouchène, Peyroulou, Siari Tengour, and Thénault: 238–44.

press, these 'Young Algerian' activists set out a wide-ranging programme whose central demand was the accession to citizenship within the personal status for the educated elites.[15] While their vision of the gradual assimilation of the indigenous population had some resonance among progressives in Paris, their influence over politics in the colony remained marginal.[16] The French government's decision, in 1912, to introduce conscription for indigenous Algerians had the potential to radically change this.

Conscription in the Colonies?

Since the advent of European empire overseas, colonial rulers had relied on the recruitment of indigenous soldiers to wage war on their behalf. The lower cost of employing indigenous troops, the higher value placed on European lives, and the greater resistance of locally recruited troops to disease all fuelled the development of indigenous-dominated military forces across the colonial world.[17] In the wars of conquest, the colonial invaders profited from the internal divisions of local populations and pitted the soon-to-be-colonized against one another on the battlefield. Indeed, the *Tirailleurs Algériens*, the military force in which most indigenous Algerians served throughout the period of French colonial rule, was founded in 1841, at the height of the 'pacification' campaign in Algeria.[18] Those who fought in the colonial forces were never simple puppets of the colonial authorities. Rather, their decision to serve was shaped by a range of push and pull factors. Coercion certainly played an important role in driving indigenous recruitment, particularly, but not exclusively, in the early colonial period. Older practices and social structures that pre-dated colonialism also influenced recruitment patterns.[19] Pre-colonial traditions of military service fed directly into the decisions made by many indigenous Algerians to sign up. For Bencherif, for example, joining the French Army allowed him to reprise the

[15] Rabah Aissaoui, 'Between Two Worlds: Emir Khaled and the Young Algerians at the Beginning of the Twentieth Century in Algeria', in *Algeria Revisited: History, Culture and Identity*, eds. Rabah Aissaoui and Claire Eldridge (London: Bloomsbury, 2017): 56–78, 59.

[16] Ibid.

[17] Fogarty, *Race and War*, 19.

[18] Belkacem Recham, *Les musulmans algériens dans l'armée française 1919–45* (Paris: L'Harmattan, 1996), 10.

[19] In sub-Saharan Africa, recruitment often reproduced the old patterns of slavery. Myron Echenberg, *Colonial Conscripts: The Tirailleurs Sénégalais in French West Africa, 1857–1960* (London: James Currey, 1991), 8–19.

familial tradition of military service.[20] The other factors that drove recruitment among indigenous populations were not, at least on the surface, that different from those that motivated European recruits. The prospect of gaining increased financial, social, and cultural capital through military service was even more important in the context of a colonial society in which the limited possibilities for social mobility were conditional on loyalty to the colonial state.[21] Whether the decision to sign up was incentive-driven, the product of coercion, or, as was probably most often the case, a combination of both, it remained, at least nominally, a choice. Conscription offered no such choice.

Although the violence and discrimination underpinning the colonial system had always driven indigenous recruitment, the prospect of introducing a legal obligation to serve for indigenous populations represented an important break with practice in the colonies. Any move toward colonial conscription implied a fundamental shift away from a model based largely on a financial contract between the subject-soldier and the colonial state. If colonial troops could no longer be categorized purely as mercenaries, how would this transform their place in the colonial order? The politics of colonial conscription were closely bound up with the different understandings of both military service and colonial rule in the three empires that would deploy significant numbers of colonial troops during the Great War: Britain, France, and Germany.

While obligatory military service had long existed in some form across human societies, legally enforceable mass conscription was an innovation of the modern state. Its origins lay in the mass mobilizations of the citizen-soldiers of revolutionary France. Ever since the citizens of France rallied to defend the *Patrie en danger*, conscription had been considered one of the bedrocks of the French social contract. Republican ideology promoted the concept of the '*impôt du sang*' or 'blood tax', which established an unbreakable link between the duty to serve the defence of the nation and the rights of the citizen.[22] Thus, not only was conscription an embedded practice in French society but it also carried with it a sense that political rights were the direct corollary of military service. In Germany, where conscription had been established in the early nineteenth century by the Prussians and subsequently extended throughout the country post-unification,

[20] Bencherif, *Ahmed Ben Mostapha*, 110.

[21] Moyd, *Violent Intermediaries*, 34.

[22] John Horne, 'L'impôt du sang: Republican Rhetoric and Industrial Warfare in France, 1914–1918', *Social History* 14 (1989): 201–23, 215.

the link between military service and civic participation in political life was radically different.[23] While German soldiers were conscripted as soldier-citizens, this did not imply the same connection between political rights and military service in an authoritarian empire as it did in democratic, republican France. Where the French barracks was supposedly used to instil the values of civic life on conscripts, the German barracks served to infuse civic life with the value system of the military, in which the responsibilities of the citizen-soldier far outweighed his rights.[24] The contrast with the United Kingdom, the other major empire to deploy colonial troops in the Great War, was even more striking. The British had no military tradition of instituting conscription during military conflicts, let alone in peacetime. Indeed, when Asquith's wartime government finally introduced compulsory military service to Britain in January 1916, the prime minister declared that the bill 'can be sincerely supported by those who…are opposed to what is commonly called conscription', a testament to the divisiveness of the issue within British society.[25] Thus, not only did conscription have a particularly strong hold on the French military imaginary, but it also reflected a specifically French understanding of the connection between political rights and military duties that would have important implications for any attempt to extend the policy to the colonies.

Debates around the conscription of subject populations were also informed by questions of colonial ideology. The British Empire's declared commitment to the protection of native customs and tradition through the system of 'indirect rule' militated against the imposition of conscription by British colonial authorities. The social contract underpinning colonial rule in the British Empire was conceived of as not between the subjects themselves and the colonial authorities but rather between the administration and the approved leaders of the 'traditional' structures of 'native' society. Of course, this form of 'decentralized despotism' meant that the 'native' agents and intermediaries of colonial rule may often have compelled local populations into military service.[26] Nevertheless, the British government rejected the suggestion that they should legally enshrine conscription in their colonies.

[23] Ute Frevel, *A Nation in Barracks: Modern Germany, Military Conscription and Civil Society* (Oxford: Berg, 2004), 2.

[24] Ibid., 220.

[25] R.J.Q. Adams and Philip Poirier, *The Conscription Controversy in Great Britain, 1900–18* (Basingstoke, Macmillan, 1987), 1.

[26] See Mahmood Mamdani, *Citizen and Subject: Contemporary Africa and the Legacy of Late Colonialism* (Princeton, NJ: Princeton University Press, 1996).

Even in 1916, when the empire was in desperate need of recruits, the Colonial Office successfully resisted the idea of instituting mass recruitment, let alone conscription, for its African subject populations.[27] The fear that arming thousands of colonial subjects and deploying them alongside white men on the battlefields of Europe would undermine the racial hierarchy of colonial rule was the driving force behind the Colonial Office's hostility to an overreliance on colonial troops, especially from settler colonies like South Africa.[28] In India, where the British had long maintained a large army of local troops, the authorities singled out the so-called 'martial races' of the subcontinent in intense recruitment drives for the duration of the war. In regions targeted by recruiters, such as Punjab, United Province, and Nepal, the authorities used a combination of financial incentives, appeals to local military cultures, and the coercive power of the colonial state to enlist thousands of Indians.[29] However, the British never formally introduced conscription in the colony, fearing that it would fuel the nascent national movement and give rise to further demands for political rights for Indian subjects.[30] Moreover, after 1915, the British kept the Indian presence on the Western Front to a minimum, preferring to deploy their Indian troops on the battlefields of Mesopotamia and East Africa.[31] While the British Empire mobilized over 1.5 million indigenous subjects during the Great War, none of these were conscripts and the vast majority were deployed outside of Europe. In the German Empire, the relationship between administrator and subject-soldier was largely perceived as transactional by both parties. The indigenous recruit to the German *Schutztruppe* hoped to gain financial, social, and symbolic capital in their local communities in return for a commitment to defend the colonial state.[32] This meant that service had to be embedded in local cultural contexts, a requirement that militated against the recruitment and conscription of indigenous troops for service overseas. Furthermore, if German reactions to the French use of colonial troops in Europe are anything to go by, the commitment to the politics of race in

[27] David Killingray, 'The Idea of a British Imperial African Army', *Journal of African History* 20, No. 3 (1979): 421–36, 435.

[28] Ibid., 425–6.

[29] Kaushik Roy, *The Army in British India: From Colonial Warfare to Total War. 1857–1947* (London: Bloomsbury, 2013), 77–87.

[30] Tan Tai-Yong, 'An Imperial Home-Front: Punjab and the First World War', *Journal of Military History* 64, No. 2 (April 2000): 371–410, 407.

[31] Robert Aldrich and Christopher Hilliard, 'The French and British Empires', in *A Companion to World War I*, ed. John Horne (London: Wiley-Blackwell, 2010): 524–39, 525.

[32] Moyd, *Violent Intermediaries*, 5.

Germany put paid to any prospect of mass mobilization of German colonial subjects within Europe.[33] For German and British indigenous subjects, neither their status as voluntary recruits nor their deployment in extra-European conflict zones shielded them from the horrors of mechanized warfare. Nonetheless, the conditions of enrolment and deployment of these troops did shape the political understandings of military service held by both colonial administrators and colonial subjects during and after the war.

French attitudes to the recruitment and deployment of colonial troops contrasted sharply with those of the British and German authorities. The French had long led the way in the use of colonial troops to expand and solidify the empire. Algerians had participated in expeditions to Madagascar as well as the conquest of Tunisia and Morocco. Much more remarkable, however, was their use in campaigns in the Crimea, in Italy, and eventually in France itself, during the Franco-Prussian War.[34] This willingness to enrol and deploy colonial troops, even in the imperial metropole, reflected the specificity of French colonial ideology. The French Empire's declared commitment to the eventual assimilation of the indigenous population through the colonial 'civilizing mission' meant that racial difference did not result in automatic exclusion from European battlefields.[35] Certain enthusiasts of the colonial project saw the conscription of colonial subjects as the ideal means of achieving assimilation, combining the traditional republican belief in the barracks as the 'school of the nation' with the unyielding conviction that France had a duty to 'civilize' her subjects.[36] In this, they were ardently opposed by conservative colonialists and the representatives of Algeria's European community, who were doubly alarmed at the prospect of conscription for colonial subjects. They feared it would give the indigenous access to firearms and enhance their claims for greater political rights.[37] While both sides advanced their competing arguments in the pages of the colonial and metropolitan press, the majority of legislators in Paris remained largely indifferent.

[33] Christian Koller, 'The Recruitment of Colonial Troops in Africa and Asia and Their Deployment in Europe during the First World War', *Immigrants and Minorities* 26, No. 1–2 (March 2008): 111–33, 123.

[34] Fogarty, *Race and War*, 17.

[35] Echenberg, *Colonial Conscripts*, 28–9.

[36] Michelle Mann, 'The Young Algerians and the Question of the Muslim Draft, 1900–14', in *Algeria Revisited: History, Culture and Identity*, eds. Rabah Aissaoui and Claire Eldridge (London: Bloomsbury, 2017): 56–78, 42.

[37] Ibid., 43.

The prospect of another war with Germany saw the once abstract debates around conscription in the colonies take on a new urgency. In the years immediately preceding the war the notion, most famously defended by Charles Mangin in his book *La Force noire* (1910), that a colonial army would make up for France's demographic deficit gained currency in Paris.[38] Policy-makers in Paris took the first tentative steps towards building the colonial army of which Mangin had dreamed by planning the introduction of conscription in Algeria and French West Africa. Civil servants had little doubt that conscription would provoke resistance from 'those who think of us as oppressors' but as one of their number pointed out, forcing a man to serve was no worse than confiscating his land, and the colonial authorities had got away with that.[39] When news of the plans to extend conscription to the indigenous population crossed the Mediterranean, it sparked a heated debate across Algerian society.[40] Both traditional elites and European community leaders were united in their rejection of a policy they believed would erode the difference between indigenous Algerian and Frenchmen. Ordinary indigenous Algerians took to the streets to denounce what they saw as yet another form of colonial expropriation with the simple slogan 'You will not have our children'.[41] Yet one group in Algerian society did endorse the extension of conscription to the indigenous population: the Young Algerians. They believed that the introduction of conscription would solidify their claim for political rights and for a liberalization of the naturalization process for colonial subjects. A Young Algerian delegation travelled to Paris to convince the then prime minister Poincaré that the implementation of conscription should be accompanied by the abolition of laws of exception and the granting of citizenship within the personal status to Muslim ex-servicemen.[42] Indigenous Algerians, they hoped, would finally take their place as citizens of the nation in arms.

In the end, the conscription law adopted in 1912 would prove the Young Algerians wrong. The forms of compensation offered in return for conscription were both extremely limited and explicitly differentiated from the republican tradition of the '*impôt du sang*'. To the dismay of the Young Algerians, the decree that regulated indigenous conscription made no

[38] Charles Mangin, *La Force noire* (Paris: Hachette, 1911, 3rd Edition).
[39] Meynier, *L'Algérie Révélée*, 90.
[40] Mann, 'The Young Algerians', 45.
[41] Meynier, *L'Algérie Révélée*, 90.
[42] Martin Thomas, *The French Empire between the Wars: Imperialism, Politics and Society* (Manchester: Manchester University Press, 2005), 69.

commitment to political rights, providing instead for the payment of a bonus on enrolment known as the *prime de mobilisation*.[43] Indeed, the governor general of Algeria assured local officials that legislators had deliberately 'conserved the mercenary character' of indigenous military service so it could not be equated to 'the blood tax'. 'The government,' he asserted, 'never intended to attribute the rights of French citizens to the indigenous.'[44] The *primes* were just one element in a whole range of specific conditions that placed indigenous Algerian and West African conscripts and recruits in an ambiguous position, 'somewhere between hired mercenaries and full French citizens'.[45] When the war came only two years later, the experience of the citizens and subjects of Algeria and the wider French Empire would simultaneously confirm and complicate this ambiguity.

Algeria in the Imperial Great War

For the inhabitants of Algeria, the Great War began closer to home than anyone would have imagined. In the early morning of 4 August 1914, just hours after the declaration of war, the port cities of Bône (Annaba) and Philippeville (Skikda) on the eastern stretch of Algeria's Mediterranean coast came under heavy shelling from German cruisers, the *Goeben* and the *Breslau*.[46] The attacks, which left seventeen dead and scores injured, marked the first non-aerial assault on French soil of the war.[47] Although Algeria would never again be directly targeted, thousands of the territory's inhabitants would lose their lives on the battlefields of northern France and south-eastern Europe. Over the course of the war, about 73,000 French citizens of Algeria served in Europe, a rate of participation roughly equal to that of metropolitan France.[48] In total, some 173,000 indigenous soldiers had served in French forces by the end of the war, with slightly more than half of these enlisting as 'volunteers'.[49] Of the indigenous contingent, 125,000 saw active duty on the battlefields.[50] Estimates for European dead range between

[43] Ibid., 96–7. [44] Quoted in Mann, 'The Young Algerians', 49–50.
[45] Fogarty, *Race and War*, 53. [46] Meynier, *L'Algérie Révélée*, 263–4.
[47] Ibid., 264.
[48] Frémeaux, *Les Colonies dans la Grande Guerre*, 55.
[49] Benjamin Stora, *Algeria 1830–2000: A Short History* (Ithaca, NY: Cornell University Press, 2001), 18.
[50] Frémeaux, *Les Colonies dans la Grande Guerre*, 63.

12,000[51] and 22,000[52] while the number of indigenous dead is usually placed at around 26,000.[53] Furthermore, thousands of indigenous workers took up positions in factories in France, freeing up men to serve at the front and playing an important role in maintaining the supply of military equipment.[54]

Algeria's contribution to the French war effort was one element of the much wider colonial participation in the Great War. Fighting alongside the inhabitants of Algeria, European and indigenous, in the trenches of northern France and south-eastern Europe were men from almost every corner of the world. The Europeans of Algeria would surely have noticed the presence of thousands of soldiers from the ranks of the white populations that had settled the colonies of the British Empire: Canadians, South Africans, Australians, and New Zealanders. Indigenous Algerians not only fought and/or worked alongside their fellow French imperial subjects from West Africa, Madagascar, and Indochina, but also shared the battlefield with the Indian subjects of the British Empire. Outside of the European zone of conflict, the British, German, and French Empires all mobilized thousands of men from the colonies to wage war in defence of imperial polities that denied them basic rights. The experience of each individual soldier from the colonies was exactly that: an individual experience. Nonetheless, the conditions in which they served, the tasks they performed, and the rewards they received were shaped by their position within the racial and political hierarchies of the different imperial polities. This was clearly the case for the thousands of men who crossed the Mediterranean to defend France.

For the Europeans of Algeria, participation as full citizens alongside metropolitan troops confirmed their full membership of the nation. The service of thousands of Spanish, Italian, and Maltese-origin settlers in the French forces removed any doubt about their loyalty to France. For many of Algeria's Europeans, the war was their first experience of the metropole, with the harsh reality of mud-filled trenches and ruined villages displacing the idealized vision of a land of rolling green countryside.[55] The encounter with metropolitan troops exposed them to the range of cultural differences that characterized Frenchmen from across the Hexagon. This confrontation

[51] Ibid., 202. [52] Stora, *Algeria 1830–2000*, 18.

[53] Frémeaux gives the figure 26,000 while Stora offers the figure 25,000 : Frémeaux, *Les Colonies dans la Grande Guerre*, 202 and Stora, *Algeria 1830–2000*, 18.

[54] See Frémeaux, *Les Colonies dans la Grande Guerre*, 73–4.

[55] Joëlle Hureau, *La mémoire des pieds-noirs de 1830 à nos jours* (Paris: Perrin, 2001), 99.

with French plurality convinced the Europeans of their legitimate membership of the national community.[56]

If the experience of the European population of Algeria was characterized by differences of culture but equality of rights and conditions, the same could not be said for the other groups of Algerians at the front. Algerian Jews were legally assimilated French citizens and thus served under the exact same regime as the European settlers and as metropolitan Frenchmen. Unlike indigenous Algerians, they did not suffer the consequences of a legally sanctioned form of discrimination. Nevertheless, the 13,000 Algerian Jews at the front were subject to high levels of anti-Semitism, with many complaining of specific incidents of discrimination and open bigotry.[57] Most served in colonial regiments, hotbeds of anti-Semitism, and comparatively few ever reached the rank of officer.[58] Their experience of the war simultaneously confirmed their status as French citizens and pointed to their fragile position within the imperial polity.

For indigenous subjects from Algeria and across the empire, their wartime experience was even more ambiguous and contradictory. The push and pull factors that always shaped indigenous enrolment in the French armed forces were greatly amplified in the context of the invasion of the imperial metropole. Conscripts were called up for service and any form of desertion or resistance was brutally crushed. Local *caïds*, paid for organizing 'voluntary' recruitment, often forced young indigenous men to sign up.[59] Nevertheless, many indigenous did volunteer, whether motivated by the imperial patriotism expressed by Bencherif, or more likely, the prospect of a steady and generous wage or simply a desire for adventure. The experience of indigenous troops was shaped by the way both the military authorities and ordinary soldiers grappled with racial difference and the fraternity of arms born in the trenches. A range of 'conflicting impulses'[60] fed into military policy toward indigenous troops. Military administrators drew on a blend of racial prejudice, paternalism, respect for difference, and a rhetorical commitment to republican equality to simultaneously acknowledge, reward, discipline, and degrade indigenous soldiers. While equality of basic pay and bonuses had

[56] Ibid., 99–100.

[57] Philippe E. Landau, *Les Juifs de France et la Grande guerre: Un patriotisme républicain* (Paris: CNRS Editions, 2008), 33–5.

[58] Ethan B. Katz, 'Jews and Muslims in the Shadow of Marianne: Conflicting Identities and Republican Culture in France (1914–1975)' (PhD Diss., University of Madison-Wisconsin, 2009), 61.

[59] Fogarty, *Race and War*, 32.

[60] Ibid., 272.

been recognized by the end of the war, indigenous troops did not receive the family allocations granted to those from the metropole and the Europeans of Algeria.[61] Similarly, the possibilities for promotion of indigenous troops that evolved over the course of the war may have been unparalleled elsewhere in the colonial sphere but did not constitute a real challenge to the idea of European supremacy.[62] The army, though it was permeated by racist discrimination, was a 'relatively egalitarian social order' compared to that which dominated in Algeria and across the empire.[63] This limited liberalism would leave a lasting impression on those who survived the war.

The encounter with both French civilians and metropolitan troops reinforced among indigenous soldiers the notion of the permeability of the racial boundaries in the metropole that were so rigid in their own society. Indigenous troops often spoke in glowing terms of the 'perfect attitudes' of the French population.[64] Within the ranks of the army, the indigenous soldier's experience of interracial relations varied wildly, with some paying tribute to the sensitivity of the officers and others denouncing racism.[65] In much the same way that the army seemed a more egalitarian institution than the colonial system, the indigenous troops' experience of interactions with the inhabitants of the metropole revealed a society less dominated by and conscious of the boundaries of racial difference.[66] This too would have lasting implications for post-war politics across the empire and, specifically, in Algeria.

In the aftermath of the war, the question of the loyalty of colonial troops would play a key role in debates around reform in the empire. While official wartime propaganda constantly trumpeted the unimpeachable imperial patriotism of colonial troops, the civil and military authorities in France were plagued by doubts over the loyalty of colonial subject-soldiers. This was particularly true in the case of Muslim troops from North Africa, who, by virtue of their religious and cultural proximity to the Ottoman Empire, were seen as vulnerable to the Central Powers' propaganda efforts.[67] The high-profile defection to the Germans of a once promising Algerian lieutenant, Rabah Boukabouya, was a prime example of the risk posed by potential deserters. His publication in 1915 of a stinging criticism of the 'racial hatred', 'pitiless violence', and 'religious profanation' that he claimed characterized

[61] Ibid., 121. [62] Ibid., 126–30. [63] Ibid., 7.
[64] Meynier, *L'Algérie Révélée*, 436.
[65] Meynier, *L'Algérie Révélée*, 421 and Fogarty, *Race and War*, 111.
[66] Fogarty, *Race and War*, 7. [67] Ibid., 110.

the French treatment of Muslim soldiers was a propaganda coup for the Central Powers.[68] Even more worrying for the French were the Central Powers' efforts to recruit among Muslim prisoners of war. The Germans incarcerated captured North African troops in a special prison camp at Zossen near Berlin, equipped with a mosque and 'Moorish baths'.[69] The so-called 'Half Moon Camp' served a dual purpose, projecting a positive image of Germany to Muslims around the world while also providing a recruiting ground for a new brigade of Muslim troops. While there is some evidence that the German denunciations of French impiety had a certain resonance, especially among Tunisian soldiers, there were no instances of mass desertion in metropolitan France during the war.[70] German efforts to recruit among the prisoners of war were not successful. Bencherif, who spent a large part of the war imprisoned at Zossen, dismisses Boukabouya and the other deserters as 'sell outs' in the pages of *Ahmed ben Mostapha, goumier*. He describes the Algerian prisoners' scepticism when faced with the grandiose claims of the deserters, with one of their number arguing that they should play along with them only 'to use their stupidity to get more bread'.[71] Although the success of this German propaganda was very limited, it did spur the French authorities on to publicize and further develop their efforts to accommodate the practice of Islam among colonial troops. The army provided halal rations, employed imams to travel the frontlines offering religious services, and, in 1916, built the first mosque in modern France in the *Jardin Colonial* on the outskirts of Paris.[72] This policy of provision fed into wider debates about how the French should reward and cultivate the loyalty of its indigenous subjects in the interwar period.

Struggles over post-war reform were also informed by the crucial role of indigenous Algerian workers in sustaining the war industries. Some 78,556 Algerian workers were drafted onto French farms and into the war factories, where they formed part of a newly diversified workforce including large numbers of women, foreign immigrants, and roughly 220,000 workers recruited from elsewhere in the empire and in China.[73] In many cases, the

[68] Rabah Boukabaya (Lt. El Hadj Abdellah), *L'Islam dans l'Armée Française* (Istanbul, 1915), 4 and 8.

[69] Fogarty, *Race and War*, 189–90.

[70] Ibid., 192.

[71] Bencherif, *Ahmed Ben Mostapha*, 236–44.

[72] Fogarty, *Race and War*, 183–9.

[73] Figures taken from Tyler Stovall, 'The Color Line behind the Lines: Racial Violence and the Great War during the Great War', *American Historical Review* 103, No. 3 (June 1998): 737–69, 741–2.

recruitment of Algerians and other colonials represented a form of 'virtual conscription' and most remained subject to military discipline within the factory gates.[74] For much of the war, their rates of pay were far below those given to metropolitan male workers.[75] The War Ministry's *Service de l'organisation des travailleurs coloniaux* closely controlled every aspect of the lives of colonial workers, coordinating their integration into the labour force and ensuring they were housed in segregated accommodation away from the local population.[76] The authorities were particularly concerned about the prospect of sexual contact between colonial workers and Frenchwomen. Colonial workers endured the harsh working conditions in the war industries, the discriminatory policies of the French government, and the hostility, even violence, of some metropolitans.[77] Nevertheless, wartime work was not an unambiguously negative experience. Their contact with metropolitan society sometimes transcended the racial divide through acquaintances, friendships, and, in rare cases, romances.[78] Such relationships would be almost unimaginable in the colonial context. Like their compatriots in the army, colonial workers saw a society, that for all its ingrained racial discrimination, appeared more equal than was the case at home in the colony. This would fuel demands for change in the post-war era.

On the Home Front, the war saw the acceleration of processes of urbanization and industrialization that were to have a transformative effect on Algeria and other colonies in the interwar period.[79] The mass participation of soldiers from across ethnic, religious, and political divides united many of the inhabitants of Algeria in the bonds of anxiety, mourning, and, eventually, celebration of victory. While the advent of an Algerian *Union Sacrée* saw the emphasis shift toward a more universalist language at the expense of the racialist discourse of the pre-war era, the experience of the conflict was not free of tension between colonial authorities, colonial citizens, and colonial subjects.[80] Gilbert Meynier points to the complexity of indigenous

[74] John Horne 'Immigrant Workers in France during World War I', *French Historical Studies* 14, No. 1 (April 1985): 57–88, 64 and 68.

[75] Ibid., 76–7.

[76] Stovall, 'The Color Line', 744.

[77] Ibid., 751–9.

[78] Tyler Stovall, 'Love, Labor, and Race: Colonial Men and White Women in France during the Great War', in *French Civilization and Its Discontents: Nationalism, Colonialism, Race*, eds. Tyler Stovall and Georges Van den Abeele (Lanham, MD: Lexington Books, 2003): 297–321, 310.

[79] Thomas, *The French Empire*, 137–8.

[80] See Jan C. Jansen, 'Une autre "Union Sacrée"? Commémorer la Grande Guerre dans l'Algérie colonisée (1918–39)', trans. Augustin Jommier, *Revue d'histoire moderne et contemporaine* 61–2, No. 2 (2014): 32–60, 34.

attitudes towards the war, which he characterizes as 'between moral resistance, *attentisme*, and loyalism'.[81] The outbreak of the war was marked by a series of patriotic declarations by indigenous officials across the colony.[82] Indigenous workers stepped in to maintain the farms of those European settlers called up to the army, in some cases even working closely with the wives of the European farmers.[83] Whether these actions can be ascribed to some form of imperial patriotism, pure self-interest, or a combination of both, they did challenge the notion that all of the indigenous population were simply biding their time and ultimately sought the expulsion of the European settlers.

This is not to say that the conflict did not result in new forms of anti-colonial violence. From the outset of the war, certain indigenous communities organized against conscription, violently resisting the efforts of the French Army to draft their young men.[84] Rural banditry increased dramatically and took on an explicitly political meaning. Draft-dodgers and armed deserters swelled the ranks of the bandits, in some cases turning the weapons they had obtained in the army training camps on European settlers and French officials.[85] They often became celebrated folk figures who represented the, however rudimentary, resistance of indigenous Algerians to the demands of the colonial regime.[86] This resistance would eventually spill over into open rebellion as the insatiable appetite of the French for new recruits proved too much for sections of indigenous society. The draft call issued in August 1916 was met with consternation by indigenous communities across the colony, culminating in a bloody insurrection in southern areas of the *département* of Constantine. The uprising, one of several rebellions that took place in the colonial world during the war, was brutally crushed by the French Army and military courts meted out harsh sentences to all the alleged participants.[87] While acts of open rebellion or desertion could be effectively repressed with military force, cultural forms of resistance to the mobilization of Algerian society were less easy to repress. For example,

[81] Meynier, *L'Algérie Révélée*, 617. [82] Ibid., 269.

[83] This cooperation with and safeguarding of settlers' farms and wives would be cited by defenders of colonial reform following the war. Baba Ali, 'Le congrès des maires', *L'Ikdam*, 11–18 June 1920.

[84] Samuel Kalman, 'Criminalizing Dissent: Policing Banditry in the Constantinois, 1914–18', in *Algeria Revisited: History, Culture and Identity*, eds. Rabah Aissaoui and Claire Eldridge (London: Bloomsbury, 2017): 20–38, 22.

[85] Ibid., 23–6.

[86] McDougall, *A History of Algeria*, 141.

[87] See Ouanassa Siari Tengour, 'La révolte dans l'Aurès', in *Histoire de l'Algérie à la période coloniale*, eds. Bouchène, Peyroulou, Siari Tengour, and Thénault: 255–60.

the folk song 'Hadj Guillaume' that celebrated the supposed conversion of the Kaiser to Islam and his coming victory against France expressed the hostility of sections of indigenous society in a traditional form that escaped the control of the colonial authorities.[88] In the wake of the war, memories of resistance and insurrection would sit uneasily with a commemorative discourse that stressed unity and loyalty.[89] Like the complex experiences of Algeria's inhabitants on the battlefields, the multi-layered reality of life on the Algerian Home Front would feed into the rival historical narratives of the colony's role in the conflict throughout the interwar period.

Legacies of the Imperial Wartime Experience

The legacy of Algeria's participation in the Great War was also shaped by the wider experience of other colonies in the war. Post-war debates about Algeria's place in the imperial polity would often look to comparisons with other colonial spaces. Key conceptions of imperial politics that informed debate in interwar Algeria frequently came from beyond the boundaries of the colony itself.

For the defenders of expanded rights for the indigenous, the wartime reform instituted in Senegal's Four Communes was a key precedent. The Four Communes of Dakar, Rufisque, Gorée, and St Louis were France's oldest settlements on the African continent and since a declaration by the Second Republic in 1848, the indigenous population of the communes, the *originaires*, were nominally citizens of France. Their real position in the imperial polity was ambiguous. Despite still holding their personal status as Muslims, subject to Koranic law for their private affairs, the indigenous inhabitants of the Four Communes enjoyed the right to elect representatives to the French Parliament, though these elections were rarely free and fair. Moreover, a whole range of limitations, practical and legal, called into question their full citizenship.[90] In the years prior to the Great War, an emergent elite of Francophone activists, similar to the Young Algerians, began to contest the dominance of local politics by the white and mixed-race

[88] McDougall, *History and Culture of Nationalism*, 105–6.

[89] For a detailed account of the tensions underlying commemorative discourse in the colony see Jan C. Jansen, *Erobern und Erinnern: Symbolpolitik, öffentlicher Raum und französischer Kolonialismus in Algerien* (Munich: Oldenbourg, 2013), 337–90.

[90] G. Wesley Johnson, *The Emergence of Black Politics in Senegal: The Struggle for Power in the Four Communes, 1900–1920* (Stanford, CA: Stanford University Press, 1971), 79–84.

minorities.[91] This led to the election, in 1914, of Blaise Diagne, the first black African to represent the communes. Diagne saw the war as an opportunity to solidify and expand the rights of the inhabitants of the Four Communes. He insisted that they be subject to the same form of conscription as metropolitan Frenchmen and that they serve in the same units as their fellow French citizens. Conscious of the French dependence on colonial troops, Diagne successfully pressured the National Assembly into passing a law that recognized the rights of the *originaires* as full citizens of France who maintained their personal status.[92] While his subsequent attempts to use mass recruitment in West Africa to expand this new category of imperial citizenship beyond the Four Communes failed, Diagne had opened a small but significant breach in the boundary between citizen and subject. The Law of 1916 not only belied the French insistence that the personal status was intrinsically incompatible with citizenship but also showed that the link between military service and citizenship held true in a colonial context. This was key for those who called for a new form of imperial citizenship for indigenous Algerians.

While the reforms in the Four Communes would clearly resonate in Algeria and the rest of the empire, political leaders in the colonies were also sensitive to the broader shifts happening in the world as a result of global conflict. In the British Empire, mass recruitment in the colonies saw power rapidly shift away from the imperial metropole and towards the administrations in the White Dominions, and to a lesser extent, India.[93] This, in turn, led to calls for a reconfiguration of the imperial polity and an embrace of new models of imperial citizenship.[94] While some defenders of greater rights for the indigenous would cite reforms in India, the British Empire would primarily serve as a point of reference for the leaders of the settler community in Algeria. They too sought a reconfigured imperial polity that remained committed to the principle of European hegemony.

Broader trends in global politics during the war also influenced how actors in Algeria understood the conflict and the possible world order that would follow it. The emergence across the Atlantic of an American president who seemed committed to establishing a new world order in

[91] Ibid., 123–53. [92] Thomas, *The French Empire*, 26.

[93] John Darwin, 'A Third British Empire? The Dominion Idea in Imperial Politics', in *The Oxford History of the British Empire. Volume IV: The Twentieth Century*, eds. Judith M. Brown and Wm. Roger Louis (Oxford: Oxford University Press, 1999): 64–87, 67–9.

[94] Daniel Gorman, 'Fractured Empire: Ideas of Imperial Citizenship in the British Empire after the First World War', *Comparitiv* 26, No. 6 (2016): 15–34.

which the voices of national minorities would be heard resonated across the colonial world, including in North Africa.[95] Both Europeans and indigenous Algerians would show some interest in the post-war 'Wilsonian Moment'.[96] Events in Leningrad in 1917 would find less of an immediate echo in Algeria, but would also play their part in shaping interwar discourses around colonial rule in North Africa. Leninist anti-imperialism would prove central to the emergence of a radical nationalist movement, first among migrants in the metropole and eventually in the colony itself. Indeed, actors across the political spectrum and the racial divide could draw on any number of wartime precedents from across the globe to legitimize their visions for post-war Algeria. The war's greatest political impact was, perhaps, the sense, in colony and metropole alike, that the conflict had fundamentally transformed the world and that a new post-war political order would have to be built.

This belief in a new post-war order did not solely apply to the field of high politics; it also implied a more practical approach to recognizing and rewarding the service of colonial citizens and subjects. The mass sacrifices of the Great War called for a new moral politics in both metropole and colony. Throughout this book, we will see how different political actors sought to impose their vision of a just post-war order by evoking their contribution to the war. In this, they were no different than the millions of men and women in Europe who sought to claim their just reward in the aftermath of the war. And yet, theirs was a colonial society, where every facet of daily life was permeated by the power relations underpinning colonial rule. How then are we to conceptualize colonial claims-making in the wake of the war?

Conceptualizing Colonial Claims-Making in the Wake of the War

Post-war debates in all belligerent territories, metropolitan and colonial, were shot through with the notion that society should replicate and vindicate the moral code that had underpinned wartime mass mobilization. The assessment of the 'worthiness' of certain individuals or groups to

[95] See Dónal Hassett, 'Reinventing Empire in the Wake of the Great War: Imperial Citizenship and the "Wilsonian Moment" in Colonial Algeria', *Comparitiv* 26, No. 6 (2016): 37–54.

[96] Manela, *The Wilsonian Moment*.

enjoy privilege in the post-war order would draw heavily on differing interpretations of the experience of the war itself. Over the course of the war, a new 'social morality' had emerged, grounded in 'a set of reciprocal moral judgements on the contribution of different groups to the national effort'.[97] At the heart of this new moral code lay the notion of sacrifice.[98] Anchoring calls for reform in the language of sacrifice allowed actors to better negotiate the terms of their participation in the war without breaking with the *Union Sacrée* and its eschewal of partisan divisions.[99] Furthermore, it facilitated the articulation of an egalitarian political language that, by focusing on inequalities of sacrifice and not those of class or race, was 'entirely compatible with the national cause'.[100] This does not mean, however, that this 'moral economy of wartime sacrifice'[101] was the preserve only of progressives.[102] Rather, a moral understanding of wartime sacrifice transcended boundaries of class, race, and political allegiance to become *the* central prism through which all actors presented their actions and interpreted those of their compatriots.[103] This emergence of a common language of politics would be of particular significance in the colonies.

The inhabitants of the belligerent societies, colonial and metropolitan, developed a 'complex moral language' that differentiated between those individuals or collectives who were fulfilling their duties and those who were not.[104] Shirkers or '*embusqués*', as they were called in French, were a prime target of criticism. The *embusqué*, in his deliberate avoidance of national service, not only weakened the war effort but also fundamentally undermined the basic moral underpinning of the war: the equal duty of all

[97] John Horne, 'Introduction: Mobilising for "Total War"', 1914–1918', in *State, Society and Mobilization in Europe during the First World War*, ed. John Horne (Cambridge: Cambridge University Press, 1997): 1–17, 11.

[98] John Horne, 'Social Identity in War: France, 1914–1918', in *Men, Women and War*, eds. Keith Jeffrey and TG. Fraser (Dublin: Lilliput Press, 1993): 119–36, 131–2.

[99] Pierre Purseigle, *Mobilisation, sacrifice et citoyenneté: Angleterre-France 1900–1918* (Paris: Les Belles Lettres, 2013), 265.

[100] Horne, 'Social Identity in War', 129.

[101] For an explanation of the use of this term, originally developed by E.P. Thompson, and its position in the historiography of the Great War see Purseigle, *Mobilisation*, 263.

[102] Bernard Waites explores the concept of the wartime moral economy solely in terms of its implication for working classes, an approach which is critiqued by Purseigle. Bernard Waites, 'The Government of the Home-Front and the "Moral Economy" of the Working Class', in *Home Fires and Foreign Fields: British Social and Military Experience in the First World War*, ed. Peter Liddle (London: Brassey's, 1985), 175–93 and Purseigle, *Mobilisation*, 265.

[103] Purseigle, *Mobilisation*, 265.

[104] Jean-Louis Robert, 'The Image of the Profiteer', in *Capital Cities at War: London, Paris, Berlin 1914–1919*, eds. Jay Winter and Jean-Louis Robert (Cambridge: Cambridge University Press, 1997): 104–32, 132.

to serve. Throughout the war, the denunciation of the *embusqué* targeted not only those who sought to avoid their responsibility but also those whose contribution to the war, vital as it may have been, kept them out of harm's way at the front.[105] The *embusqué* thus came to symbolize the 'constellation of unequal wartime sacrifice' that marked the experience of the war and would continue to resonate long after the Armistice.[106]

The same was true of the hated figure of the profiteer. He had placed his personal interest above that of the nation and thus embodied the 'extremes of deplorable behaviour in wartime'.[107] In the context of a society in which the struggle for the most basic provisions was constant, the profiteer was to blame for the 'improper distribution of material hardship in wartime'.[108] Although the profiteer was a particular target of scorn for the left,[109] his transgression of the 'wartime social morality' was condemned across society. Thus, the profiteer served as a figure against which wartime society could unite, with this consensus grounded in a shared 'notion of fairness defined not in precise terms but revealed by its gross abuse'.[110]

When the war ended, the wartime consensus as to what constituted a breach in 'fairness' disintegrated. Although conflicts had abounded during the war over where exactly the frontiers of this moral code lay, the political truce instituted by the *Union Sacrée* in France and its equivalents elsewhere ensured that they never boiled over into full-blooded partisan political disputes. Once the existential threat to the nation receded, the various *Unions Sacrées* faltered and the struggle to shape the post-war order became distinctly political. In many parts of Europe, this struggle descended into violence as paramilitary groups sought to impose their vision of post-war society.[111] In a victorious France political parties and civil society groups rushed to claim the mantle of symbolic legitimacy conferred by the wartime sacrifice. Rival actors openly mobilized the labels of 'profiteer' and '*embusqué*' to denigrate their opponents and support their visions of a moral post-war order. While the evocation of the 'moral economy of wartime sacrifice' varied widely across time and between different movements, it became a defining feature of political discourse in interwar France.

[105] Horne, 'L'impôt du sang', 217. [106] Robert, 'The Image of the Profiteer', 130.
[107] Ibid., 104. [108] Ibid., 125.
[109] Horne, 'Social Identity', 128.
[110] Robert, 'The Image of the Profiteer', 125.
[111] For details see Robert Gerwarth and John Horne, 'Vectors of Violence: Paramilitarism in Europe after the Great War, 1917–1923', *Journal of Modern History* 83, No. 3 (September 2011): 489–512.

Whether the 'moral economy of wartime sacrifice' ever permeated colonial societies to the extent it did in the metropole is debatable. The instances of resistance to recruitment and conscription in the colonies would suggest that the colonial subject's sense of duty to serve the imperial polity was not the same as that felt by the citizen toward the nation-state. Furthermore, the equality of all citizens before the draft, a key feature that underpinned the 'moral economy' in the metropole, had less resonance in territories where conscription and recruitment were enforced unevenly and arbitrarily. Finally, the existential threat to the metropole that played a key role in uniting society behind the war was less immediately relevant to colonial subjects, who often had far more to fear from the colonial state than a foreign aggressor. Thus, the centrality of the 'moral economy of wartime sacrifice' to life in the colonies seems less inevitable than in the metropole. And yet, throughout this book, we see a whole range of political actors in Algeria trumpet their fulfilment of the wartime moral code. This colonial evocation of the 'moral economy of sacrifice' was inextricably bound up with the coercive nature of the colonial state. In a colony such as Algeria, stressing compliance with the wartime moral code not only improved the chances of securing reform but also reduced the threat of violent repression at the hands of the state. While the loyalty of certain groups of citizens in the metropole may occasionally have been called into question, the level of suspicion directed toward indigenous subjects and political subversives in the colonies was much more consistent and intense. As a result, publicly declaring and proving loyalty to the colonial state was a prerequisite for all but the most radical activists. The stakes of being labelled an *embusqué*, a profiteer or, even worse, a traitor, were much higher in the colonies. This meant that the 'moral economy of sacrifice' became a powerful, if heavily contested, concept in Algerian society.

The centrality of the Great War to claims-making in Algeria and the wider colonial world was not solely motivated by a desire to forestall the coercive power of the colonial state. Like their erstwhile brothers-in-arms in the metropole, subjects and citizens across the empire had come to conceive of their contribution to the war in terms of 'a reciprocal national obligation': they had fulfilled their duty to the colonial state, now it was up to the colonial administration to fulfil its duty to them.[112] For most colonial veterans, subjects, and citizens, this primarily meant the provision of

[112] John Horne, *Labour at War: France and Britain, 1914–1918* (Oxford: Clarendon Press, 1991), 351.

pensions, healthcare, and enhanced employment opportunities. The veterans' demand for an improvement in social and economic conditions was also shared by many non-combatants across the empire. Other political actors would go much further in their demands, asserting that the state could only repay the debt incurred in the war by radically restructuring the imperial polity. All post-war demands in the colonies, whether these were economic, social, or political, implied some form of reconfiguration of the relationship with the metropole.[113] Over the course of the interwar period, actors across the French Empire would attempt to redefine their position in the imperial polity by claiming participation in the war had changed the terms of their social contract with the state. However, the three principal groups implicated in the post-war reconfiguration of colonial politics—colonial administrators, citizens, and subjects—could rarely agree among themselves, let alone between each other, as to how the state could adequately recognize the new political reality.

This 'gap of expectations' in the post-war colonial world gave rise to what the colonial historian Gregory Mann has called 'idioms of mutual if uneven obligation' between the colonial state, its citizens, and its subjects.[114] Political actors from all sides of the triangular colonial divide recognized the new relationship forged by the war and sought to advance their claims in a common language born of the war. Nevertheless, the use of a shared system of references did not necessarily result in mutual intelligibility between political actors and their claims. As Mann points out, the 'language of mutual obligation and interdependence is and has always been fraught with misunderstandings, *malentendus* and moments of false confidence, in which one group or another believes that it is finally being heard and understood'.[115] The debates around reform in post-war colonial Algeria, whether in the economic, social, or political sphere, bear witness to this fundamental ambiguity.

Mann's analysis is the product of the study of the French Soudan (Mali), a sub-Saharan African colony with an almost non-existent European population. Undoubtedly, the participation of indigenous Algerians in the war gave rise to a similar 'uneven idiom of mutual obligation' between subject and colonial state, but what of the citizen-soldiers of the European

[113] Ibid.

[114] Gregory Mann, *Native Sons: West African Veterans and France in the Twentieth Century* (London: Duke University Press, 2006), 65.

[115] Ibid.

community? Surely, their status as citizens fighting for the nation of which they were full members excluded them from the kind of specific colonial 'blood debt' evoked by Mann.[116] And yet, the debates recounted in this book seem to suggest that for many in the European community it was quite the contrary. The disparity in power relations between the indigenous and the colonial state was far greater than that which characterized the European community's relationship with the state. Nonetheless, the belief that the power to shape Algeria's present and future lay in the hands of the officials and representatives of metropolitan institutions, and not with the European community, gave a sense of asymmetry to the power relations between colonial citizen and imperial state. The fact that, rightly or wrongly, large swathes of the European community felt that metropolitan politicians and bureaucrats cared little for their interests meant that they too would articulate post-war claims in 'a contentious political language of mutual obligation'.[117]

The effects of these 'idioms of mutual if uneven obligation' extended far beyond the boundaries of colonial high politics, encompassing a whole swathe of social and economic demands. Throughout the interwar period, a range of other claims, not directly pertaining to questions of citizenship and subjecthood, would be advanced by groups encompassing both Europeans and indigenous. Often their unity of purpose was framed in terms of participation in the Great War. In certain cases, this sentiment converted into acts of cross-community political solidarity, in others communal, individual, or ideological interests either obscured or reconceived the fraternity of arms in ways that challenged political solidarity. The ethno-legal divide that underpinned the colonial system remained *the* crucial axis for political debate in the period. And yet, the explosion in civil society groups coupled with the growth of mass political organizations, some of which claimed to be transcommunal, opened a space where common claims (if not always common goals) could be articulated in a shared language.

Conclusion

In the pages of *Ahmed Ben Mostapha, goumier*, Mohamed Bencherif offers a lyrical account of his emotions on his arrival in metropolitan France in

[116] Ibid., 3. [117] Ibid., 2.

1914. As the train carrying him and his brothers-in-arms to the battlefields pulls out of the station in Marseille, he looks wistfully at the 'long blue ribbon of the Mediterranean' and contemplates how 'it laps the shores of my double *Patrie*'. The eventual disappearance of the sliver of blue over the horizon leads, he claims, to the 'fusion of the land of France and that of Africa' in his 'poetic soul'.[118] Bencherif's romantic hyperbole undoubtedly obscures the mix of fascination, fear, and fatalism that marked the arrival of most colonial troops in Europe. Nevertheless, his evocation of the 'double *Patrie*' constituted by metropolitan France and its empire, especially Algeria, does reflect a real sense that the shared sacrifices of the war would radically alter the imperial polity. Declaring the 'fusion' of metropole and colony was not simply a rhetorical expression of the unity of the empire behind the war effort. It reflected the belief held by Bencherif and his friends among the indigenous educated elites that their community's wartime service would result in their full integration into the French national community. They, like many actors across the colonial world, were convinced that the war had radically transformed the relationship between colony and metropole and between colonial citizen, colonial subject, and colonial administrator. While these actors rarely shared a common view of what the colonial post-war order should look like, they did pursue the same strategy to secure it: evoking the Great War.

The complex and multi-layered experience of the war for the inhabitants of Algeria and the wider colonial world lent itself to multiple, often contradictory, interpretations. Throughout the interwar period political actors would offer alternative visions of the past in an effort to defend their rival visions of the future. Colonial versions of the 'moral economy of wartime sacrifice' became central to political debate, as interest groups in the colonies competed for the legitimacy that only the war could confer. Whether defending the extension of citizenship to colonial subjects or calling for a pay increase for disgruntled dockers, political actors in Algeria and further afield anchored their campaigns in the rhetoric of the Great War. The war permeated political discourse, resulting in the emergence of a shared language that was used to articulate ideas that were often contradictory, if not radically opposed to each other. The wide range of experiences that marked colonial participation in the war and the many different ways in which they could be understood allowed for the emergence of this common

[118] Bencherif, *Ahmed Ben Mostapha*, 220.

but contested language. While the same phenomenon can also be traced in metropolitan France and in other European countries, it was more significant in the colonial context, where, as Cooper and Stoler have pointed out, the maintenance of difference was key to the preservation of colonial rule.[119] The existence of this common language would facilitate all kinds of attempts to blur the lines of demarcation underpinning the colonial system, something that would be vigorously resisted by a wide range of interest groups in the imperial polity.

Although the experience of the Great War provided citizens and subjects in the colonies with a new and powerful language of claims-making, this was not without a cost. The language of the Great War, like all other forms of language, was 'shot through with intentions and accents'[120] that would structure claims-making in the colonies, often in ways that escaped the control of those who used it. The colonial and military ideologies that had shaped wartime service for the inhabitants of Algeria were infused into this language, as were the multitude of experiences that had characterized both the colony and the wider empire's involvement in the war. Those who mobilized its memory in pursuit of their post-war goals would have to grapple with this unwieldiness. Nowhere was this truer than in the divisive debates around political reform in Algeria.

119 Cooper and Stoler, 'Between Metropole and Colony'.

120 Bakhtin, 'Discourse in the Novel', in *The Dialogic Imagination*, 293.

2
Remaking the Post-War Colonial Order

In May 1919, the European representatives of the General Council of the Department of Oran passed a motion demanding that 'the French population of Algeria, who had, through the sacrifice of their children, proven their attachment to France, enjoy the same rights as the Frenchmen of the metropole'.[1] Some eighteen years later, a group of indigenous political activists issued an appeal for reform to the French government asserting that 'since the end of the war, Algerian Muslims who, like all Frenchmen, responded to the call to defend the invaded territory, await the basic rights so solemnly promised them'.[2] The striking similarity in the language employed by radically opposed political groups in very different political contexts underlines the centrality of the Great War to discourse in interwar Algeria. Throughout the interwar period, attempts to redefine colonial rule, whether they sought to enhance European hegemony or expand indigenous rights, were consistently articulated in the language of the Great War.

This chapter considers how radical strategies for pursuing a transformation of the colonial order, especially the embrace of Wilsonian principles, lost out to arguments for a reconfiguration of the imperial polity. It examines how colonial citizens and subjects framed their demands for reform as compensation for their wartime service, talking up their contribution to the war and minimizing that of their opponents to secure the best deal for the constituencies. Finally, it discusses how actors assessed the efforts (or lack of the same) of the French authorities to fulfil its 'mutual obligation' to the inhabitants of the colony and asks how this shaped their perception of the social contract underpinning colonial rule in Algeria.

[1] 'Le Conseil Général d'Oran', *La Dépêche Algérienne*, 2 May 1919.
[2] 'Comité Parisien du Congrès Musulman', *La Défense*, 12 February 1937.

Legislating for Colonial Reform

Throughout the period of French rule in Algeria, different governments in Paris sought to impose their own visions of the reciprocal relationship between colony and metropole. The interwar years were marked by two great moments of reform. The impetus for the first reform project came from the need to recognize the contribution of indigenous Algerians to the Great War. During the war, colonial reform had been championed by those who saw the salvation of France in its recruitment pool in the colonies. With victory secured under Clemenceau, a strong advocate of indigenous recruitment and of colonial reform, it seemed sweeping changes were in store for the colonial system in Algeria. The *Loi Jonnart*, named after Charles Jonnart who Clemenceau reappointed to his old post of governor general of Algeria, extended a limited form of franchise for local and departmental elections to certain categories of the indigenous population, including all veterans. 421,000 indigenous men now enjoyed the right to vote, albeit in a restrictive system that never called into question European hegemony in the colony.[3] The expansion of the political rights of a significant proportion of the male indigenous population would gradually foster the development of a new political sphere in which the dominance of the traditional allies of the colonial regime would be challenged.[4] The law also abolished the punitive levies applied only to the indigenous population, known as the '*impôts arabes*'. While the Jonnart reform may have granted thousands of indigenous men a circumscribed form of influence over politics in the colony, the pressure of the colonial lobby ensured that it left the essential boundary between citizen and subject intact. The fundamental principle of European supremacy remained unchallenged.

The second great reform programme, the Blum-Viollette Project, was also the brainchild of a reforming prime minister, Leon Blum, and a former governor general of Algeria, Maurice Viollette. Articulated in the wake, not of a military conflict but, rather, of a distinctly political conflict, it represented the Popular Front's vision of reform in Algeria. It also reflected the transformation of the political scene in the colony. In the wake of the triumphalist celebration of the centenary of the French invasion in 1930, disgruntled activists began to organize the indigenous community, bringing mass politics

[3] Charles-Robert Ageron, 'Une politique algérienne libérale sous la troisième République (1912–1919): Étude historique de la loi du 4 février 1919', *Revue d'histoire moderne et contemporaine* 6, No. 2 (April–June 1959): 121–51, 144.

[4] Ibid., 148.

to Algeria's colonial subjects.[5] A range of new indigenous reform movements emerged while indigenous workers and activists also swelled the ranks of the left in the colony. The project, the fruit of collaboration between the Algerian left and movements of indigenous reform, envisaged the extension of citizenship within the status to a small portion of the indigenous elite (circa 21,000). These new citizens would vote in a common electoral college with the European community and were to be drawn from the ranks of the indigenous who had proven their loyalty and capacity to serve France, especially during the Great War. Members of the indigenous educated elite, elected officials, and some, but by no means all, veterans stood to benefit from the project's provisions.[6] Although the project was limited in scope, it opened up the possibility of citizenship within the personal status in Algeria, a radical change to the power structure of the colonial system. This, coupled with the incessant attacks on the Popular Front in both metropole and colony, meant that the Blum-Viollette Project, unlike the *Loi Jonnart*, would never make it on to the statute books. Nevertheless, it structured debate around colonial reform at a particularly tumultuous time in the colony's political history.

While the Jonnart reforms and the Blum-Viollette Project reflected metropolitan understandings of colonial reform, political actors on the ground in Algeria articulated their own visions of a new imperial polity. In some cases, these dovetailed with the government's proposed reforms; in others, they directly opposed them. What they all shared, however, was a sense that the war had transformed the relationships underpinning the colonial system and this represented an opportunity to make the colonial order anew. But exactly what form a new settlement for Algeria and the rest of the empire should take was not clear. Actors from both communities in Algeria would have to come up with their own programmes that could effectively mobilize the memory of the Great War to achieve the change they sought.

The Wilsonian Temptation

In the wake of the war, actors from across the colonial world placed their hopes for a new settlement in the colonies in the figure of the American president, Woodrow Wilson. While colonial populations were a 'largely

[5] Jean-Robert Henry, 'Le centenaire de l'Algérie, triomphe éphémère de la pensée algérianiste', in *Histoire de l'Algérie à la période coloniale*, eds. Abderrahmane Bouchène, Jean-Pierre Peyroulou, Ounassa Siari Tengour, and Sylvie Thénault (Paris: La Découverte, 2012): 369–75.

[6] For complete text see Benjamin Stora, *Histoire de l'Algérie Coloniale (1830–1954)* (Paris: La Découverte, 2004), 108.

unintended' audience for Wilson's doctrines, some eagerly adopted his rhetoric as a means to challenge the status quo.[7] Wilson's stipulation, in the fifth of his famous Fourteen Points, that the 'interests' of colonial populations 'must have equitable weight' with the interests of their colonial masters, appealed across the broad spectrum of those who supported expanding indigenous political rights.[8] Meanwhile, settler communities across the colonial world embraced a narrower interpretation of Wilson's vision focused on the national rights of people of European origin, a position entirely compatible with Wilson's own commitment to white racial hegemony.[9] Political elties from across the colonial empires saw that the new post-war order and their place in it was being shaped in Paris. They hoped to secure a voice, or at the very least, a sympathetic ear for their cause at the conference table. But to what extent did this 'Wilsonian Moment', so vividly described by Erez Manela,[10] resonate in post-war Algeria?

The figure most closely associated with Wilsonian thought in Algeria is the Emir Khaled. Khaled, the grandson of Abdelkader, the leader of the resistance against the French invasion, had served with distinction in the French Army during the Great War. He was the only indigenous soldier to reach the rank of captain without renouncing his personal status to become a French citizen. On his return to Algiers after the war, he led a group of activists in a campaign for the extension of greater rights to indigenous subjects. They saw the reforms of the *Loi Jonnart* as 'a step forward'[11] but advocated a more radical overhaul of the colonial system. At the heart of the emir's philosophy stood a commitment to a form of 'equality in difference' that would recognize and protect the culture of Algerians without subordinating them to an oppressive and discriminatory system of rule.[12] What this doctrine meant for the emir's vision of post-war reform is ambiguous. On the one hand, the demand for equality in difference could be interpreted as a plea for citizenship within the personal status. On the other, the emir's doctrine could also align with Wilson's advocacy of a world order defined by the equal recognition of the rights of national groups. Wilson's contestation of the existing world order, even if it was, in reality, only concerned with Europe, opened a space for the expression of more radical political ideas that challenged the imperial status quo. The French colonial authorities recognized this and

[7] Manela, *Wilsonian Moment*, 4. [8] Ibid. [9] Ibid., 26. [10] Ibid.

[11] 'A nos lecteurs et amis', *L'Ikdam*, 7 March 1919.

[12] Ahmed Koulakssis and Gilbert Meynier, *L'Emir Khaled: premier za'îm?* (Paris: L'Harmattan, 1987), 198.

expressed fears that Wilsonian self-determination would 'awaken racial pride and hope of a national revenge among the peoples who had long since lost their independence'.[13] Would the actions of the emir and his supporters in Algeria prove them right?

In May 1919, the emir and his closest allies submitted a petition addressed to 'the honourable President of Free America' to the American delegation at the Paris Peace Conference.[14] The emir's appeal is archetypical of the 'flood of declarations, petitions and memoranda' that various anti-colonial groups sent to the delegation in early 1919.[15] Khaled's adulation of Wilson as the 'standard-bear of law and justice' for the peoples of the world reflected the personal connection politicians from the colonial world felt with the American president.[16] His denunciation of the usurpation of Algerian sovereignty by the French 'occupation' and his use of Wilson's own past declaration that 'no people should be forced to live under a sovereignty it repudiates' shows a conscious effort to frame the Algerian activists' demands in the legalistic language of self-determination. Khaled's call for French sovereignty in the colony to be replaced by the stewardship of the League of Nations and for Algeria's future to be decided at the Peace Conference by 'delegates freely chosen' by the population suggests a clear embrace of Wilsonian principles.[17] The emir and his allies hoped to make Wilson a powerful advocate for their radical vision for a new settlement for Algeria.

For the Emir, like so many of the other petitioners who sought Wilson's support, the experience of the Great War was key to justifying the transformation of the colonial world. Throughout his petition, the emir evoked the notion that this 'immense war' was fought to 'extend' freedom and justice 'to all peoples'. He underlined that Wilson's famous Fourteen Points had been 'accepted by the Allies and the Central Powers' as the basis for peace and thus argued that the post-war settlement must enshrine 'the emancipation of all oppressed peoples, regardless of race or religion'. The emir railed against the fact that indigenous Algerians, who were already 'impoverished, subjugated and debased', were forced to carry the burden of military service without enjoying 'all the rights' of citizenship. Here we see a

[13] 'Report on the Administrative and Political Situation of the Indigenous of Algeria, 1st November 1920–1st February 1921', quoted in Aissaoui, 'Between Two Worlds', 65 and 76, footnote 69.

[14] Charles Robert Ageron, 'La pétition de l'Emir Khaled au Président Wilson (mai 1919)', in *Genèse de l'Algérie algérienne* (Algiers: Editions Bouchène, 2005): 165–78, 168 and 173.

[15] Manela, *The Wilsonian Moment*, 4.

[16] Ageron, 'La pétition de l'Emir Khaled', 174.

[17] Ibid., 171–4.

hint at the contradictory nature of the emir's programme, which seemed, at least in the petition, to advocate an end to French sovereignty while also lamenting the exclusion of the indigenous from the privileges of French citizenship. His summation of indigenous Algerians' experience of the war was, however, more stridently anti-colonial. The emir asserted that 'hundreds of thousands of our sons fell on the battlefields, fighting, against their will, peoples who wished them no ill'.[18] This profoundly subversive statement, which fundamentally challenged the French narrative of the war, sought to tie Algeria's war experience into Wilson's wider critique of multi-national empires, which ruled without popular consent, as agents of conflict.[19] If Algeria was extended the freedom to make its own decision, the emir implied, it would not involve itself in bloody wars on the European continent. Algeria's contribution to the Great War allowed the emir and his allies to stake a claim for inclusion in Wilson's new post-war order of nation-states.

While the emir's petition, like so many others from around the colonial world, went unanswered, it remains an important document for understanding post-war claims-making in Algeria. Both its tone and its content mark a dramatic break with previous forms of political contestation by indigenous elites. The emir did not trumpet the indigenous community's compliance with the 'wartime moral economy of sacrifice' to claim new rights within the empire. Nor did he evoke the 'mutual obligation' established between France and her indigenous subjects to legitimize a reconfiguration of the imperial polity. Rather, he and his allies used the petition to claim that French rule was illegitimate in Algeria and that in the post-war world order Algeria had the right to take her place among the nations. Algeria's leading indigenous activists had, it seemed, turned their back on the quest for citizenship within the status and embraced anti-colonial nationalism.

However, if the petition can be considered evidence of an Algerian Wilsonian Moment, this was both fleeting and muted. The emir and his allies tried to hide their attempts to win over Wilson to their cause. One month prior to the submission of the petition, an article in the group's newspaper *L'Ikdam* rejected 'Wilsonian principles', insisting on Algerians' commitment to the empire, as proven by 'the spilling of their blood' on the battlefields of France.[20] While the fear of the coercive power of the colonial state contributed to this public rejection of self-determination, it also reflected an ideological and strategic divide within the indigenous elite. Most indigenous politicians

[18] Ibid. [19] Manela, *Wilsonian Moment*, 24.
[20] 'La guerre continue', *L'Ikdam*, 5 April 1919.

owed their position in Algerian society in part to the education and/or the public office they had secured under the colonial regime. Many did not share the emir's deep commitment to an Islamic cultural identity.[21] They were uncomfortable with, even hostile toward, any political programme that questioned French sovereignty in Algeria.[22] Their political foes in the European community sought to exploit these divisions in the press, condemning the emir's appeal to Wilson as part of a wider 'insidious campaign to spread disaffection' and eventually secure 'the expulsion of the French'.[23] The emir and his allies distanced themselves from the petition, variously denying or minimizing their attempts to engage with Wilson. Khaled went as far as to challenge his critics to 'prove that I invoked Wilsonian principles to call for the independence of Algeria'.[24] Even if the emir and his closest supporters remained committed to self-determination, and this is a source of much historiographical debate,[25] they realized that Wilsonian principles had little chance of success in the specific colonial context of Algeria. Rather than provoking the ire of the colonial authorities by calling for self-determination, they focused on evoking their war record in defence of a radically different vision of colonial reform: imperial citizenship.

This moderation of his policy platform was not enough to spare the emir from the repressive force of the colonial state. Driven into exile in 1923, he briefly returned to the political scene in 1924 in an alliance with the anti-colonial French Communist Party. Although his address to Algerian migrant workers in Paris denounced the 'pauperization' of the indigenous population, it stopped short of demanding self-determination for the colony. Even in this radical setting, the emir shied away from evoking Wilsonian principles. Instead, he sought to mobilize the memory of Algeria's participation in the Great War to stress the bond of 'mutual obligation' between the colonial state and the subjects who had defended it and to demand new political, civil, and social rights within the empire.[26] The emir's tone was more extreme than most evocations of the war, arguing that France's failure to extend new

[21] Mahfoud Kaddache, *Histoire du nationalisme algérien, Tome I 1919–1939* (Algiers: EDIF, 2003; 1st Edition 2000), 76–8.

[22] Aissaoui, 'Between Two Worlds', 67–8.

[23] Ageron, 'La pétition de l'Emir Khaled', 166.

[24] Ibid., 167.

[25] Ahmed Koulakssis and Gilbert Meynier, *L'Emir Khaled: premier za'îm?* (Paris: L'Harmattan, 1987) and Kaddache, *Histoire du nationalisme algérien Tome I*, 86–102.

[26] Charles-Robert Ageron, 'Enquête sur les origines du nationalisme algérien. L'émir Khaled, petit-fils d'Abd El-Kader, fut-il le premier nationaliste algérien?' *Revue de l'Occident musulman et la Méditerranée* 2, No. 1 (1966): 9–49, 44.

rights after the war meant that Algerians may as well have been fighting for 'the King of Prussia'.[27] He did not, however, call for national independence or a total break with empire. This was not a rerun of indigenous Algeria's brief Wilsonian Moment.

For the remainder of the interwar period, traces of Wilsonian thought were evident in the rhetoric and the programmes of indigenous political movements in Algeria. The emergent nationalist movement, rooted in the Algerian migrant community in the Paris region, had its origins in the radical anti-colonialism of the French Communist Party. The initial programme of the *Étoile Nord-Africaine* (ENA), founded in 1926, blended often contradictory demands influenced by the quest for imperial citizenship, the drive for Wilsonian self-determination, and a Leninist vision of revolutionary anti-colonialism. It simultaneously called for 'equal political rights for indigenous Frenchmen', 'self-determination', and 'the nationalisation by the Algerian state of all property expropriated by the conquerors'.[28] In April 1927, the Wilsonian current in the party pushed for self-determination, asserting that: 'Algerians, like all other peoples, should decide their own future, in line with the declarations of President Wilson and the principles for which the Algerian and French peoples fought side by side from 1914 to 1918'.[29] This type of Wilsonian rhetoric was increasingly sidelined, however, as memories of the post-war 'Wilsonian Moment' receded and the party embraced the revolutionary anti-colonialism favoured by its charismatic and radical leader Messali Hadj.

Under Messali, the party developed an Islam-inflected form of revolutionary nationalism that favoured direct action over the genteel petition writing of the Wilson Moment.[30] His address to the Congress of the International League against Imperialism in Brussels in 1927 set out the movement's commitment to securing 'national independence' through the 'permanent action by all means' of the 'working population' of the colony.[31] It was through a mass nationalist revolution, not a bourgeois quest for Wilsonian self-determination, that Algeria would achieve its independence. This became the central tenet of the ENA and its successor organization, the *Parti du*

[27] Émir Khaled, *La Situation des Musulmans d'Algérie: Conférences faites à Paris les 12 et 19 juillet 1924*, ed. Victor Spielmann (Algiers: Éditions du Trait-d'union, 1924), 4 and 16.

[28] Stora, *Messali Hadj*, 69–70.

[29] Kaddache, *Histoire du nationalisme algérien Tome I*, 176.

[30] Carlier, *Entre Nation et Jihad*, 13 and 38.

[31] 'Discours de Messali Hadj au Congrès de la Ligue contre l'Impérialisme (1927)', in Claude Collot and Jean-Robert Henry, *Le mouvement national algérien, Textes 1912–1954* (Paris: L'Harmattan, 1978), 25–9.

Peuple Algérien (PPA), for the rest of the interwar period. By 1939, the nationalist movement's newspaper *El Ouma* was evoking Wilsonian doctrine solely as a means of highlighting the treachery of imperialism. Those who believed that a post-war settlement would apply 'the principles of Wilson' to the case of Algeria had been 'duped'. Such rights would never be conceded to those sent to 'the butchery of the battlefields' by an empire that was built on 'brutal force', 'plunder', and the 'negation of all justice'.[32] For the nationalists, the goal of self-determination remained central to their political programme, but this was never understood, either strategically or ideologically, in Wilsonian terms. National liberation could not be obtained from a coercive imperial polity through petitioning and parliamentary activity. It required revolutionary action by the masses.

While Wilsonian doctrine proved too weak for the nationalist movement, it was too radical for the indigenous reform movements. The notables of the *Fédération des Elus Musulmans Algériens* (FEMA), a successor movement to the Young Algerians founded in 1928, rejected any form of language that envisaged an end to French rule in the colony, preferring to call for the extension of citizenship within the personal status to indigenous elites. Ferhat Abbas, a leading member of the FEMA,[33] famously rejected the existence of an Algerian nation declaring 'if I had found the Algerian nation, I would be a nationalist... this fatherland does not exist'. He argued that the future of the Algerian people was 'tied definitively to the French project in this land'.[34] For the moderates, evoking the wartime service of Algeria's indigenous community was the best way of promoting a more equal union between the people of Algeria and the French Republic.

Both the rhetoric and the ideology of the Islamic reformists of the *Association des 'Ulama Musulmans Algériens* (AUMA), founded in 1931, seemed to lend itself to the evocation of Wilsonian principles. The organization, which promoted a distinctly Arab and Islamic vision of Algerian identity, condemned Abbas' dismissal of the existence of an Algerian people. The AUMA leader and founder Cheikh Ben Badis wrote a stinging reply to Abbas, asserting 'the Algerian Muslim people is not France, it cannot be and does not want to be... it is a people very distant from France, by language, customs, origins and religion'.[35] This defence of the existence of a distinct

32 'Les Crimes Impérialistes aux noms de Missions civilisatrices', *El Ouma*, May–June 1939.

33 Abbas would later embrace nationalism and serve as the president of the National Constituent Assembly in post-independence Algeria.

34 Ferhat Abbas, 'La France, c'est moi', *L'Entente franco-musulmane*, 27 February 1936.

35 *Ach-Chibab*, April 1936, quoted in Kaddache, *Histoire du nationalisme algerien Tome I*, 395.

Algerian people chimed with the Wilsonian rhetoric deployed by Emir Khaled in May 1919. Indeed, on Khaled's death in 1936, Ben Badis wrote a glowing tribute to the 'venerable Emir' in the AUMA's Arabic-language newspaper, specifically celebrating the petition he sent to Wilson on behalf of the Algerian people.[36] However, the AUMA never adopted Wilsonian rhetoric or policy wholesale. Although its leaders remained hostile towards any form of assimilation that would water down indigenous Algerians' commitment to Islam and Arab culture, they sought the recognition of rights within the existing imperial polity.[37] The AUMA would 'strive to tie bonds of friendship' with France so that the 'weak and backward nation' of Algeria could develop 'under the wing of a strong, just and civilised nation'.[38] The AUMA's public discourse suggested that imperial rule in Algeria was sustained by a social contract of mutual obligation under which indigenous Algerians owed loyalty to the colonial state in exchange for the modernization of their homeland and the protection of their culture. They joined the FEMA and the organizations of the left in the colony in a coalition in support of the Blum-Viollette Project, the *Congrès Musulman Algérien*, where they too would evoke the indigenous communal contribution to the Great War to demand compensation from the colonial state.

While Emir Khaled's brief flirtation shows that indigenous Algerian activists were not immune to the siren calls of the 'Wilsonian Moment', the drive for self-determination never became the dominant force in Algeria that it was elsewhere in the colonial world. A form of self-censorship in the face of a unitary and coercive colonial state certainly played a role in discouraging the use of Wilsonian rhetoric. However, its absence from most political debate in the colony is primarily a reflection of the centrality of notions of citizenship and subjecthood to French colonial politics. The promise of a future possible assimilation of the indigenous population into the ranks of the French citizenry turned most indigenous actors away from calls for self-determination. Instead, they placed their faith in France and hoped for a reconfiguration of the imperial polity in their favour. Those who did dream of a break with empire also largely eschewed Wilsonian rhetoric as they were convinced that the means of winning popular support was not through the petitioning of international legal bodies but rather through mass agitation, by showing the Algerian people that the colonial state was unwilling

[36] *Ach-Chibab*, February 1936, quoted in Ageron, 'La pétition de l'Emir Khaled', 167.
[37] McDougall, *History and Culture of Nationalism*, 64–6.
[38] 'Khitatna', *Al-Muntaqid*, 2 July 1925, quoted in McDougall, *A History of Algeria*, 165.

and unable to change. For indigenous activists, whether they wanted to remain within the empire or not, the question of the rights and responsibilities of all parties within the imperial polity proved far more important than new Wilsonian concepts of the rights and responsibilities of nation-states. They continued to conceive of the relationship between colonial state and colonial subject in terms of 'mutual obligation'. This, inevitably, placed the Great War at the centre of demands for change to the imperial polity.

Algerian Autonomy

If Wilsonian principles were largely absent from the post-war claims-making of indigenous Algerians, what place, if any, did they have in the rhetoric of European community leaders? It might seem counterintuitive to suggest that these staunch opponents of majoritarian rule would embrace Wilsonian doctrine. Surely, the principle of self-determination, if applied in Algeria, would automatically bring an end to their hegemonic position in the colony? Nevertheless, as the American president's personal commitment to racial segregation in America showed,[39] Wilsonian principles were not necessarily incompatible with a political regime based on racial exclusion. While the leadership of the European community never directly appealed to Wilson, and indeed roundly condemned Emir Khaled for having done so,[40] their campaign for enhanced autonomy bore some of the hallmarks of the 'Wilsonian Moment'.

Resentment toward the interference of Paris in the affairs of the colony had fuelled demands for Home Rule among the leaders of the European community since the late nineteenth century.[41] The colony's contribution to the Great War gave new impetus to the quest for autonomy. In the immediate aftermath of the war, figures from the European political class evoked their community's sacrifices to stake a claim for representation at the Paris Peace Conference, the epicentre of the 'Wilsonian Moment'. An article in *L'Echo d'Alger* in February 1919 set out a clear case for the seating of an Algerian delegation alongside those of the British Dominions. After all, was Algeria not 'worth the same as Australia, New Zealand, and Canada?' Were her

[39] Manela, *Wilsonian Moment*, 26.

[40] 'Le Problème de l'Entente et de la Coopération des Races', *La Dépêche Algérienne*, 15 November 1922.

[41] McDougall, *A History of Algeria*, 108.

'sacrifices' in men and money 'less than that of the Dominions of England?'[42] The author also stressed the importance of a settler presence to ensure the colony was not 'sacrificed in the wheeling and dealing of the diplomats'.[43] Like their equivalents across the colonial world, subjects and citizens, the leaders of Algeria's European community understood that a new global political order was being shaped in Paris. Their exclusion from the conference was held up as evidence of the 'little attention' paid to their concerns by those in the metropole. The denunciation of the 'close control' exercised by the metropole, which supposedly amounted to a form of 'subjugation', would not have been out of place in any of the petitions that poured into the American bureau in Paris from across the colonial world.[44] It seemed as though Wilsonian rhetoric had entered the vocabulary of the leaders of Algeria's European community.

The drive to secure a place at the negotiating table in Paris was just one element of the much wider campaign to expand settler autonomy in the colony. Here again the language employed by the European leaders echoed the petitions sent to Wilson. In an editorial entitled 'Algerian Freedoms: Autonomy', the newspaper *L'Évolution Nord-Africaine* evoked participation in the Great War to assert that 'Algeria has reached the age of majority and can no longer live under [the metropole's] guardianship' with its 'odious regime of exception that, all too often, enforce all the duties without giving all the rights'. Defending its claim for an autonomous Algeria, the newspaper rejected accusations of separatism by drawing comparisons with the British Empire, asking 'have the freedoms enjoyed by the English Dominions made separatists of them?'[45] The evocation of the relative autonomy of the British Dominions may seem quite distant from the soaring rhetoric of Wilsonian self-determination. It does, however, bear testimony to the settler leadership's desire to negotiate some form of sovereignty for the colony's European population and its recognition that the post-war moment offered a potential global audience to their cause.

This flirtation with quasi-Wilsonian rhetoric was short-lived among the leadership of Algeria's settler community. The demographic position of the European community as a small minority made them dependent on the coercive power of the French state to maintain their racial hegemony in the colony. In colonial Algeria, the protection of settler primacy always took

[42] 'La représentation de l'Algérie à la conférence de la paix', *L'Echo d'Alger*, 6 February 1919.
[43] Ibid. [44] Ibid.
[45] 'Libertés algériennes: l'autonomie', *L'Évolution Nord-Africaine*, 5 July 1919.

precedence over efforts to expand settler sovereignty.[46] This was not the case in Australia, Canada, and New Zealand, where the eliminatory logic of settler colonialism had established a polity in which settler hegemony was a given and settler sovereignty a goal. These dominions would defend their own specifically imperial vision of self-determination in the wake of the Great War to successfully expand on their already significant autonomy.[47] Such concessions were unimaginable in an Algeria that was both an integral part of the French Republic and a majority-indigenous settler colony. Given the limits of the political space in which they operated, the partisans of autonomy in Algeria would prove far less comfortable with imperial adaptations of Wilsonian rhetoric, choosing to frame their demands in a way that more clearly rooted them in the empire.

Faced with the rise of mass politics among the indigenous population in the 1930s, the leaders of the European community all but abandoned the quest for autonomy, seeking instead to shore up their position within the imperial polity. The Algerian branches of French far-right movements such as the *Croix de Feu*, its successor movement the *Parti Social Français*, and its rival the *Parti Populaire Français* all called for a restoration of discipline in the colony and a new authoritarian imperial polity based on the 'intimate hierarchy' forged in the trenches.[48] Far from seeking to distance Algeria's European community from the empire, these organizations sought to place them at the heart of a new imperial system.[49] The Europeans of Algeria, who had fought alongside the indigenous on the battlefields, were best placed to build this new 'reconciled' empire.[50] Like their rivals in the indigenous community, they too would seek to mobilize their participation in the Great War to justify this reconfiguration of empire.

For the majority of both indigenous and European community leaders throughout the interwar period, the change they sought could only be achieved within a reformed imperial polity. Ideas of Wilsonian self-determination seemed both unrealistic and undesirable. Both groups aspired to a form of imperial citizenship that would enhance their power without

[46] For more on the distinction between these concepts see Dónal Hassett, 'Proud Colons, Proud Frenchmen: Settler Colonialism and the Extreme Right in Interwar Algeria', *Settler Colonial Studies* 17, No. 1 (2017): 1–19, 3–4.

[47] Darwin, 'A Third British Empire?', 68–75.

[48] Sandrine Sanos, *The Aesthetics of Hate: Far-Right Intellectuals, Anti-Semitism and Gender in 1930s France* (Stanford, CA: Stanford University Press, 2013), 223.

[49] See Chapter 4.

[50] Colonel de La Rocque, 'La Plus Grande France', *La Flamme: Organe Nord-Africain de la Réconciliation Française*, 28 January 1939.

compromising their traditional privileges under colonial law. They shared a common belief that the best way to secure this was through the mobilization of the memory of their service in defence of the empire during the Great War. By proving their compliance with the 'moral economy of wartime sacrifice' and insisting on the 'mutual obligation' between the colonial state and its colonial citizens and/or subjects, they could stake a claim for a new, more just post-war colonial order. And what better way to do this than to evoke Algeria's thousands of war dead.

Quantifying the Communal Contribution to the Great War

For any political actor seeking to mobilize a language of 'mutual obligation' in debates surrounding colonial reform, valorizing their own vision of Algeria's contribution to the war was key. Although the campaigns around colonial reform saw the participation of members of both communities on both sides of the debates, the centrality of questions of citizenship and subjecthood resulted in a debate articulated largely in ethnic terms. Thus, when political actors sought to legitimize their programmes, they would stress the compliance of the community they sought to empower with the wartime 'moral economy of sacrifice'. Unsurprisingly, the frontline of this debate would focus on quantifying the contribution of Algeria's ethnic communities to the war.

The supporters of indigenous reform in the immediate aftermath of the war placed their community's sacrifice at the heart of their campaign. The first issue of *L'Ikdam*, the group's newspaper, published 7 March 1919, contained no fewer than four separate articles calling for citizenship within the personal status in terms that evoked the indigenous war dead.[51] In July 1919, a leading collaborator of the emir, Sadek Denden, denounced the *indigénat* in the pages of *l'Ikdam* by specifically evoking the 'more than 200000 indigenous troops, 88000 of whom now sleep eternally'.[52] A week later, an article in the same newspaper would indirectly contradict Denden by citing a set of figures that had appeared in the metropolitan newspaper, *Le Temps*, referring to 177,800 indigenous troops and 56,000 dead. In this article, the stress was on the percentage of deaths among the indigenous contingent, put at '32%', supposedly 'exactly double' the losses experienced by metropolitan contingents, a claim followed by the comment 'this evidence eloquently speaks for

[51] *L'Ikdam*, 7 March 1919.

[52] Sadek Denden, 'L'indigénat', *L'Ikdam*, 5 July 1919.

itself'.[53] The statistical veracity of the death toll was not the central concern of the partisans of indigenous reform. Their goal was to maximize the indigenous contribution and thus legitimize their programme of reform.

When the emir attempted to launch a new political movement, *la Fraternité Algérienne*, he explicitly advocated such a strategy, declaring that the 'first task should be to underline the participation of the indigenous Muslims in the Great War that finished gloriously for our adopted fatherland'.[54] He would go on to offer a statistical reading of the war that inflated the contribution of the indigenous community, claiming the participation of 500,000 indigenous troops, of whom 100,000 died and 20,000 were injured or disappeared. This sacrifice had created 'a sacred debt' which only radical reform could satisfy.[55] His followers were not averse to evoking even higher figures in vague rhetorical terms, with one election candidate demanding reform in the name of 'our brothers who fell in their hundreds of thousands on the battlefields of Charleroi, the Marne, Verdun'.[56] Maximizing the communal compliance with the wartime 'moral economy of sacrifice' served also to maximize the state's obligation to the indigenous community.

The opponents of indigenous reform would also seek to shroud their projects for Algeria's future in the legitimacy conferred by the war dead. Where the emir's supporters focused on headline figures of casualties, their opponents stressed percentage figures, contrasting the proportion of the European population who fell on the battlefields to that of the indigenous community. In June 1919, Ferdinand Ancey presented a report to a settler organization, the *Congrès des Colons*, claiming that, in the department of Algiers, where 24 percent of the European community had been mobilized, that figure stood at only 3 percent for the indigenous community.[57] Ancey used these percentages to ask whether such a level of participation could justify extending to 'all the Muslim people of Algeria' the right to 'merge politically into the mass of the French people'.[58] In September 1920, the column 'Les Propos du Bled' in *La Dépêche Algérienne*, a recurring feature that presented a satirical narrative of life in a small settlement town, sought to introduce the statistical debate to an everyday setting. It recounted the tale

[53] 'Ce que la guerre nous a couté exactement en hommes', *L'Ikdam*, 12 July 1919.
[54] 'Appel de la Fraternité Algérienne aux Musulmans d'Algérie', *L'Ikdam*, 11 August 1922.
[55] Ibid.
[56] Sadek Denden, 'Les prochaines élections', *L'Ikdam*, 30 November 1919.
[57] Ferdinand Ancey, 'La Question Indigène au Congrès des Colons', *L'Evolution Nord-Africaine*, 21 June 1919.
[58] Ibid.

of a young Arab who complains to a European veteran that indigenous youths are banned from the local festival, framing his grievance in terms of his community's wartime contribution: 'You treat us like rotten fish and you, who speak of fraternity; you practice it in your own way by ostracising us and holding us in contempt. However, is it not true that we, the Arabs, saved France?'[59]

The response of his European neighbours is telling. The archetypal war veteran character, *Trois-Quarts de Poilu*, agrees that the indigenous did make an important contribution to the war effort but declares himself sick of hearing them 'go on about it'.[60] His friend, who just happens to have the official numbers on hand, points out, with the help of a detailed table of figures, that 20 percent of the European population were mobilized, while that figure stands at just 3 percent for the indigenous. The Arab is told he does his cause no good by exaggerating his part in the war.[61] This apocryphal scene from the Algerian countryside indicates the extent to which the war and particularly the comparative sacrifice made by each ethnic community now formed part of the quotidian struggle to define power relations in the colony.

Many of the statistical arguments against reform hoped to use the diminution of the indigenous contribution to the war to reduce the state's obligation to the indigenous community. This strategy involved acknowledging the debt born of the indigenous contribution but asserting that the compensation offered by the colonial state was disproportionate. In July 1919, an article by Ancey appearing in the virulently anti-indigenous reform newspaper *La Voix des Colons*, accepted that 'regardless of the number of dead... nothing can diminish the merit of the indigenous troops who did their duty' but asked 'if the compensation, which came quickly, is proportionate to the sacrifices made, however large these were?'[62] This issue of proportionality was echoed by long-time *colon* representative and advocate of autonomy Gustave Mercier. Mercier supplied his own set of percentage figures before arguing that low levels of mobilization had allowed the indigenous to grow rich off the land while the *colon* fought at the front.[63] The implication was clear: the indigenous had profited from his failure to serve, a clear breach of the 'moral economy of sacrifice'. And yet, according to both Mercier and Ancey, the magnanimous *colon* had acknowledged the indigenous contribution to

[59] 'Les Propos du Bled', *La Dépêche Algérienne*, 5 September 1920. [60] Ibid.
[61] Ibid.
[62] Ancey, 'La Question Indigène', *La Voix des Colons*, 20–7 July 1919.
[63] Gustave Mercier, 'L'Autonomie Algérienne, Le Contrôle Métropolitain', *L'Echo d'Alger*, 21 January 1920.

the war and taken upon himself the financial burden of the abolition of the *impôts arabes*.[64] Thus, the Europeans and the state had met their 'mutual obligation' to the indigenous community. Now it was time for the state to tend to the European community.

The manipulation of figures on both sides of the debate did not go unchallenged. Many of the figures produced in the publications hostile to indigenous reform were framed as direct responses to those proffered by Emir Khaled,[65] while Khaled's supporters in turn often reprinted these tables with detailed critiques and yet another set of figures.[66] For political actors in a society still deeply affected by the loss of thousands of men on the battlefields, proving compliance with the wartime 'moral economy of sacrifice' was key to securing political legitimacy. Twisting the figures in one's favour, a practice common across political and ethnic boundaries, was an essential strategy to recalibrate the 'idioms of uneven if mutual obligation' in favour of a particular vision of post-war reform.

In the debates around the Blum-Viollette Project, the proliferation of political movements and the attenuation of the memory of the war displaced the evocation of wartime sacrifices from the hegemonic place it had enjoyed in the immediate post-war moment. Nevertheless, the dispute over the war dead of each community did feature in the polemics of the 1930s. The main defenders of an inflated death toll for the indigenous community came from two groups that had not existed during the Jonnart debates: indigenous veterans' organizations and the nationalists of the ENA/PPA. It is not surprising that indigenous veterans, the self-appointed guardians of the indigenous community's contribution to the war, would seek to inflate the numbers of their fallen comrades, thus maximizing their own claims to legitimacy.[67] This legitimacy would then be lent to the wider campaign in favour of the Blum-Viollette Project, in which indigenous veterans' organizations played an active role (see Chapter 5, The Emergence of the Indigenous Veterans' Associations). The case of the nationalist movement is, perhaps, more surprising,

The nationalists' attitude to participation in the Great War had always differed radically from that of the movements of indigenous reform. Since its foundation, the ENA had developed its own nationalist vision of Algeria's

[64] Ibid. and Ancey, 'La Question Indigène', *La Voix des Colons*, 20–7 July 1919.
[65] 'La Question Indigène: Quelques chiffres précis', *L'Echo d'Alger*, 4 August 1920.
[66] 'La conscription indigène', *L'Ikdam*, 20 January 1922.
[67] See for example the letter from the *Ligue des Anciens Combattants Musulmans de l'Oranie* to the governor general, published in *La Défense*, 23 October 1936, where a death toll of 150,000 is evoked.

past. An article in an early edition of the movement's newspaper, *L'Ikdam Nord-Africain*, offered a new narrative of Algerian history, stressing the armed resistance of indigenous Algerians to French occupation over the communal contribution to French military campaigns. Expressly condemning the strategy of the moderates of the FEMA, who cited the Great War as proof of indigenous loyalty in order to 'better bow down' to the colonial state, the ENA rejected the notion that the indigenous owed any loyalty to a foreign colonial occupier. Rather, it used the failure of the French state to fulfil even the limited promises made to the indigenous Algerians who had defended it as proof of the colonial system's contempt for its subjects.[68]

The ENA's historical vision of Algeria was centred on a blend of military opposition to French occupation through insurrection and socio-cultural resistance through Islam.[69] In this narrative, the indigenous Algerian war dead were not *morts pour la Patrie* who had secured or potentially could secure rights for the indigenous within the empire but rather victims of French colonial oppression. Algeria's future lay in the mobilization of the nation politically, and if need be, militarily. A quote ascribed by police services to Messali Hadj in 1934 may well be apocryphal but it does reflect the ENA's belief in both the right and the duty of Algerians to win back their own sovereignty: 'We want to become the absolute masters in our country that you took by force... Muslim soldiers should be our soldiers and not yours'.[70] In such a narrative, the figure of the indigenous soldier fighting under the French flag was at best a tragic hero, at worst an inconvenient reminder of Algerian submission. The nationalists were, thus, disinclined to employ the evocation of the Great War in their political language as anything other than a symbol of betrayal. Unlike their rivals in the movements of indigenous reform, they were not fighting primarily for political, social, and economic rights within the empire but rather for the right to leave the empire. They rejected the understanding of participation in the war as a *quid pro quo*, an enhanced position for the indigenous in the imperial polity.

Nevertheless, the nationalists did occasionally seek to maximize the numbers of indigenous war dead in their political rhetoric. Their exaggeration of the indigenous death toll served to highlight the enormity, not only of the

[68] 'Contre la représentation au Parlement Français pour un Parlement Algérien', *L'Ikdam Nord-Africain*, December 1927.

[69] Carlier, *Entre Nation et Jihad*, *passim*.

[70] Report of the office of Indigenous Affairs of the Residency General of Morocco, 1–15 October 1934, Archives Nationales d'Outre-Mer, Aix-en-Provence (hereafter ANOM), GGA/3CAB/41.

debt owed by the French state to its indigenous subjects but also of the betrayal that its failure to meet this obligation represented. Writing in the nationalists' newspaper *El Ouma* in January 1934, the ENA leader Messali Hadj condemned the repressive measures of the French state by evoking the '200000 North Africans who died for promises of freedom'.[71] Speaking in Paris later that year, Emilie Busquant-Messali, the French radical and wife of the then imprisoned Messali, seemed to contradict these figures when framing her calls for the 'French people' to show solidarity with the 'oppressed of North Africa' in terms of the 'more than 100000 dead in the war of 14–18'.[72] By October 1938, the nationalists had inflated this figure to several hundreds of thousands, asserting that the only compensation received in exchange for this 'immense sacrifice' was the 'flowery speeches' of French officials.[73] For the nationalists, the exact figures of war dead were unimportant. What mattered was France's betrayal of those who fought and died for the empire. The ENA mobilized this betrayal to dismiss the contention that there was any form of reciprocity of duty in the colonial relationship.

The kinds of numerical disputes that had characterized the Jonnart debates were much less frequent in the political discourse around the Blum Viollette Project. The only major instance of this kind of dispute was as notable for its exceptionality as for the response it elicited. On 14 February 1937, Armand Lemoine, a local elected official, published an article in *La Dépêche Algérienne* under the title 'Truth, Come to the Rescue of France!'.[74] Lemoine attacked what he perceived to be the exaggeration of the indigenous contribution to the war: 'We need to put an end for once and for all with this legend that, all too often, represented the indigenous as having provided to the cause of National Defence during the war a contribution that was an important factor in the victory'.[75] The first response came in an editorial appearing in *La Défense*, a newspaper close to the AUMA, five days later.[76] The author launched a blistering personal attack on Lemoine, dismissing the 'lies and slander' he had used to 'make 190000 Muslim soldiers disappear'.[77] The main rebuttal came from the ranks of the indigenous ex-servicemen with the prominent veterans' activist Tahar Aouidad, a key figure discussed

[71] Messali Hadj, 'Lettre du Comité Central de l'ENA', *El Ouma*, January 1934.
[72] 'Discours de Mme Messali à La Mutualité', *El Ouma*, December 1934.
[73] 'Les derniers évènements internationaux et l'Afrique du Nord', *El Ouma*, 25 October 1938.
[74] Armand Lemoine, 'Vérité, viens au secours de la France', *La Dépêche Algérienne*, 14 February 1937.
[75] Ibid.
[76] 'Patriotisme des embusqués', *La Défense*, 19 February 1937.
[77] Ibid.

in Chapter 5, taking to the pages of both the indigenous and the veteran press to refute Lemoine's claims.[78] Aouidad's article denounced Lemoine as 'an ad-hoc statistician' whose claims 'could not be taken seriously' before asserting that no figure could truly represent the horrors inflicted on those who fought and died for France.[79]

The Lemoine controversy offers two principal insights into the contrast between the role of the war in the debates around the Blum Viollette Project and the *Loi Jonnart*. Firstly, the fact that this seems to have been the only major dispute over the death toll in the mid- to late 1930s is indicative of the diminishing importance of the 'moral economy of sacrifice' over the course of the interwar period. Secondly, the centrality of the indigenous veterans to the campaign against Lemoine showed to what extent these newly politicized actors had become the guardians of the indigenous community's contribution to the war. In the Jonnart debates, politicians, most notably Emir Khaled, had been the primary defenders of both the communal contribution to the war and the general campaign for indigenous reform. As the importance of the link between these two elements of political discourse decreased and as politicians' field of reference points expanded dramatically, the indigenous veterans' movement alone maintained the constant evocation of the war, and thus became the principal defenders of the communal contribution.

Qualifying the Communal Contribution to the Great War

Juggling figures was not the only way in which political actors in post-war Algeria would seek to claim the mantle of the fallen as their own; they would also employ distinct historical visions, both of the war specifically and of Algerian history in general, to optimize the communal contribution which they sought to evoke.

The defenders of reform in the immediate aftermath of the war used a variety of strategies to valorize the indigenous contribution. European supporters of reform praised the fact that the indigenous community had taken on the duties of the citizen to defend the *Patrie* despite not enjoying the privileges of citizenship.[80] Emir Khaled echoed this claim in his famous

[78] *La Défense*, 26 February 1937; *La Justice*, 20 February 1937 and 27 March 1937; *La Voix des Humbles*, January–February 1937; and *La Tranchée*, Second Fortnight, February 1937.

[79] Ibid.

[80] 'Français et musulmans algériens dans la guerre', *La Revue Indigène*, October–December 1921 and the former minister for war and long-time *indigénophile* M. Messimy in 'Banquet Fraternel', *L'Akhbar*, 27 February 1919.

lecture series, following his return from exile to Paris, evoking the 'hundreds of thousands...who died for a country that always considered them "subjects"'. This meant that 'they had to fight to defend rights that they themselves had never possessed'.[81] While there was a difference in tone between the evocation of this argument by Khaled and its use by European supporters of reform, the intent was the same: to simultaneously enhance the indigenous contribution to the war and underline the connection between military service and citizenship rights.

The advocates of reform also emphasized the Great War as the central piece in a wider historical meta-narrative of 'mutual obligation' built up through indigenous participation in French military campaigns. Previous colonial campaigns as far afield as Tonkin and Madagascar and the indigenous involvement in the Franco-Prussian War were linked to the great sacrifices of 1914–18.[82] A particular stress was put on those conflicts, including the Great War, which had pitted indigenous Algerians against other Muslims.[83] By virtue of the long history of their service in the defence of the empire, in which the Great War stood out by virtue of the sheer scale of the sacrifice, the indigenous had earned the right to participate in the French nation.

The opponents of reform offered their own counter-narratives of the wartime experience, minimizing the indigenous contribution and maximizing that of their community. Their rhetoric focused on the range of special regulations governing indigenous recruitment and conscription in an effort to undermine indigenous attempts to equate their service with that of the European and metropolitan contingents. The '*primes de mobilisation*' received by indigenous soldiers was a particularly popular reference point for the anti-Jonnart camp. The existence of the '*primes*' allowed them to portray the indigenous troops as mercenaries, fighting for money, not for the defence of the nation.[84] Furthermore, the wealth garnered from the '*primes*' fed into a growing fear in the post-war period that the indigenous, having profited from the war, were buying up European-owned land.[85] Yet again, European political leaders insisted that the lesser contribution of the

[81] Khaled, 'La Situation des Musulmans d'Algérie', 16.

[82] 'Représentation des Indigènes Algériens au Parlement', *L'Ikdam*, 13 January 1922 and 'Protestation M. Tyeb Guedda, sous-officier en retraite, mutilé de guerre', *L'Ikdam*, 9 February 1923.

[83] 'Les grands problèmes coloniaux: l'Islam et la politique des Alliés', *L'Ikdam*, 18 March 1921 and 'Représentation des Indigènes Algériens au Parlement', *L'Ikdam*, 13 January 1922.

[84] 'La masse indigène et la guerre', *L'Afrique Latine*, 15 July 1922, 124.

[85] Ancey, 'La Question Indigène', *La Voix des Colons*, 20–7 July 1919.

indigenous community was being unduly rewarded at the expense of the state's greater obligation to the Europeans.

For the opponents of indigenous reform, the loyalty of most of the indigenous community was tempered by incidents of resistance that occurred during the war. The mainstream settler press was careful not to undermine the image of overwhelming loyalty, which they held up as evidence of the indigenous satisfaction with the status quo. They presented the revolts of 1916 as exceptional but still representative of the potential violence of the indigenous and their susceptibility to agitation.[86] Radical opponents of reform were much more open in their condemnation of indigenous treachery during the war. Speaking before the settler organization the *Congrès des Colons*, Ferdinand Ancey claimed that indigenous unrest during the war was the product of pan-Islamist propaganda and insisted that Emir Khaled's campaign was simply a continuation of these revolts by other means.[87] *L'Afrique Latine*, in its extensive dossier of allegations seeking to minimize the indigenous contribution, combined an evocation of wartime unrest with a reference to the case of Boukabouya, the indigenous officer who had defected to the Germans. It concluded that these examples, when taken with the whole range of 'evidence' of indigenous treachery, denied the indigenous community the right to claim any form of compensation.[88] For both the radicals and the mainstream press, the instances of unrest during the war served to recalibrate the relationship of 'mutual obligation' against the indigenous community.

In the Blum-Viollette debates, questions about how to define and qualify the communal contribution took a radically different form. The kinds of arguments presented by the opponents of the *Loi Jonnart* did occasionally resurface but the vigilance of the indigenous veterans' movements saw any attempt to question the quality and quantity of the indigenous contribution to the war vigorously rebuffed.[89] Crucially, a new debate was emerging within the indigenous community, as both the nationalists and the supporters of Blum-Viollette sought to reshape understandings of the communal contribution to French military campaigns. The war remained an important reference point for movements seeking indigenous reform, but was now more firmly placed in a wider narrative about indigenous service in the French

[86] 'Le Problème de l'Entente et de la Coopération des Races', *La Dépêche Algérienne*, 27 August 1922.
[87] Ancey, 'La Question Indigène', *La Voix des Colons*, 20 July 1919.
[88] 'La masse indigène', *L'Afrique Latine*, 15 July 1922, 129.
[89] 'Communiqué—Nos anciens combattants protestent', *La Défense*, 29 March 1935.

military, with a particular stress on participation in the Riff, Syrian, and Lebanese campaigns.[90] Undoubtedly, the fact that these campaigns were more recent than the Great War fed into their prominence, but also the increased awareness of Algeria's place in a wider Muslim and Arab world played a part in the reframing of the narrative of military service. The specific Islamic nature of the conflicts was underlined by partisans of further reform, whether these were pro-Blum-Viollette campaigners or the radical nationalists of the ENA.

For the supporters of Blum-Viollette, the fact that indigenous troops served against their Muslim brothers underlined their total commitment to their obligation to the French imperial state. Dominique Cianfarani, a senior figure in the department of Constantine's Popular Front, evoked the fact that 'they had not hesitated to take up arms against their coreligionists' not only to counter anti-reform hysteria around pan-Islamism, but also to underline the state's duty to respond to its obligations.[91] A November 1937 article in *L'Entente Franco-Musulmane* stressed that the 'hundreds of thousands of Muslims' were willing 'despite their personal status' to serve and even 'to kill their brothers in Morocco, in Syria etc., so that French sovereignty would live'.[92] Evoking indigenous participation in French military campaigns that pitted Muslim against Muslim, including but not limited to the Great War, was a key strategy to recalibrate the measure of 'mutual obligation' in their favour and to highlight the compatibility of the personal status with the duties of citizenship.

For the nationalists of the ENA/PPA, indigenous service against other Muslims exposed the oppressive nature of the colonial state, where obligation was never mutual. The Algerian nationalist movement had always viscerally opposed indigenous participation in military campaigns in the service of French imperialism, especially when this implied conflict with other Muslims.[93] The ENA's political programme demanded 'full respect for the Koranic sura, that says: "he who deliberately kills a Muslim is bound for Hell for eternity and should be cursed"'.[94] The French state's failure to honour these precepts was just the latest in the litany of betrayals, including the failure to reward the sacrifices of the Great War, that formed the

[90] 'Notre Statut Electoral', *La Défense*, 12 February 1937 and 'En marge du Projet Viollette', *L'Entente Franco-musulmane*, 4 November 1937.

[91] Police Commissioner of Batna to the Sous-Préfet, 26 March 1937, ANOM/91/2I/39.

[92] 'En marge du Projet Viollette', *L'Entente Franco-Musulmane*, 4 November 1937.

[93] See Kaddache and Guennanèche, *L'Etoile nord-africaine 1926–1937*, 43–5.

[94] 'Programme de l'ENA', May 1933, in ibid., 59.

nationalist's narrative of colonial rule.[95] Thus, the Great War was tied into a wider meta-narrative of colonial rule in which the economy of wartime sacrifice was far from moral and obligation was unidirectional, the product of the coercive power of the system.

Assessing Personal and Group Sacrifice

While establishing the communal contribution to the war had important implications for the wider justification of programmes of reform, the war record of individual or collectives of political actors could potentially enhance or diminish their legitimacy to represent their community. The challenges to communal contributions were also replicated on a personal and/or group level as political rivals sought to undermine their opponents by calling into question their compliance with the 'moral economy of wartime sacrifice'.

In the years after the war, it became a truism for opponents of reform that indigenous intellectuals had shirked their responsibility to fight.[96] Anti-reform editorialists asserted that the only indigenous demanding civil and political rights were those Young Algerians who had shirked their wartime duties.[97] While these attacks fed into the general attempt to minimize the indigenous communal contribution, the principal aim was to undermine the intellectual elite's right to express the indigenous community's post-war demands. These effeminate intellectuals, with 'their long finely-combed hair in the latest style', were attempting 'to harvest' the crop that 'the landless labour, the share-cropper…their poor Muslim brothers' had fertilized with their blood.[98] By excluding the Young Algerians as a group because of their alleged failure to comply with the 'moral economy of sacrifice', the opponents of indigenous reform hoped to reorient the debate on the post-war colonial order away from dangerous political reforms and towards a social and economic programme that would not challenge European hegemony.

The attack on the war record of the educated indigenous elite or *évolués* was to resurface in the Blum-Viollette debates. Under the project's provisions, only those veterans who had been awarded both the *médaille millitaire* and the *Croix de Guerre* were to receive citizenship within the status. The bulk of

[95] 'Les derniers évènements internationaux et l'Afrique du Nord', *El Ouma*, 25 October 1938.

[96] 'La Question indigène', *L'Echo d'Alger*, 17 August 1919; *La Voix des Colons*, 31 August 1919; and *L'Afrique Latine*, 15 July 1922, 124–9.

[97] 'Fantaisie sur les fess', *L'Évolution Nord-Africaine*, 17 April 1919.

[98] 'Un professeur qui a son franc-parler', *L'Évolution Nord-Africaine*, 19 July 1919.

indigenous veterans would not benefit at all. Thus, it is hardly surprising that its opponents would contrast the war record of those set to benefit from the project with that of the veterans, who were largely excluded from it. In January 1937, *La Dépêche Algérienne* denounced the fact that the indigenous elites, 'few of whom had fought in the war' but many of whom had profited from it by occupying the jobs left by mobilized Europeans, would benefit from the project's provisions while indigenous veterans were left empty-handed.[99] The newspaper repeated this accusation against 'M. Ferhat Abbas and friends' the following year and the theme was taken up by campaigners against the project.[100] This strategy not only attacked the elite's worthiness to benefit from reform on the basis of its war record, but also cast the intellectuals as war profiteers, living off the back of the suffering of their compatriots, indigenous and European. Thus, the Blum-Viollette Project, far from complying with the 'moral economy of sacrifice', was rewarding the profiteers and *embusqués* of the indigenous intellectual elite over those indigenous who had actually fought in the war.

The supporters of indigenous reform in the Popular Front period were not above attacking their political opponents' war records. Again, such critiques were both diminished in number and altered in nature by the context in which they occurred. In these debates, individual war records were almost only ever evoked as part of wider discussions around the war, usually involving veterans. While veterans were present as an abstract group in the rhetoric of the opponents of the project, they represented an active and important collective in the pro-Blum-Viollette campaign. Drawing their legitimacy from their contribution to the war, they were quick to attack the war records of their opponents. The Lemoine controversy was a prime example of this. In his rejection of Lemoine's attack, the veteran leader Tahar Aouidad's was quick to point to his opponent's dubious war record: 'It is, for us, an unpleasant surprise that he, the strapping young fellow of 1914 who did not hesitate to hide behind his job title and whose knowledge of the war came only from reading official communiqués, now loudly declares his delayed and ill-timed patriotism.'[101] The editorials in the indigenous press

[99] 'Le projet du gouvernement sur la représentation des indigènes', *La Dépêche Algérienne*, 10 January 1937.

[100] 'Le Salut des Algériens dépend de la fermeté qu'ils mettront à défendre leurs droits de citoyens', *La Dépêche Algérienne*, 5 March 1938.

[101] *La Défense*, 26 February 1937, 'A Lemoine l'embusqué', *La Justice*, 20 February 1937 and 27 March 1937, *La Voix des Humbles*, January–February 1937 and 'Encore un détracteur', *La Tranchée*, Second Fortnight, February 1937.

echoed this argument, seizing on Lemoine's absence from the front to dismiss him as an '*embusqué*' and thus strip his claims of any legitimacy.[102]

For the nationalists, convinced that any 'mutual' relationship was impossible within the framework of the colonial system, the figure of the *embusqué* served to convey the injustice underpinning colonial rule to the metropolitan French. In the nationalists' direct appeals to the French public, the *embusqué* occasionally appeared alongside other key French reference points such as the rhetoric of the French Revolution or the language of the revolutionary and republican left. Following the arrest of Messali Hadj in early 1938, *El Ouma* printed an appeal to the people of France complaining that those who evoked the nation to resist the extension of rights to the indigenous were the same people who had failed to defend the nation in the Great War. Whereas the Algerians 'gave such brave soldiers in 1914', the 'self-proclaimed patriots of 1938', the 'rapacious Lemoines' who sought only 'to maintain the totality of their privileges', had been '*embusqués* in 1914'.[103] The following month the Central Committee of the PPA issued an appeal to the 'Republicans of France' to support the nationalists against 'settler profiteers and fascist *embusqués* of 1914'.[104] The condemnation of the *embusqué* opponents of reform highlighted for a metropolitan audience that the colonial regime was unwilling, if not unable, to respect the 'moral economy of wartime sacrifice'. While the *embusqué* was a minor reference point in nationalist discourse, it is nevertheless interesting to note the continued scorn expressed by those who challenged French sovereignty for those who had failed to defend it during the war.

The multitude of ways in which political actors in interwar Algeria attempted to define, defend, and denigrate communal contributions is testament to the potential legitimacy to be gained from the war sacrifice. Unsurprisingly, such tactics were omnipresent in the debates in the immediate post-war period. The Jonnart reforms were universally understood as some form of recognition of the 'mutual obligation' between the colonial state and its subjects. The supporters of reform sought to enhance the indigenous contribution with a view to deepening the state's obligations to its subjects and thus opening the door to far wider reform. For opponents

[102] 'Patriotisme d'un embusqué', *La Défense*, 19 February 1937 and 'Le pacifisme et la question indigène', *La Voix des Humbles*, May 1937.

[103] 'Les atrocités de l'administration algérienne', *El Ouma*, 22 April 1938.

[104] 'Un manifeste du PPA', *El Ouma*, 27 May 1938.

of indigenous reform, undermining the indigenous contribution not only weakened the case for wide-ranging reforms but also paved the way for the European community to evoke their own relationship of 'mutual obligation'. By the mid- to late 1930s, the war no longer dominated understandings of the relationship between colonial state, subject, and citizen. The memory of the conflict had attenuated and the nature of politics had fundamentally changed, with the massification and internationalization of political culture, particularly among the indigenous. And yet, debates over communal and individual contributions to the war endured. The rise of the indigenous veterans' movements, charted in Chapter 5, meant that at least one significant interest group would continue to think of reform in the terms of 'mutual obligation' born of the war. This in turn would ensure that the war remained a reference point available for actors on all sides of the political debate to manipulate and evoke to serve their own agendas. Nevertheless, the radical differences in the contexts of each project would have important implications. The increasing awareness of international politics and particularly of a wider Islamic identity fed into the attempts by both pro- Blum-Viollette campaigners and the nationalists to redefine 'mutual obligation' in light of indigenous participation in conflicts against other Muslims. The specific provisions of Blum-Viollette would see anti-indigenous reformers embrace the veteran cause in a way unimaginable in the Jonnart debates. In the end, the most enduring feature of the struggle to define, defend, and denigrate communal contributions was the very flexibility of 'idioms of uneven if mutual obligation'.

Evaluating the Reciprocal Relationship

Over the course of the interwar period, political actors not only asserted their compliance with the 'moral economy of wartime sacrifice' but also constantly assessed the French government's efforts to compensate them for their wartime service. The extent to which France was seen to be meeting its responsibility to those who had served it shaped attitudes toward colonial reform across the political spectrum in the colony.

Critiques of France's failure to meet her 'mutual obligation' were often comparative, questioning why others, perhaps less deserving, had been rewarded while the indigenous population remained subject to an unjust colonial administration. In support of their claim for naturalization within the status, the proponents of radical indigenous reform constantly cited the imperial precedent: the case of the *originaires* of Senegal.[105] As one activist put it 'we are not asking for special treatment' but rather 'justice', a fulfilment of the 'many promises of republican and democratic France' through the 'assimilation of our status with that of our coreligionists from Senegal'.[106] Their argument was not grounded in some abstract concept of universal racial equality. Rather, pleas for the extension of citizenship within the status were framed in terms of the increasingly dominant concept of Greater France, a multi-racial empire with its different racial families gathered under the tricolour, as they had been on the battlefields.[107] The imperial precedent was not simply a justification for naturalization within the status; it also represented an overt criticism of the French government's failure to recognize its 'mutual obligation' to the indigenous population of Algeria as it had done for their colonial brothers.

The naturalization *en masse* of 5,000 Maltese settlers in Tunisia in November 1921 once more highlighted the French government's failure to pay its debt to Algeria's indigenous population. *L'Ikdam* drew a contrast between the indigenous, who 'had been in the trenches' and 'were first in the line of fire and last everywhere else', while the Maltese-Tunisians, who had 'stayed at home', were granted the vote and citizenship.[108] Whereas Clemenceau had famously declared that 'veterans have rights over us', Khaled's supporters argued that the granting of citizenship to Maltese-Tunisians meant that they had 'rights over' indigenous veterans.[109] For the *Khaledistes*, a form of European racial kinship had won out over the sacred bond forged on the battlefield.

Above all, however, it was the perceived collaboration between the colonial authorities and the political leadership of the European community that most incensed the supporters of indigenous reform. Their campaign against reform made a mockery of the wartime moral code, suggesting to indigenous Algerians that their 'excellent service only served to increase the hatred, the animosity of the Europeans of Algeria against' them.[110] As a

105 'Réponse à l'Echo d'Alger', *L'Ikdam*, 29 March 1919, Emir Khaled, 'Ne pourrions-nous pas avoir voix au chapitre?', *L'Ikdam*, 27 January 1919, Emir Khaled, 'Riposte de l'Emir Khaled au journal 'L'Algérie', *L'Ikdam*, 9 June 1922, and 'Problèmes Musulmans d'Algérie, une conversation avec l'Emir Khaled', *L'Ikdam*, 22 December 1922.

106 'L'ère Nouvelle', *L'Ikdam*, 4 August 1922.

107 Wilder, *The French Imperial Nation-State*, 24.

108 *L'Ikdam*, 6 January 1922, *L'Ikdam*, 13 January 1922, and *L'Ikdam*, 3 February 1922.

109 *L'Ikdam*, 20 January 1922.

110 'Le Peuple faible, ignorant et oppressé n'est pas fautif', *L'Ikdam*, 20 October 1922.

transformation of the colonial system grew increasingly unlikely, the most radical *Khaledistes*, including the emir, began to condemn the whole structure of imperial rule. In late 1922, the emir openly condemned the *Loi Jonnart* as window-dressing on the part of the colonial regime.[111] By the following year, he was denouncing the 'desperate mirage' of reform, arguing that those 'who fought to save the country' had become the 'pitiful playthings' of the colonial administration.[112] For the emir, the French had betrayed those who had served her during the war.

The treachery of the colonial state was also a motif in the campaign against indigenous reform. As early as March 1919, *L'Echo d'Alger* charged the French government with 'taking advantage' of wartime conditions to impose a reform that would have serious consequences for the European community. While the men of the European community 'were still at the front', the government 'treacherously dealt us a hammer blow' by introducing a reform that was 'just the beginning' of a wider effort to undermine European hegemony.[113] The following year, the indigenous press reported on a speech allegedly given by a European politician in which he denounced colonial reform as a betrayal of settler soldiers, quoting him as saying 'while we are riddled with bullets from the front, they shoot us in the back'.[114] European political leaders constantly evoked this settler version of the 'stab-in-the-back legend' throughout the anti-reform campaign in the immediate aftermath of the war.

By the 1930s, the rise of contestatory mass politics among the indigenous shifted the emphasis for opponents of radical colonial reform onto the state's duty to meet its obligation to the indigenous population. For some among the staunchest opponents of indigenous reform, the *Loi Jonnart*, which they had once fiercely opposed, had sufficiently rewarded the indigenous communal contribution and, thus, no further reform was needed. This was the position adopted by the deputy for Constantine, Emile Morinaud, who claimed that the post-war promises to the indigenous had 'been fulfilled by the law of 1919'.[115] Other leaders in the anti-indigenous reform camp were willing to concede that greater efforts were required of the colonial state.

[111] Emir Khaled, 'Ni française, ni arabe mais étrangère', *L'Ikdam*, 3 November 1922.

[112] 'L'Emir Khaled rappelle la situation privilégiée des Européens en Algérie', *L'Ikdam*, 16 March 1923.

[113] 'Le Réveil des Consciences', *L'Echo d'Alger*, 26 March 1919.

[114] 'La Question Indigène au Conseil Supérieur', *L'Ikdam*, 6 January 1922.

[115] 'M. Morinaud montre que le projet Viollette constitue une monstruosité', *L'Echo d'Oran*, 4 February 1938.

They contended, however, that the provisions of the project, far from satisfying the debt born of the war, represented a betrayal of the wartime 'moral economy of sacrifice'. By privileging a tiny elite, the Popular Front government was abandoning the vast majority of the indigenous community and in particular those who had fought for France.[116]

The range of alternative projects proposed by the opponents of Blum-Viollette claimed to balance the different obligations of the state to the people of Algeria. They included a form of parliamentary representation, elected from a special college, which would allow the indigenous community to defend its interests while maintaining its cultural difference.[117] They gave priority to economic and social measures as a means of effecting tangible improvements on the lives of the allegedly politically apathetic and ignorant masses.[118] Above all, the opponents of Blum-Viollette left the barrier between the personal status and citizenship intact. Fulfilling the state's obligation to the indigenous community could not come at the cost of its deeper obligation to the European community.

Many of the motifs that had shaped the rhetoric of the campaigns of the immediate post-war period were once more present in the language of the supporters of Blum-Viollette. The Senegalese precedent remained an important point of reference both in the press[119] and in the public meetings[120] of the FEMA, the AUMA, and the other organizations of the *Congrès Musulman*. Similarly, the defenders of the project again highlighted groups, who they felt had unjustly been prioritized over them. They targeted Europeans of non-French origin, a major support base for their political opponents, asking why a 'Calabrian just off the boat' had the right to vote while those who had 'defended the territory, the honour and the prestige of France in 1914' had not.[121] United under the banner of the *Congrès Musulman*, the mass movements of indigenous reform anchored their joint programme in a demand for equality that would honour the French government's obligation to the indigenous, demanding 'that the same duties, especially *l'impôt du sang*, be rewarded with the same rights'.[122]

[116] 'Le Projet Blum-Viollette n'est qu'un don de la démagogie', *La Dépêche Algérienne*, 28 December 1937.

[117] 'L'opinion algérienne est hostile au projet Viollette', *La Dépêche Algérienne*, 8 January 1937.

[118] 'La question indigène et les réformes nécessaires', *La Dépêche Algérienne*, 29 May 1936.

[119] 'La Représentation Parlementaire', *La Défense*, 19 June 1936 and G. Laux, 'Les revendications des Anciens Combattants Musulmans Nord-Africains', *L'Entente Franco-Musulmane*, 2 June 1938.

[120] Police Commissioner of Aïn-Beïda to the Prefect, 3 May 1937, ANOM/91/2I/39.

[121] 'Bluff et Chantage', *La Défense*, 10 March 1938.

[122] 'Le peuple musulman fête l'anniversaire du Congrès', *La Défense*, 9 July 1937.

The content of the proposed reforms was not the only change in context between the Jonnart and Blum-Viollette debates: the intervening period had seen the rise of mass political movements among the indigenous community and an increasing impatience with the lack of governmental reform. Political actors from across the pro-indigenous reform camp constantly evoked the failure of the state to meet the obligations born of the war. In its first issue, *La Défense* was unambiguous in its attitude to the governmental reform record, highlighting a long history of the administration repaying wartime service with great promises and then acting 'in absolute contradiction to it words'.[123] The pro-reform *La Justice* was even more forthright in its criticism. An article that appeared in the paper in November 1934 powerfully contrasted the sacred sacrifice of the Algerian war dead with the post-war treatment meted out to their community by men who had spent the war far from the front:

> Sixteen years of promises and lies. Over there [in the metropole], the rain falls heavily on the Muslim graves of the front; here, the millions earned through pride and infamy pay for the chains that oppress you, Governors insult you, cowardly scum confront you... They scammed their way through the war.[124]

While not all actors shared *La Justice*'s sense of anger and cynicism, there was certainly an element of truth in the assertion by the newspaper's editor that 'the indigenous man of 1934 is no longer that of 1914'.[125] The supporters of indigenous reform carried with them the weight of a series of broken promises that served as both a cautionary tale about the trustworthiness of governmental reform projects and a further justification for the need for an immediate and comprehensive reform. They would be vigilant in their campaign to hold the Popular Front to its promises.

While the supporters of the Blum-Viollette Project continued to hope that total emancipation could come through the government in Paris, Messali Hadj's nationalists were clear in their rejection of that possibility. An appeal launched by the ENA in 1927 left little doubt as to the credence it lent to French promises which had been used 'in 1914–1915 to lure us into the war' only for the government to 'take back all they had given once the immediate

[123] 'Procédés d'un autre âge', *La Défense*, 2 February 1934.
[124] 'Après la Victoire en Commun', *La Justice*, 15 November 1934.
[125] 'A nos frères européens d'Algérie', *La Justice*, 4 March 1935.

danger had passed'.[126] Nevertheless, the group had initially aligned itself with the Popular Front, won over by its commitment democratic and social emancipation. The 'great disappointment' that followed simply reinforced the notion that French politicians were not to be trusted.[127] The group's rejection of the Blum-Viollette Project shared a common thread with the European opponents of the reform, in arguing that it did not represent a just compensation for the state's obligation. Their vitriolic attacks on elements of the reform's supporters as a self-serving elite willing to sacrifice the masses in pursuit of their own ambitions would not have been out of place in the *colon* press.[128] And yet, the nationalists carried their critique in a radically different direction to their European foes. They cited the limitation of the project to a small section of the population as further proof of the colonial state's unwillingness and incapacity to expand the rights of the indigenous. The project represented yet more 'tragic trickery' on the part of the French political class who served only their own interests.[129]

Political actors in both the Jonnart and Blum-Viollette debates displayed a keen awareness of the state's obligations born of participation in the Great War. Communal understandings of the duties of the colonial state allowed political actors to judge the state's record in comparative terms, pitting their vision of the treatment they received from the state against the favours accorded to others. The Great War and the relationship of reciprocity it had supposedly fostered between colonial state, colonial citizen, and colonial subject thus became a key point of reference in the constantly shifting debates around colonial reform in interwar Algeria.

Conclusion

The mass mobilization of hundreds of thousands of Algeria's inhabitants during the Great War inevitably left its mark on debates over the colony's place in the post-war imperial polity. As this chapter has shown, for the majority of political actors in the colony, the most promising strategy for securing new rights was to highlight the colonial state's duty to compensate

[126] 'Un appel de l'Etoile Nord-Africaine', in Kaddache and Guenaneche, *L'Etoile nord-africaine 1926–1937*, 46–7.

[127] Messali, 'Le Front Populaire et le Problème Nord-Africain', *El Ouma*, May–June 1936.

[128] 'Peuple algérien où vas-tu?', *El Ouma*, August–September 1936 and 'Peuple Algérien, Dresse-toi contre le Projet Viollette', *El Ouma*, January 1936.

[129] 'Congrès algérien et Front Populaire', *El Ouma*, 1 July 1937.

those who had served in its defence. And what better way to do this than maximize their own wartime contribution and minimize that of their opponents. The result was a political debate shot through with references to the 'moral economy of wartime sacrifice' and centred on the notion of a 'mutual obligation' between the inhabitants of Algeria and the colonial system that governed them.

Colonial reform in Algeria would always be discussed in communal terms. And yet, even in this most Manichean aspect of political life in Algeria, one of the key languages employed by political actors was shared across ethnic lines. Both the supporters and the opponents of indigenous reform in interwar Algeria employed a common language articulated around notions of 'mutual obligation' and the 'moral economy of sacrifice' to support directly opposing political programmes. Ethnicity, and its corollary legal status, still had a major bearing on the extent to which the demands expressed in this language would be met. The restriction of the *Loi Jonnart* and the failure of the Blum-Viollette Project speak for themselves in this regard. Nonetheless, the Great War served as a common and potentially polysemous point of reference through which political actors in interwar Algeria would frame their demands for colonial reform.

The notion, shared across ethnic and ideological boundaries, that the imperial polity could be restructured to reward those who had ensured its survival on the battlefields, shaped demands for colonial reform throughout the period. While certain actors did flirt with the idea that their community's contribution to the war should pave the way for the loosening of, if not liberation from, the bonds of empire, most politicians in Algeria believed their future lay in a renewed relationship of 'mutual obligation' within a reformed imperial polity. Even those who secretly petitioned Wilson for his support for an independent Algerian state or hoped to make of Algeria a new Canada, or more appropriately, South Africa, dedicated most of their efforts to securing and improving their respective constituencies' positions within the existing colonial framework. The nationalists, alone in their commitment to ending empire in Algeria, recognized that mass support could only come once the Algerian people were convinced that the colonial state would not and could not meet its duties to them. The concept of 'mutual obligation', so closely tied to the colony's wartime contribution, was thus at the heart of the discourse even of those who sought to end French rule in Algeria. Like more mainstream political actors in the colony, they too would seek to impose their narrative of the Great War to legitimize their vision of Algeria's future.

The use of a certain language was, as Bakhtin underlined, never neutral. In both the immediate post-war debates and those that took place under the Popular Front government, evoking the war was a means of speaking to the colonial administration and, indeed, to society at large, in a language that was recognized as legitimate. This legitimacy, however, came at a certain cost. For the partisans of further colonial reform from the indigenous elite, their defence of the indigenous community's fulfilment of the 'moral economy of sacrifice' left them open to charges that they themselves could not proffer a glowing war record. This reinforced the long-standing argument employed by their opponents who asserted that elite demands for citizenship were driven by self-interest, with no regard for the indigenous masses. The specific provisions of Blum-Viollette, which excluded many veterans, would further compound this. By anchoring their vision of Algeria in the glory days of the *Union Sacrée*, mainstream opponents of extensive colonial reform had to recognize the state's duty to in some way reward indigenous participation in the war. While they sought to minimize this obligation, they would, at least by the time of the Blum-Viollette debates, have to offer an alternative vision how the indigenous community's position in the post-war order could be improved. Their position became intrinsically defensive: their own hopes of reshaping the relationship between metropole and colony in their favour faded as the defence of European hegemony took priority. For the nationalists, the evocation of the Great War may have served to highlight French betrayal of the indigenous community but it also undermined their attempt to build a historical narrative grounded in the resistance of indigenous Algerians to French colonial rule. And yet, despite all the disadvantages and unforeseen consequences of framing their demands in the language of the Great War, political actors on all sides of the debate on colonial reform continued to speak in terms of 'mutual obligation' and the 'moral economy of sacrifice', to greater or lesser extents, throughout the interwar period. For all its unwieldiness, a language of claims-making grounded in the Great War was still perceived by actors across political and racial divides in the colony to be particularly effective.

3
Social Claims in the Shadow of the Fallen

On 1 May 1919, crowds of workers gathered on the streets of Algeria's major cities to celebrate the first May Day since the Armistice. Marching side by side, workers of all ethnic and religious backgrounds called for the transformation of society. In the wake of a war in which death and suffering had known no racial boundaries, the Algerian left united in a class-based front to demand economic, social, and political compensation for the participation of the working class in the defence of the nation. The left's support for a post-war settlement based on the wartime moral code mobilized thousands under the banner of the labour movement across the colony in the years immediately after the war. This was countered by the mass mobilization conservative forces in Algeria, who presented an altogether different vision of the war and its legacy. Into this already explosive mix was thrown the contentious issue of the post-war rights of indigenous workers and their place both in the labour movement and in colonial society as a whole. This chapter explores this post-war moment of social conflict in the colony, exposing the competing visions of the Great War that underlay the clash between left and right.

At the heart of my analysis lies the contention that right and left understood the legacy of the Great War in fundamentally distinct ways. For the right, the war was about the 'fraternity of arms', a national unity forged on the battlefield that respected social and colonial hierarchies. For the left, the war necessitated a reordering of society on the basis of the 'equality of sacrifice', ensuring that the working class claimed their stake in the post-war settlement. The place of the indigenous worker in this vision was, as we shall see, both ambiguous and controversial. In the years immediately after the war, these rival visions were pitted against each other on streets and factory floors and in newspapers and ballot boxes across the colony.

Algeria's Left and the Great War

The Great War had an 'accelerator effect' on the Algerian labour movement.[1] During the war, the contact of European and indigenous soldiers and workers with their metropolitan equivalents fostered a new understanding of the universal mission of socialism.[2] In its immediate aftermath, the prevailing social conditions favoured an expansion of the left's extremely limited influence among the urban working classes. The local branch of the French Socialist Party (SFIO) in Algeria, with an estimated total of 750–1,000 members in large urban areas across the colony,[3] had signed up to Algeria's version of the *Union Sacrée* in the early days of the war. As the conflict dragged on, the French left grew increasingly sceptical of continued participation in the *Union Sacrée*, reflecting the war-weariness of the population in general and the working class in particular. In 1917, this led to an upsurge in industrial action on the Home Front,[4] paralleled by the mass mutinies at the frontlines.[5] In Algeria, a land far from the front where the demographics and political structure of colonial rule militated against collective action among the masses, the echoes of this discontent were much more restricted. Nevertheless, a shared hatred of speculators and profiteers gave rise to a limited class front between poorer Europeans and elements of the indigenous masses, particularly in the west of the colony. Protests against profiteers brought together Europeans and indigenous in the cities and towns of Oran, Sidi-Bel-Abbès, Mostaganem, Saint-Denis-du-Sig (Sig), and Perrégaux (Mohammadia), all areas of a high working-class European population.[6] The sense that the suffering was not being shared equally drove workers to take direct action, with or without the coordination of the labour movement.

For troops returning to Algeria after the lengthy demobilization process, the effects of four years of war were plain to see. Prices had more than

[1] Ahmed Koulakssis and Gilbert Meynier, 'Sur le mouvement ouvrier et les communistes d'Algérie au lendemain de la Première Guerre mondiale', *Le Mouvement social* 130 (January–March 1985): 3–32, 4.

[2] Ibid.

[3] Emmanuel Sivan, *Communisme et nationalisme en Algérie 1920–1962* (Paris: Presse de la Fondation Nationale des Sciences Politiques, 1976), 20.

[4] Jean-Louis Robert, *Les ouvriers, la patrie et la révolution: Paris 1914–1919* (Paris: Annales Littéraires de l'Université de Besançon, 1995): 137–56.

[5] Leonard V. Smith, *Between Mutiny and Obedience: The Case of the French Fifth Infantry Division during World War I* (Princeton, NJ: Princeton University Press, 1994), 175–214.

[6] Meynier, *L'Algérie Révélée*, 614.

tripled, crippling the purchasing power of lower-class Europeans and the indigenous, while popular perception held that the profits of the war had accrued to a small minority of *colons* and businessmen.[7] The Algerian left would do its best to capitalize on this malaise, seeking to transform it into a wider critique of capitalist society. Even prior to the Armistice, the Algerian branch of the Socialist Party had begun to attack the National Unity government for its failure to eradicate profiteers. Activists in the region of Bône (Annaba) published a short-lived newspaper, *Le Droit du Peuple Nord-Africain*, in March 1918, denouncing those who used the *Union Sacrée* to undermine, rather than defend, the republican order.[8] In the dying days of the war, the paper set the tone for the post-war left in Algeria, singling out the figure of the profiteer as the very epitome of capitalism. His monopoly over the market allowed him to make 'scandalous profits' on the most basic necessities. The coming post-war order would 'force all of you who have speculated on the sweat and blood of others to cough up your ill-gotten gains'.[9] The battle lines were drawn for a conflict over how to build a just post-war society in Algeria.

The political contestation in Algeria reflected wider debates in the metropole and across the belligerent countries. In France, the pro-National Defence majority within the labour movement believed that their participation in the capitalist state's war effort entitled them to a special role in the reorganization of the post-war economy. The majority of the leaders of the left, especially within the trade union body the *Confédération Générale du Travail* (CGT), came to believe that the labour movement's role was to direct and restructure the economy for the maximization of production and the improvement of the lives of the proletariat.[10] Within the left, the main challenge to the statist-managerial model came from the minority that remained committed to revolutionary syndicalism. Their belief in the revolutionary potential of the general strike as a tool to overthrow capitalism would have an important bearing on post-war strikes.[11] Finally, events in Russia, where the Bolsheviks had recently seized power, also weighed heavily on the ideological and strategic debates within the labour movement in the immediate aftermath of the war.[12] Although the lines of division would soon harden, in the months that followed the war the situation was still in flux

[7] Ibid., 690.
[8] D. Vidi, 'L'Union Sacrée', *Le Droit du Peuple Nord-Africain*, 17 March 1918.
[9] D. Giovacchini, 'Aux Commerçants', *Le Droit du Peuple Nord-Africain*, 10 March 1918.
[10] Horne, *Labour at War*, 128–30. [11] Ibid., 189–90. [12] Ibid., 172.

and the left was united in the belief that dramatic change was coming for the working classes.[13]

The 'Syndicalist Spring': Algeria's Labour Movement in Early 1919

As the slow-moving demobilization process finally saw the repatriation of significant numbers of soldiers to their homes in Algeria, the left moved to organize the Algerian labour force. The Socialist Party's newspaper in the department of Oran, *La Lutte Sociale*, re-emerged from wartime censorship in April 1919 with a stinging criticism of the horrors of war, the failures of the demobilization process, and the betrayal of the *poilus*. Its first editorial asserted that the working class would never again 'be duped by the lies of the reactionary press' whose only fruits were 'ruins, poverty, mourning, and blood'.[14] The absence of any specific reference to the demobilization of indigenous troops here is notable. The conditions of service for indigenous troops stipulated that they would remain in service 'for the duration plus six months'. This meant that priority in demobilization was given to citizens, who were far more likely to complain and assert their rights than indigenous subjects who feared the coercive power of the colonial state.[15] This injustice would go unmentioned by the left in Algeria, subsumed into a wider discourse of frustration at the slow rate of demobilization. *La Lutte Sociale* demanded a dramatic speeding up of the process so that the 'long martyrdom of the *poilus*' could be brought to an end and they could reclaim their positions on 'the land, in the factory, and in the workshop'.[16] The paper sought to rally workers by affirming that the war had crippled the trade union movement, giving the profiteers free rein.[17] The only way to defeat the greed of the capitalist, it asserted, was to flock *en masse* to the organizations of the labour movement.

This call to arms met with a certain degree of success. Trade unions proliferated across the colony. In Oran, the number of small trade unions increased dramatically, from a handful at the end of the war to over twenty by the end of 1919.[18] These unions were more than willing to pursue strike

[13] Edward Mortimer, *The Rise of the French Communist Party, 1920–1947* (London: Faber and Faber, 1984), 46.

[14] *La Lutte Sociale*, 20 April 1919.

[15] Fogarty and Killingray, 'Demobilization', 114.

[16] 'A nos lecteurs, à nos Amis', *La Lutte Sociale*, 20 April 1919.

[17] 'La Vie Syndicale', *La Lutte Sociale*, 20 April 1919.

[18] Marynower, 'Être socialiste', 93.

action. In February 1919, as contingents of demobilized troops arrived in the city, the sandal-makers of Oran went on strike, complaining of spiralling prices and low wages.[19] They were soon followed by the dockers' union, a bastion of the most militant section of the indigenous workforce.[20] The *Union des Syndicats du Département d'Alger* justified these strikes by arguing that: 'The working-class, conscious of its duty and obligations, is also conscious of its rights, the fruits of its conduct and its sacrifices in defence of the country'.[21] The seeds were sown for the 'syndicalist spring',[22] when workers from both the European and indigenous communities mobilized together to claim their just reward for participation in the Great War.[23]

As the first hints of the coming industrial unrest appeared in Algeria, the leaders of the labour movement in the metropole were engaged in an open struggle with the post-war government. The government's rejection of any fundamental restructuring of the economy fuelled the resentment of organized labour.[24] The introduction of the eight-hour day was the only significant concession granted in recognition of the wartime service of the working classes. Promulgated on 23 April 1919 in the face of massive opposition from business owners, the CGT's campaign in favour of the eight-hour day had stressed the participation of workers in the war and the need to compensate them immediately.[25] Whether it was considered a sop to the restless proletariat or a glorious conquest of the labour movement, the eight-hour day was seen as *the* primary compensation bestowed on workers for their participation in the Great War.

Like so many of the post-war reforms, the status of the eight-hour day in Algeria was complicated. The provisions of the law were not officially extended to Algeria until March 1924.[26] Even in the metropole, the law was more recognized in the breach than in its application.[27] Nevertheless, industry-wide conventions enforced at a national level and agreements negotiated at a local level meant that the benefits of the law were shared by

[19] 'Lettre du Président du Syndicat des patrons fabricants d'espadrilles', *Le Soir: Journal Quotidien d'Oran*, 20 February 1919.

[20] Marynower, 'Être socialiste', 93.

[21] 'Le Droit de Grève', *La Dépêche Algérienne*, 6 April 1919.

[22] Marynower, 'Être socialiste', 93.

[23] Marynower, 'Être socialiste'. 91.

[24] Horne, *Labour at War*, 359.

[25] Ibid., 360.

[26] Réglementation de l'application de la loi du 23 avril 1919, 5 Mar 1924, *Bulletin Officiel du Gouvernement Général de l'Algérie* 2652 (1924), 622–5.

[27] Gary S. Cross, 'The Quest for Leisure: Reassessing the Eight-Hour Day in France', *Journal of Social History* 18, No. 2 (Winter 1984): 195–216, 200–2.

some workers in Algeria. It is not surprising, given the perception that this provision was the principal compensation extended to workers after the war, that the labour movement's campaign in favour of the eight-hour day should make extensive reference to the wartime contribution of Algeria's workers. *Demain*, the Algiers Socialist Party's newspaper, launched a strong defence of the reform in May 1919. The paper offered a detailed and harrowing account of the horrors of 'modern warfare' before asserting that the returned worker, 'having accomplished his duties', was ready to finally secure the eight-hour day.[28] It fell to the labour movement to ensure that this hard-won concession would be applied. The full application of the eight-hour day thus became one of the central demands of the 'syndicalist spring'.

May Day 1919 was the most symbolically significant moment of the 'syndicalist spring'. Across the major urban centres of the colony, large crowds, almost always including both Europeans and indigenous Algerians, took to the streets to express support for the cause of labour. In Oran, the centrist newspaper *Le Soir* spoke of an 'immense column' of some 'three to four thousand' marching through the city behind the red flag. It noted the presence of a group of indigenous dockers marching behind a flag they had fashioned for themselves. Speeches were given in French, Spanish, and Arabic proclaiming the end 'of the old rotten world' and demanding that 'workers conquer their place in society'. Calls for the application of the eight-hour day, pay rises, world peace, and the unity of action of workers were omnipresent in the rhetoric of the speakers and on the signs carried by the marchers.[29] In the colony's capital, the *Union des Syndicats du Département d'Alger* published a rallying call for May Day, asserting that the workers' demands, including a worker-directed economy and the immediate application of the eight-hour day, were the only way to compensate 'the cruel experiences of the war'.[30] The march that followed in the city on 1 May saw 6,000 workers,[31] around a third of whom were indigenous Algerians,[32] take to the streets to demand the compensation to which they felt entitled. Similar scenes occurred on a smaller scale in all the important urban areas across the colony.[33] Not only was the left on the move in Algeria, but it also seemed to have successfully organized across the boundaries of race for the first time.

[28] 'Les 8 heures: Objections Officielles Patronales', *Demain: Journal Socialiste et de Défense Syndicaliste*, 17 May 1919.
[29] 'A Oran, La manifestation des Syndicats', *Le Soir*, 2 May 1919.
[30] 'Appel aux Ouvriers Organisés', *Demain*, 1 May 1919.
[31] 'Le Premier Mai à Alger', *La Dépêche Algérienne*, 1–2 May 1919.
[32] Meynier, *L'Algérie Révélée*, 691.
[33] Ibid., 693–4.

Although the May Day marches were a dramatic visual representation of the growth of the labour movement in the colony and its seeming ability to transcend racial divisions, the real thrust of the 'syndicalist spring' lay in strike action. The mass rallies of 1 May gave new impetus to the strike movement and by 8 May *Le Soir* was reporting a figure of 6,000 on strike in the city of Oran alone.[34] *Lutte Sociale* sought to justify this strike by underlining the poverty faced by those workers returning from the battlefields to a society that rewarded profiteers over *poilus*.[35] This theme was echoed in a poster distributed in late May calling construction workers in the eastern city of Constantine to a discussion of a possible strike. It drew a direct correlation between the *patron*, who 'turns a deaf ear' to the 'needs' of his veteran workers, and 'those who profited so much from the war, who refuse to do anything to improve the lot of those who gave so much'.[36] The labour movement was seeking to cloak strike action in the shroud of legitimacy of the Great War. It demanded that the 'equality of sacrifice' of the war dead be transformed into tangible social and economic equality for the living.

The radical rhetoric espoused by the labour movement in Algeria's 'syndicalist spring' did not prevent many unions signing agreements with management securing pay rises and the application of the eight-hour day.[37] By the end of the month of May, a combination of internal division, employer concessions, and repression had brought the strikes to an end. Although the Algerian labour movement had succeeded in mobilizing workers, their inexperience and lack of organizational structures had compromised efforts to direct sustained industrial action.[38] The evocation of the war may have served as a justification for the strikes and a rallying point for workers, but it did not convince the population at large, European and indigenous, to weigh in behind the workers.

Mobilizing against *La Vie Chère*: Capitalizing on the Cost of Living

Although the left's campaign to recruit, organize, and mobilize workers met with a success that was unprecedented in colonial Algeria, it remained primarily restricted to industrial workers: a minority of the European

[34] 'Le Mouvement gréviste s'est accentué, hier', *Le Soir*, 8 May 1919.
[35] 'Vers la Grève Générale', *La Lutte Sociale*, 11 May 1919.
[36] Poster, 'Aux Ouvriers du Bâtiment', 21 May 1919, ANOM/93/B3/579.
[37] Marynower, 'Être socialiste', 95.
[38] Meynier, *L'Algérie Révélée*, 692.

population and a tiny percentage of the indigenous population. Efforts to rally other sectors of the workforce to the cause of labour would centre on a campaign against the high cost of living. Here, even more so than in the strikes, the rhetoric of the 'moral economy' of post-war society had pride of place. Colonial administrators themselves recognized that the deep-seated nature of popular discontent about the 'imbalance between the social classes' was feeding support for the left.[39] Socialists and trade unions hoped to capitalize on this popular anger to turn the masses against capitalism.

The left's campaign against the high cost of living began in earnest in early 1919, when the Socialist Party, the trade unions, and the left-affiliated *Ligue des Droits de l'Homme* organized a joint meeting in Oran. The poster publicizing the meeting listed the difficulties facing the inhabitants of the city who, 'despite the end of the war', remained at the mercy of 'tricksters and speculators'.[40] Salomon Tordjmann, the local secretary of the SFIO, opened the meeting by asking why a government that had proved so effective in mobilizing millions of men to protect the wealth of businessmen and industrialists was now incapable of mobilizing that same wealth to protect the families of the fallen and the ex-combatants.[41] Similar sentiments featured prominently on May Day, with marchers in Algiers bearing signs with ironic denunciations of those who profited from their poverty:

> To the newly rich, the gratitude of poverty,
> Bread is not expensive enough, increase the price,
> Nouveau riche don't turn red with embarrassment, others
> turned the trenches red [with their blood] for you.[42]

For the left in Algeria the crusade against *la vie chère* offered an opportunity to broaden support outside of the small industrial working class by turning popular discontent around high prices and the hatred of profiteers into a more general condemnation of capitalist society.

Conscious that the mass strikes of May 1919 had been overambitious, the Algerian left focused on demanding price controls on basic goods. Trade unions and the Socialist Party participated in the foundation of local 'Committees of Vigilance against High Prices' in towns and cities across the colony. These committees published detailed tables showing the hefty

[39] Report of Police Commissioner of Philippeville, 7 April 1919, ANOM/93/B/3/560.
[40] SFIO Poster, 'Contre la Vie chère', March 1919, ANOM/92/2541.
[41] Head of Departmental Security to the Prefect, 9 March 1919, ANOM/92/2541.
[42] 'Le Premier Mai à Alger', *La Dépêche Algérienne*, 1–2 May 1919.

mark-ups charged by suppliers to local businesses on essential goods. They sought to win over small business owners to the campaign against the unjust post-war social order.[43] In Bône (Annaba), the local trade unions rallied 1,700 workers against the high cost of living 'of which the working class is the sole victim'. Their solution was simple: the replacement of the 'bosses', who 'make scandalous fortunes while Frenchmen wallow in famine', with worker self-management.[44] The boycotts and strikes that swept across the ports and industrial centres further west eschewed such radical declarations, primarily demanding the reduction of the cost of essential goods.[45] In late September, the 3,500 dockers of the port of Algiers, including an important indigenous contingent, refused to handle any alcohol products until the price of wine was reduced.[46] The campaign against the high cost of living had succeeded in rallying workers of different classes and races behind the banner of the labour movement.

For some within the movement, however, the primary goal of the campaign against the high cost of living was not to win followers over from the centre ground but rather to challenge the basis of capitalism, the right to private property. Writing in *La Lutte Sociale*, Gaston Monmousseau, a prominent revolutionary in the metropole and member of the Railwaymen's Union, typified this approach. His article identified private property as the root cause for both the slow rate of demobilization and the mass unemployment that were the driving forces of the crisis of post-war society.[47] This structural analysis of the class struggle in Algeria sat uneasily with the attempts to use the campaign against the cost of living to build a broader alliance for the left in the colony. The extent to which Monmousseau's message resonated in both the metropolitan and Algerian labour movements would only become clear in early 1920.

The cost of living was central to the Socialist Party's campaign for the legislative elections of November 1919 in Algeria. The party faced the elections with a certain optimism. Its leaders believed that it was in a unique position to capitalize on public anger about war profiteers and the cost of living. An article in *La Lutte Sociale* three months prior to the electoral contest highlighted what it perceived to be the socialists' advantage: 'Socialism

[43] Meynier, *L'Algérie Révélée*, 692.
[44] Police Commissioner of Bône to the Sous-Préfet, 27 September 1919, ANOM/93/B3/579.
[45] Meynier, *L'Algérie Révélée*, 692.
[46] Koulakssis and Meynier, 'Sur le mouvement ouvrier', 24.
[47] Monmousseau, 'La démobilisation, le Chômage et les Profiteurs', *La Lutte Sociale*, 8 June 1919.

emerges from this cruel ordeal enhanced, but the capitalist parties, perched atop the piles of gold gathered shamelessly, will collapse dismally'.[48] The party's programme demanded the restoration of economic justice to post-war society through the economic intervention of the state and the punishment of the profiteers.[49] Its moral argument was put into sharp relief days before the election, when *Demain* published an article promising that a socialist victory would see the war dead wreak revenge on the war profiteers.[50] The socialists alone could ensure that the wartime 'moral economy of sacrifice' would be respected.

In the end, the socialists' campaign failed to convince a majority of the (European-only) Algerian electorate. Nevertheless, the party achieved unprecedented results, with the socialist lists receiving an average of 15 percent of the vote in the departments of Algiers and Constantine, and over 20 percent in the department of Oran.[51] The party had managed to capitalize on popular discontent over the perceived injustice of the post-war economic order, establishing, for the first time, a significant electoral base in the colony's main urban areas. The campaign against the high cost of living had been a qualified success. By evoking a sense, shared to some extent across class and racial boundaries, that the post-war economic order was rewarding the least deserving, the left won support for its wider demand for a restructuring of the economy and of society. The campaign did, however, hint at the principal pressures that would eventually stunt the growth of the left. Firstly, it provoked a virulent response from their opponents, of which there were many in the colony. They not only condemned and organized against the activities of the left, but also proffered a counter-narrative that rejected any attempt by the labour movement to monopolize popular discontent around the post-war settlement. Alongside this external challenge, the labour movement was also hampered by serious internal divisions. It remained, as ever, divided on the so-called 'indigenous question', preferring to focus on the politics of class over an attempt to establish an agreed position on those of race. And yet, even the politics of class did not unite the left in Algeria. While party and union members may have initially rallied around the campaign against the high cost of living, they did not necessarily share a common view of what its strategic and ideological goal should be. These tensions reflected wider divisions on the French and, indeed, the global left,

[48] 'Le Parti Socialiste et les Elections', *La Lutte Sociale*, 17 August 1919.
[49] 'La Révolution Sociale', *La Lutte Sociale*, 24 August 1919.
[50] 'Les Profiteurs de la Guerre', *Demain*, 6 November 1919.
[51] Koulakssis and Meynier, 'Sur le mouvement ouvrier', 5.

divisions that would eventually result in a split. Before that could happen, the French labour movement and its affiliated organizations in North Africa would embark on a mass strike campaign in 1920 that would play a key role in both the radicalization of its opponents and the exacerbation of internal conflicts.

Reform, Revolution, and Railwaymen: The Strikes of 1920

By the winter of 1919–20 the French state's policy towards labour had shifted significantly. The *chambre bleu-horizon* returned in the 1919 election was hostile towards further concessions to workers. While victory in the elections had strengthened the resolve of conservatives to resist the left, it had, conversely, radicalized both the demands and the strategy of the labour movement, now largely persuaded that change could not be achieved through parliamentary action.[52] The radical minorities within both the Socialist Party and the trade unions grew in strength.[53] Even the majoritarian leaders within the CGT moved to the left, no longer hoping to use their wartime participation to negotiate a place for labour in the post-war state but rather seeking to impose their vision of the post-war order through a campaign of strikes.[54] In this climate, a confrontation with the government seemed unavoidable.

In the end, it was the railwaymen who would light the powder keg of industrial dispute. Traditionally, railway workers had been viewed as dependable and moderate, loyal to the hierarchical and paternalistic rail companies.[55] The extreme pressure placed on the rail network during the war, coupled with the general economic difficulties of the post-war period, radicalized the workforce. The newly founded *Fédération Nationale des Travailleurs de Chemins de Fer* capitalized on this discontent, achieving a unionization rate in the industry of 80 percent by late 1919 and counting over 350,000 members in January 1920, making it the largest union in France.[56] Thus, the railway workers' decision to go out on strike in the spring of 1920 had significant implications for both the labour movement and the government.

[52] Mortimer, *The Rise of the French Communist Party*, 48–9.
[53] Ibid., 46–50.
[54] Horne, *Labour at War*, 377.
[55] Roger Magraw, 'Paris 1917–1920: Labour Protest and Popular Politics', in *Challenges of Labour: Central and Western Europe, 1917–1920*, ed. Chris Wrigley (London: Routledge, 1993): 125–48, 142.
[56] Magraw, 'Paris 1917–1920', 142 and Annie Kriegel, *La grève des cheminots: 1920* (Paris: Armand Colin, 1988), 34.

In Algeria, the railway workers had played an active role in the cost-of-living strikes of the summer of 1919. The staff of the *Paris-Lyon-Méditerranée* (PLM) company declared a strike in August 1919 but were forcibly mobilized by the military authorities and subsequently compelled to return to work having accepted an arbitration process. The colonial administration's actions were bitterly criticized in the pages of *La Lutte Sociale*. The paper denounced forced mobilization as outrageous given that, during the war, the railwaymen had 'saved France' through their maintenance of the rail network and their service as 'brave soldiers' at the front.[57] This condemnation of the abandonment of the wartime 'moral economy of sacrifice' was accompanied by an appeal to railway workers to realize that the only true division in society was that of class and, thus, embrace revolutionary internationalism.[58] The radicalization of the railway workers had begun.

The outbreak of a mass strike among the railway workers of the PLM in the metropole in late February 1920 offered the *cheminots* of Algeria their first chance to pursue their new strategic and ideological agenda. What began as a local strike in a Parisian suburb in mid-February soon spread across the PLM network in the metropole, with the *Fédération Nationale* finally declaring a general strike on 28 February.[59] The CGT called for the nationalization of the railways as part of its wider campaign for increased state intervention in the economy.[60] In Algeria, the regional Union of Railway Workers addressed an appeal to the public on 21 February condemning the French state's treatment of the worker who had fought to defend the *Patrie*. It denounced the 'hypocritical' bourgeoisie that 'only days before...honoured the brave worker, the glorious soldier...with garlands of flowers' but now condemns him once more as 'the dirty worker, the vile poor, good only for exploiting' and seeks to 'strip' him of the right to the eight-hour day. The ruling classes were, it claimed, placing 'their interests, their money, above else, even this fatherland in whose name they demanded your blood and that of your family'.[61] In this narrative, the strikers, far from betraying the nation, were saving it from the profiteers and capitalists whose only goal was the accumulation of wealth.

In the end, the radical rhetoric of the union's Algerian branch was countered by the pragmatism of the moderate majority in the *Fédération des*

[57] 'Syndicat national des Travailleurs des Chemins de Fer: Une grève brisée', *Demain*, 16 August 1919.

[58] Ibid.

[59] Kriegel, *La grève des cheminots*, 52–6.

[60] Ibid., 59.

[61] 'Les Cheminots Algériens au Public', *Demain*, 21 February 1920.

Cheminots, who signed up to a government-brokered agreement with the employers. The radicals were harshly critical of the decision to settle the strike.[62] In the months that followed, dissent spread among railway workers, culminating in the election of a radical majority under Gaston Monmousseau at the national congress in late April.[63] When the new revolutionary leadership of the *Fédération* called for a nationwide strike on 1 May, the moderate majority in the CGT quickly declared a general strike in an effort to take control of the movement.[64] Thus, the *Fédération*, the CGT, and thousands of workers across France and the empire embarked on a strike with the shared goal of nationalizing the railways but with radically different conceptions of where such a nationalization should lead and how it could be achieved.

On the ground in Algeria, the goals of the strike were also unclear. Although rail workers across the colony responded in great numbers to the strike order, they did not present a common programme of demands.[65] Representatives of the 1,037 striking railway workers of Bône (Annaba), a radical stronghold, combined demands for trade union recognition, the eight-hour day, and the nationalization of the railways with a call for the nationalization of the means of production, the normalization of relations with Soviet Russia, and an end to colonial warfare in Syria.[66] In contrast, the *sous-préfet* of Sétif claimed that striking workers in his city had sent a delegation to assure him that their demands were restricted to 'the defence of their material interests' and that they 'refused to express solidarity with revolutionary elements'.[67]

While confusion reigned among the strikers, the opponents of the left in the colony mobilized to smash the strike. Once more, the defenders of strike action evoked their recent participation in the Great War to legitimize their cause and denigrate their adversaries. An open letter published in *Demain* on 10 May framed the class conflict in Algeria in terms of the 'wartime moral economy'. While the striking workers 'did their duty from 1914 to 1918 at the frontline and on the Home Front', the 'property owners, the extremely rich farmers… the big businessmen, the industrialists' were 'war profiteers'. And yet, in post-war Algeria, those who 'gave everything to France' remained

[62] Kriegel, *La grève des cheminots*, 64–7. [63] Ibid., 75.

[64] John Horne, 'The State and the Challenge of Labour in France 1917–1920,' in *Challenges of Labour: Central and Western Europe 1917–1920*. ed. Chris Wrigley (London: Routledge, 1993): 239–261, 253.

[65] Meynier, *L'Algérie Révélée*, 692.

[66] Report on the Railwaymen's Strike, May 1920, L'Arrondissement de Bône, ANOM/93/1349.

[67] Annual Report on Strike, 1920, Sous-Préfecture de Sétif, 27 January 1921, ANOM/93/1349.

at the mercy of elites who, the letter asserted were 'no better than the *boches*'.[68] This effort to mobilize the wartime participation of the rail workers and their proletarian brothers highlights once again the understanding, shared across political divides, that the Great War was *the* central font of political legitimacy.

The rhetorical flourishes of *Demain* were not sufficient to counter the concerted actions of the state and large swathes of civil society to crush the strike. The combination of brutal repression and internal division led to the strike's collapse by the end of May, a defeat from which the left in Algeria would not recover for over a decade.[69] The strike further exacerbated tensions within the labour movement, accelerating the split between the communists and the socialists. In the years that followed, the embittered railway workers would form the backbone of the Algerian section of the Communist Party, with the party's local branches almost mapping directly onto the train network.[70] The strike would remain a bone of contention between socialists and communists, both of whom blamed the other for the failure of the last great movement that sought to radically change the post-war settlement.

If the general strike of 1920 was a disaster for the labour movement in France and in Algeria, it also represented a great success for the adversaries of the left, who organized and mobilized to crush the strike action and maintain the integrity of the capitalist imperialist state. The evocation of the Great War played an important role in this success, as Algerian conservatives rallied to defend the hard-won victory on the battlefields.

'Defending Victory': Opposing the Left's Vision of Post-War Algeria

For the opponents of the left in Algeria, the programme of radical reform supported by the labour movement represented the betrayal of the fallen soldiers.[71] While they may have shared some of the left's concerns about the post-war abandonment of the wartime moral code, they did not share its

[68] 'Lettre Ouverte', *Demain*, 10 May 1920.

[69] Koulakssis and Meynier, 'Sur le mouvement ouvrier', 5.

[70] Jacques Choukroun, 'L'Internationale Communiste, le PC français et l'Algérie (1920–1925)', *Cahiers d'histoire de l'Institut Maurice Thorez* 25–6 (1978): 133–59, 147–50.

[71] John Horne, 'Defending Victory: Paramilitary Politics in France, 1918–1926: A Counter-Example', in *War in Peace: Paramilitary Violence in Europe after the Great War*, eds. Robert Gerwarth and John Horne (Oxford: Oxford University Press, 2012): 216–35.

commitment to a transformation of the status quo. From the outset, the mainstream press, leading local political figures, and a whole range of civil society organizations in the colony challenged the left's vision for post-war Algeria. They believed that the left's programme represented a grave danger for the future of the colony and of France. The implication was clear: support for the left's radical programme would see France and Algeria snatch defeat from the jaws of victory.

The mainstream press played a key role in articulating a vision of post-war Algeria that refuted the left's class narrative. In its editorial on 1 January 1919, *L'Echo d'Oran* employed an argument that would become a constant in the rhetoric of the left's opponents. Demanding an end to the 'hideous class struggle, the fratricidal struggle', the article called for a future grounded in the 'collaboration and association of Capital and Labour'.[72] A similar editorial in *L'Echo d'Alger* in March of that year echoed this argument, asserting that 1919 represented a crossroads for Algeria and that 'an era of prosperity' could only be secured by 'uniting the interests of Capital and Labour'.[73] The demand for a perpetuation of the *Union Sacrée*, and the subjugation of social claims to the necessities of national reconstruction that this implied, was central to the post-war counter-narrative of the enemies of the left.

The events of the 'syndicalist spring' served to reinforce and radicalize this counter-narrative. The mainstream press continued to present an idealized view of the social unity occasioned by the war and denounced those who now seemed ready to betray it. Columnists in the leading settler newspapers celebrated the 'fraternity of arms' that had defined the war and contrasted it with the 'fratricidal struggles', 'criminal class struggles', and 'political strikes' that were now threatening 'rob France of the fruits of victory'.[74] Their spirited defence of the *Union Sacrée* ignored the important role played by the leaders of the left in the war effort. Instead, they presented the left as the enemy of national unity, arguing that its attempts to claim some form of compensation for the working classes were simply a cover for its desire to overthrow capitalism and imperil the hard-won victory in the Great War.

Within civil society, it was the emergent veterans' movement that led the charge against the left. The more conservative organizations aligned themselves with the *Union Nationale des Combattants* (UNC), which had firmly

[72] '1918–1919', *L'Echo d'Oran*, 1 January 1919.

[73] E. Bailac, 'La Situation Politique', *L'Echo d'Alger*, 3 March 1919.

[74] Jules Rouanet, 'Le devoir de s'aimer', *La Dépêche Algérienne*, 17 July 1919 and Alfred Cazes, 'Avant la Signature', *L'Echo d'Oran*, 14 June 1919.

opposed the left from the early days of 1919.[75] In advance of May Day, the UNC issued an appeal, carried in the pages of *La Dépêche Algérienne*, calling on workers and *patrons* to remain 'united like at the frontlines' and thus ensure that the 'immense sacrifice of the living and the dead was not in vain'.[76] At the forefront of the veterans' associations' campaign stood their particular understanding of the 'moral economy' of post-war society, grounded in the 'primacy of the veteran' (see Chapter 5). Thus, while they too preached the conciliation of workers and *patrons*, they were more inclined to critique the post-war order and its failure to guarantee a livelihood for returning veterans. The local UNC-affiliated newspaper in the department of Algiers, *Le Mutilé de l'Algérie*, acknowledged the difficulties facing demobilized soldiers, particularly the high cost of living, and railed against the injustice of a system that failed to reward those who fought to preserve it. However, its principal target remained the left, which it claimed restricted the right to work by imposing the 'obligatory strike' on workers, a tactic that was judged 'as ineffective as it is odious'.[77] In contrast, the more centrist associations, including the *Amicale des Mutilés du Département d'Alger*, the central focus of Chapter 5, remained, for the time being, focused on the demands of veterans and reserved their attacks for the war profiteers and their 'scandalous fortunes'.[78] It would take the revolutionary strike wave of spring 1920 to rally these organizations against the left in Algeria.

Conscious of the threat that veterans' organizations could pose to the collective action of the labour movement, the left's propaganda courted working-class veterans by combining its calls for a new moral basis for the post-war economy with attacks on bourgeois veteran leaders. As early as April 1919, *La Lutte Sociale* was warning veterans not to entrust their future to bourgeois philanthropists whose good intentions could not affect the change necessary for a just post-war order.[79] Class struggle was the only solution. By late 1919, with the increasing sense that conservative veterans' associations constituted a bulwark of the established order against the left, socialists in Algiers asked veterans not to compromise their 'just cause' by delegating their moral authority to 'stooges who seek only to secure

[75] Chris Millington, *From Victory to Vichy: Veterans in Interwar France* (Manchester: Manchester University Press, 2012), 25–35.

[76] 'Le Premier Mai', *La Dépêche Algérienne*, 29 April 1919.

[77] 'Le Remède à la Vie Chère', *Le Mutilé de l'Algérie*, 13 July 1919.

[78] 'Bénéfices de Guerre', *Bulletin de l'Amicale des Mutilés du Département d'Alger*, July 1919.

[79] 'Les Amochés de la Grande Guerre', *La Lutte Sociale*, 27 April 1919.

positions, resources and even revenue for themselves'.[80] The first skirmishes between the left and veterans' associations had begun.

The events of early 1920 provoked a mass mobilization in the colony against the strikers that deliberately recalled the mobilization of 1914. The administration, the mainstream press, and most veterans' associations organized jointly against the labour movement by arguing that the future of France, and in particular that of Algeria, was in peril. Faced with the first railway strike of late February/early March, a group of businessmen who had served in the war and were now organized in the *Fédération des Commerçants et Industriels Mobilisés* built a broad coalition of veterans' associations to counter the threat from the left. This new alliance, which incorporated supposedly centrist organizations such as the *Amicale des Mutilés du Département d'Alger*, issued a 'manifesto of the Algerian patriotic groups' under the title 'Veterans and the Demobilised against the General Strike' that was carried in the pages of the mainstream conservative press. It affirmed the 'right and the duty' of those 'who had made supreme sacrifices' for France 'to make their voices heard when the *Patrie* is under threat'. A general strike would, it argued, 'ruin our industry and commerce under the mocking eye of the satisfied *boche*', leading to the 'decline of victorious France'. The actions of ordinary members of the labour movement were, it claimed, based on a misunderstanding of the true meaning of the great motto of the Republic:

> If there is not a single Frenchman, worthy of the name, whose heart is not imbued with the ideas of Liberty and Equality, let us not forget that these two words are nothing without the third, the greatest: Fraternity.[81]

For the veterans' associations and the wider forces opposed to the left in Algeria, the 'fraternity of arms' had to take priority over 'the equality of sacrifice' if France's glorious victory was not to be thrown away.

This attempt by the veterans' associations to monopolize the memory of the war and mobilize it in defence of the capitalist system did not go unanswered. The Oran branch of the leftist *Association Républicaine des Anciens Combattants* (ARAC) attacked the manifesto as the work of organizations that 'under a disguised form, are, for the most part controlled by employers', claiming that they served only to provide strike-breaking labour. The ARAC alone would protect the interests of those workers who had

[80] 'Aux mutilés et pour les mutilés', *Demain*, 16 August 1919.

[81] 'Combattants et Démobilisés contre la Grève Générale', *La Dépêche Algérienne*, 2 March 1920.

fought for France.[82] Where the coalition of veterans' associations had grounded their appeal in the language of the *Union Sacrée* and class collaboration, the ARAC sought to mobilize the working-class veterans behind an egalitarian vision of a post-war order grounded in the 'moral economy of wartime sacrifice'.

When revolution seemed to loom on the horizon, with the outbreak of the general strike of May 1920, the 'patriotic groups' quickly swung into action. Across France, business owners, conservative politicians, and veterans' associations had begun to form 'civic unions' to prepare the resistance to the coming strike.[83] Two days after strike action began in Algeria, an editorial in *La Dépêche Algérienne* cited the precedent of the 'strike-breaking leagues' in metropolitan France, calling on the 'citizens, friends of work and order' to follow their example and organize against the 'antipatriotic, anti-Algerian, revolutionary' labour movement.[84] That evening an assembly of veterans met in Algiers to form an organization that would provide 'an army of civil volunteers' to replace striking workers. The veterans declared themselves 'ready to sacrifice our lives for France' to ensure that 'our victory will not be sabotaged'. They claimed total ownership of France's success in the Great War, ignoring the fact that many of the striking workers were themselves veterans of the conflict.[85] The assembly even went as far as to draw a direct parallel between the strikers and the Germans, asserting that they would remain 'as united against the enemy within as they had been against the enemy without'.[86] The adversaries of the left, with the veterans' associations at their head, were seeking to reproduce not so much the moral unity of purpose of the *Union Sacrée* as its strictly hierarchical discipline.

The foundation of the *Ligue Civique d'Alger* 'under the auspices of various associations of veterans of the Great War' was soon replicated in all the major towns and cities across the colony. The declared goal of mobilizing society, and in particular veterans, to 'once again save the Patrie' was shared across the range of organizations that sprang up in towns and cities throughout Algeria.[87] The *liguers* of the town of Isserville (Boumerdès) condemned the strike as the work of revolutionaries who had been '*embusqués*' during

[82] 'Association Républicaine des Anciens Combattants', *La Lutte Sociale*, 13 March 1920.

[83] Horne, 'Defending Victory', 223.

[84] 'Le Mouvement Révolutionnaire des Cheminots: Pour briser la grève', *La Dépêche Algérienne*, 3 May 1920.

[85] 'Pour briser la grève: La Mobilisation Civile', *La Dépêche Algérienne*, 4 May 1920.

[86] Ibid.

[87] 'Pour briser la grève: Ligue Civique', *La Dépêche Algérienne*, 5 May 1920.

the war and now sought to 'sabotage the victory'.[88] In Tiaret, the local *Ligue Civique* was directed by a retired officer who had played a key role in the repression of the 1916 revolt in the Sud-Constantinois. He showed a similar zeal for violence in his dealings with local striking railway workers, leading 400 men in a vicious attack against them and driving them out of the town.[89] Indeed, in many of the smaller towns across the colony, where striking workers were few in number and relatively isolated from their comrades, the mobilization of the civil population and especially ex-combatants took on a militaristic and often violent character.[90] The colonial context in which any threat to the existing social order was also perceived as a subversion of European hegemony facilitated a greater recourse to violence than would have been tolerated in a metropolitan setting.

In the colony's capital, the *Ligue Civique* claimed to have recruited 6,000 members by 7 May.[91] Article 6 of the *Ligue Civique*'s statutes stipulated that only veterans who had seen action during the war could serve on the group's executive committee. Maurice Van Ghèle, the first president of the *Amicale des Mutilés du Département d'Alger*, was elected to preside over the *Ligue*. In his acceptance speech, Van Ghèle vowed that the members of the *Ligue* would act as the 'interpreters of the 1,700,000 dead *poilus*', intervening when necessary to ensure the defeat of those who sought to 'deprive the Nation of the benefits of a victory so dearly bought with the blood of her children'.[92] The meeting closed with the formation of a 'civic guard', an auxiliary force that would use former combatants to maintain public order in the city.[93] The conservative veterans of Algiers had appointed themselves guardians of the security of the state, conferring the legitimacy their wartime service had granted them on the repression of the labour movement in the colony.

By 14 May, the *Ligues Civiques* had federated at a colony-wide level as the *Ligue Civique Algérienne*, claiming some 20,000 members,[94] a similar membership to that of the CGT in the colony.[95] This umbrella structure continued to shroud itself in the cloak of legitimacy of the veterans, rejecting claims

[88] 'Les poursuites contre la CGT', *L'Echo d'Alger*, 13 May 1920.
[89] Meynier, *L'Algérie Révélée*, 693.
[90] Ibid.
[91] 'Chez les Cheminots: A Alger', *La Dépêche Algérienne*, 7 May 1920.
[92] 'A La Ligue Civique', *L'Echo d'Alger*, 8 May 1920.
[93] Ibid.
[94] 'Les briseurs de grève: Ligue Civique Algérienne', *La Dépêche Algérienne*, 14 May 1920. The *Ligue Civique Algérienne* was registered with the authorities on 18 February 1921 with the stated goal of 'fighting, with all legal means available, all movements that seek to throw into disarray services and public life' and 'assuring the freedom to work', AWA 1Z/17/811.
[95] Meynier, *L'Algérie Révélée*, 690.

that it was a front for the interests of big capitalists: 'Constituted and directed by the War-wounded and Veterans who remain faithful to the ideal of law and liberty for which they fought and suffered during the last war, the *Ligue Civique* is in nobody's pocket!'[96] However, the *Ligue* and its affiliated organizations had received support from both the administrative authorities and the representative bodies of commerce and finance in the colony. The *Conseil Général* of the department of Algiers voted to grant a subvention of 3,000 francs to assist its 'defence of the freedom to work'.[97] That same day the governor general issued a communiqué praising the *Ligues Civiques* as the embodiment of the population's 'reprobation of the revolutionary movement'.[98] While the *Ligues*' success in mobilizing thousands across the colony is beyond question, the protestations of its leaders that they were independent of both the interests of big business and the administration were, at best, disingenuous.

Unsurprisingly, the left bitterly rejected the attempt of the conservative veterans in the *Ligues* to monopolize the political legitimacy of the wartime sacrifice. An open letter addressed to the colony's veterans and authored by a 'decorated veteran' appeared in the pages of *Demain* on 8 May denouncing the leaders of the *Ligues Civiques* as 'a handful of clowns' who did not represent the 'mass of veterans'. The 'true veterans', 'who had learned from the war', emerged from the horrors of the trenches ready to fight not only those who 'forced them into the carnage' but also those 'who had not denounced the profiteers of death'. They were firmly on 'the side of the exploited'.[99] *La Lutte Sociale* echoed this attack, dismissing Oran's *Union Civique* as a 'collection of cretins' in the service of the Chamber of Commerce and suggesting it should be renamed '*Union Cynique*'.[100] The *Union des Syndicats du Département d'Alger* launched a stinging attack on what it called the 'League of Swindlers', denouncing the manipulation of the memory of the war by a 'handful of schemers' who used the veterans' movement 'as a launching pad' for their personal ambitions. These 'new self-styled Patriots' were motivated, it argued, primarily by their belief that 'the word Patrie is a synonym of Purse'. In contrast, the 'true veteran marches with' the left, the only movement that remained committed to the construction of a just post-war order.[101] Far

[96] 'Les briseurs de grève: Ligue Civique Algérienne', *La Dépêche Algérienne*, 14 May 1920.
[97] 'Motion du Président note d'un crédit à la Ligue Civique', *L'Echo d'Alger*, 8 May 1920.
[98] 'Une Communication du Gouvernement Général', *L'Echo d'Alger*, 7 May 1920.
[99] 'Les Anciens Combattants', *Demain*, 8 May 1920.
[100] 'Questions Indiscrètes', *La Lutte Sociale*, 5–11 June 1920.
[101] 'Une Affiche: Union des Syndicats du Département d'Alger', *Demain*, 28 May 1920.

from redressing the failings of post-war society, the left argued that the *Ligues* were working to preserve, even expand, them, by using a false new-found patriotism to mobilize society in the defence of the property of the profiteers. This was the ultimate betrayal of those who had served France.

Although neither the left nor the right managed to completely impose their vision of the Great War across Algerian society in the immediate post-war moment, the conservatives emerged victorious from the conflict of 1920. There is little doubt that the 'fraternity of arms' grounded in class collaboration won out over the drive for a post-war economy based on the 'equality of sacrifice'. At a national level, a hostile government, working in tandem with a mobilized and conservative civil society, took decisive action to crush the labour movement. In this, they were facilitated by the internal divisions of the left itself. In Algeria, each of these factors was compounded for the left by the reality of the colonial situation. The ever present 'indigenous question' would complicate the left's attempt to build a coherent vision for a post-war Algeria while allowing the right to expand its claim to be defending the victory of France, to encompass 1830 as well as 1918. A call to reconstruct society on a moral and egalitarian basis was all the more difficult to sustain in the colonial context where even the European working class enjoyed the perks of racial privilege. The left was then faced with the thorny question: Where did the indigenous population fit in its vision of a new post-war Algeria?

Fraternity of Arms or Equality of Sacrifice: The Left and the 'Indigenous Question'

The place of the indigenous both within the movements and within the ideology of the left in colonial Algeria has been the subject of extensive research by historians. However, with the notable exception of the work of Gilbert Meynier and Ahmed Koulaksiss, these studies have largely focused on the period following the split between the communists and the socialists at the Congress of Tours in 1920.[102] The left's position on the indigenous in the immediate post-war moment has hitherto been largely overlooked.

[102] Koulakssis and Meynier, 'Sur le mouvement ouvrier' and Meynier, *L'Algérie Révélée*. For works focused on the post-Tours 'indigenous question' see: Charles-Robert Ageron, 'Les Communistes français devant la question algérienne de 1921 à 1924', *Mouvement Social* 78 (January–March 1972): 7–37, Choukroun, 'L'Internationale Communiste', Allison Drew, *We Are No Longer in France: Communists in Colonial Algeria* (Manchester: University of Manchester Press, 2014), Marynower, 'Être socialiste', and Sivan, *Communisme et nationalisme*.

In the dying years of the war, socialists in Algeria may have embraced the notion that the social order was set to change radically, but they did not envisage such a transformation of the colonial order. The pre-war SFIO's programme had called for an end to the most abusive elements of the colonial system, the expropriation of land, and the *Indigénat*, while stressing the role education should play in 'civilizing' the indigenous masses.[103] In light of the mass participation of indigenous Algerians in the war, both as soldiers and as workers, it seemed possible that a government nominally committed to colonial reform would implement this programme of limited reform. An article in *Le Droit du Peuple Nord-Africain* in March 1918 suggested that the 'fraternity of arms' between indigenous and Europeans should pave the way for a 'social fraternity' and 'political fraternity'.[104] The concept of equality was studiously avoided. The article endorsed the reforms proposed by Clemenceau in January 1918, the basis of the subsequent *Loi Jonnart*, hardly a disavowal of European supremacy. As the events of the immediate post-war period in Algeria would demonstrate, the left understood 'social fraternity and political fraternity' in much the same way as soldiers had understood the 'fraternity of arms': unity of action not equality of status. Here the parallel with the right's rhetoric towards the working classes is striking, with the broad notion of fraternity taking precedence over the specific concept of equality.

The left's reticence to embrace radical colonial reform did not quell the alarm among the fringes of right-wing opinion in the colony who denounced the prospect of a left-nationalist alliance. As soon as wartime censorship was relaxed, extreme settler journalists evoked the threat posed by the mobilization of indigenous workers behind the banner of the labour movement. While the mainstream press continued to speak of 'our indigenous brothers',[105] the populist right-wing publicist Charles Collomb railed against 'the Islamic CGT', who sought to unionize indigenous workers to form 'a sort of war machine against the Frenchmen of Algeria'.[106] Collomb's rhetoric was ahead of the curve in an immediate post-war Algeria where the desire to perpetuate the *Union Sacrée* ensured that open hostility to the indigenous was not employed by the mainstream right. It did hint, however, at the rhetorical strategies that would subsequently be employed by the mainstream press and by colonial administrators during the strikes of 1920.

[103] Sivan, *Communisme et nationalisme*, 31.

[104] Mama, 'Politique et Réformes Indigènes', *Le Droit du Peuple Nord-Africain*, 17 March 1918.

[105] Meynier, *L'Algérie Révélée*, 689.

[106] 'La CGT islamique', *L'Evolution Nord-Africaine*, 10 April 1919.

The irruption of the indigenous worker into the public consciousness in the colony came with the mass mobilization of May Day 1919. While indigenous workers had previously taken part in May Days in Algeria, the large numbers who turned out across the colony on 1 May 1919 were unprecedented.[107] The conservative press reported the indigenous participation with a certain trepidation, while the more radical right openly denounced the presence of 'Arabs' alongside Europeans.[108] In contrast, the socialist press stressed the 'fraternal' nature of the marches that grouped together not just 'Arabs' and 'Frenchmen' but also 'Jews and Spaniards', 'all those with calloused hands'. United in action, they abandoned any 'hatred and prejudice' they once held in their hearts.[109] The agendas adopted by the marchers in both Algiers and Oran did not specifically mention the demands of indigenous workers, choosing instead to subsume them into the wider call for a more economically just post-war settlement.[110] In Oran, the crowd was addressed by three indigenous speakers. First to speak was Saïd Façi of the Union of Primary School Teachers, a naturalized French citizen married to a Frenchwoman. He addressed the crowd in French. This was followed by speeches in Arabic by the dockers Sahroui and Zétouni.[111] Façi's speech, the only one of which a record remains, paid no special attention to indigenous grievances, denouncing in general terms 'social iniquities, the oppression of Capital' and calling for unity in service of the 'common ideal'.[112] In a striking parallel with the activities of the veterans' movements, who would become the sworn enemies of the labour movement in the years that followed, specifically indigenous demands were obscured in the protests of 1 May 1919 in favour of a wider discourse denouncing the government's failure to provide for the working class in general (see Chapter 5).

Despite its symbolic importance, there is little trace in the sources of indigenous participation in the strikes of 1919 and the campaign against the high cost of living. The dominance of a 'class struggle' narrative largely obscured any differentiation between striking workers. Cases of class trumping race did occur. Famously, the indigenous dockers of Algiers refused to handle

107 Marynower, 'Être socialiste', 99.

108 'Le Premier Mai', *La Dépêche Algérienne*, 1–2 May 1919 and 'Le 1er mai à Oran', *L'Echo d'Oran*, 1–2 May 1919.

109 'Le 1er mai à Oran', *La Lutte Sociale*, 4 May 1919.

110 'Le Premier Mai', *La Dépêche Algérienne*, 1–2 May 1919 and 'Le 1er mai à Oran', *L'Echo d'Oran*, 1–2 May 1919.

111 Marynower, 'Être socialiste', 100.

112 'A Oran, La manifestation des Syndicats', *Le Soir*, 2 May 1919.

wine imports until the price of this European staple was reduced.[113] The European-dominated *Amicale des Instituteurs* called for equal pay conditions for their indigenous comrades. The dockers of Mostaganem, in contravention of the law of 21 March 1884, elected a majority of indigenous members to the central committee of their union, who in turn voted to strike for the reduction of wine prices.[114] This solidarity, however, was neither universal nor permanent. In May 1919, indigenous workers in the mining town of Mokta-el-Hadid joined the strike of their European comrades, refusing to obey their *caïd*'s order to return to work.[115] Months later the Europeans, who enjoyed superior salaries and working conditions, returned to work while the indigenous continued their strike, condemning the 'cowardice' of their European colleagues.[116] The employment of indigenous workers as strike-breakers also had the potential to undermine cross-community solidarity.[117] Thus, the primacy of the class struggle was neither a rhetorical invention of the left nor an accurate reflection of the complexity of the intersection between race and class in the industrial unrest of 1919.

The language of claims-making adopted by the left in this immediate post-war moment, blending socialist internationalism with the 'moral economy of wartime sacrifice', was universal in its potential. It encompassed all those communities who had contributed to the war effort. It also, however, allowed for the possibility that communities whose wartime participation had been carried out differently could be rewarded differently. Thus, while the trade unions pursued a campaign of class struggle that claimed to unify European and indigenous workers, the political left offered a vision of reform that did not extend equality and citizenship status to the indigenous. The Socialist Party called for the abolition of measures of exception and for the naturalization of 'all those who spilled their blood for France', but insisted on the need to educate the masses before allowing them to accede to citizenship.[118] This policy platform, an expanded *Loi Jonnart*, allowed the left to set aside the 'indigenous question' and focus on a class struggle that obscured the very real racial discriminations facing indigenous workers.

[113] Koulakssis and Meynier, 'Sur le mouvement ouvrier', 24.

[114] Meynier, *L'Algérie Révélée*, 695–6.

[115] Report of the Political and Administrative Situation of the Indigenous, May 1919, ANOM/GGA/11H/46.

[116] Marynower, 'Être socialiste', 94.

[117] 'Le Mouvement Social: Grèves et difficultés', *Le Soir*, 7 May 1919.

[118] 'Le statut indigène: Rapport fait au nom de la section oranaise de la Ligue des Droits de l'Homme', Report by the Police Inspector of Oran, 28 April 1919, ANOM/92/2541.

The role of indigenous workers in the strikes of 1919 and the campaign against the high cost of living is difficult to assess. Indigenous Algerians were legally entitled to join (but not to lead) a trade union, a right not accorded to subjects elsewhere in the empire.[119] However, the constant threat of punishment under the *Indigénat* for a 'hostile act against French sovereignty' militated against indigenous participation in union activity.[120] Furthermore, the vast majority of the indigenous population, tied to labour on the land, remained largely unaware of a labour movement that was confined to major urban areas. The authorities' attitude to indigenous involvement in the left's class struggle campaign proved somewhat confused. A May 1919 report described indigenous involvement in trade unionism as 'passive' and 'without political significance'. It expressed satisfaction that May Day had seen 'no exclusively indigenous' marches but worried about the presence of indigenous workers alongside their European comrades in the marches of 1 May and in strikes throughout the month.[121] Action taken by indigenous workers alone was considered potentially subversive of the colonial hierarchy. However, European trade union leaders, it was feared, could radicalize the supposedly naive indigenous workers, converting them to the cause of revolution.[122] Reports in the months that followed underlined the continued support of urban indigenous workers for the trade unions, increasing propaganda activity in the countryside and the role of returned colonial workers in spreading radical ideas.[123] In particular, as the municipal elections drew closer, and with them the prospect of an alliance between the left and the *Khaledistes*, colonial administrators looked with concern at the labour movement's engagement with indigenous workers.[124] This was coupled with a fear that worsening conditions in the countryside, where administrators were witnessing the first indications of the famine that would afflict the colony from mid-1920 until 1922, were leading the indigenous to embrace violence. Yet the widespread sense that indigenous workers 'remained indifferent to the political suggestions of certain European agitators' meant

[119] 'Loi relative à la création des syndicats professionnels', *Journal Officiel*, 22 March 1884, 1577–8.

[120] Marynower, 'Être socialiste', 404–5.

[121] Report on the Political and Administrative Situation of the Indigenous, May 1919, ANOM/GGA/11H/46.

[122] Jean-Louis Planche, 'Grèves en Méditerranée Maghrébine', *Cahiers du GREMAMO* 4 (1987): 67–72, 67.

[123] Monthly Reports on the Political and Administrative Situation of the Indigenous, May–September 1919, ANOM/GGA/11H/46.

[124] Monthly Reports on the Political and Administrative Situation of the Indigenous, August–October 1919, ANOM/GGA/11H/46.

that for colonial administrators the real threat to European hegemony came not from the urban indigenous proletariat but rather from the new indigenous elite.[125] Conscious of the mobilizing potential among the European community of the image of the mass of indigenous workers and peasants challenging the existing social and political structure, the colonial authorities and the wider opponents of the left in the colony would evoke this threat when faced with the revolutionary strikes of 1920.

The strikes of 1920 bore witness to the continuing cross-community solidarity among Algeria's working class. Although indigenous workers joined their European comrades in strike action in both February and May of that year, the pages of the socialist press made little express mention of indigenous involvement. The May Day marches of 1920, which attracted larger crowds and a higher proportion of indigenous workers than the previous year, are prime examples of the primacy of class over race in the left's discourse.[126] The pages of *La Lutte Sociale* presented the class unity on display in Oran's march as the direct result of the horrors of the war, which had proven to the working classes that 'behind the mask of patriotism' lurks the 'insatiable appetite' for profit of the capitalists.[127] Indigenous participation was framed in terms of a wider class consciousness that drew heavily on the experience of the war.

If the left's discourse around indigenous participation changed little between the 'syndicalist spring' of 1919 and the revolutionary strikes of 1920, the same cannot be said for the rhetoric of its opponents. Whereas in 1919 the evocation of the threat posed by indigenous strike action to the colonial hierarchy had been confined to the margins of political debate, the 1920 strikes saw the figure of the radicalized indigenous worker move centre stage. In what would become a recurring trend throughout the interwar period (see Chapter 4), the opponents of the left in Algeria combined metropolitan discourse, condemning the strikes as a threat to the nation's post-war unity and survival, with a specifically colonial reference to the menace the indigenous represented for the empire's survival. The mainstream press denounced the striking workers as 'traitors to France and Algeria' who were failing to meet their 'mutual obligation' to the colonial state by abandoning

[125] Report on the Political and Administrative Situation of the Indigenous, September 1919, ANOM/GGA/11H/46.

[126] Meynier, *L'Algérie Révélée*, 692.

[127] 'Le 1er Mai à Oran', *La Lutte Sociale*, 8–14 May 1920.

'their duty to safeguard French supremacy'.[128] *L'Echo d'Alger* suggested that the alliance of the left and the 'Muslim nationalists' posed an even greater existential threat to France and Algeria than the Germans had in 1914:

> The danger is as grave for Algeria as it was for France at the time of the declaration of war. But this time, the threat is all the more acute because the enemy comes from within and he could carry along with him in his anti-French action the indigenous whose attitude does nothing to allay our fears.[129]

The governor general echoed this parallel in his address to the *Délégations Financières* during the strikes. Evoking a long history of sacrifice for victory encompassing not only the 'harrowing ordeal' of the Great War but also the struggle against 'hostile nature' in the taming of the Algerian countryside, he expressed confidence that the European community would never surrender to 'the Sirens of Anarchy'.[130] In Oran, the head of the department's *Union Civique* denounced the 'agitators' who 'in the two years since Victory' had undermined France, declaring that his organization would 'prevent anyone from compromising the hard work accomplished by French settlers in this land of Algeria'.[131] The threat posed by an imagined alliance of revolutionaries and indigenous nationalists served to rally large sections of Algeria's European community behind the forces opposing the labour movement, simultaneously legitimizing and reinforcing the efforts to crush the strikes. The resulting alliance between sections of civil society, the mainstream press and politicians and colonial administrators was framed as a continuation of the *Union Sacrée*, defending Algeria against the dual menace of left-wing revolution and indigenous nationalism. The whole swathe of forces opposing the left in Algeria understood their actions in 1920 as a defence not only of the victory of 1918 but also of the victory of 1830.

The defeat of the strikes of 1920 threw the Algerian labour movement into disarray. In the recriminations that followed, the unity of the left behind the cause of class struggle gave way to bitter partisan divisions in which the 'indigenous question' would play an important role. Late 1920 saw the

[128] 'Le Mouvement Révolutionnaire des Cheminots: Pour briser la grève', *La Dépêche Algérienne*, 3 May 1920 and 'Après la Grève: Les revendications des Cheminots de l'Ouest-Algérien', *L'Echo d'Oran*, 13 May 1920.

[129] Pierre-Edmond, 'L'Effort Révolutionnaire', *L'Echo d'Alger*, 4 May 1920.

[130] 'Discours de M. Abel, Gouverneur Général', *L'Echo d'Oran*, 19 May 1920.

[131] 'Union Civique de l'Oranie', *Le Petit Oranais*, 3 June 1920 and 'Union Civique de l'Oranie', *L'Echo d'Oran*, 12 July 1920.

Algerian left vigorously debate the Twenty-One Conditions laid down by the Comintern against the backdrop of a famine afflicting the rural indigenous population. While the left unanimously condemned the neglect of the indigenous masses and the arbitrary rule of law in the colony, such unity was not evident in wider debates around the 'indigenous question'. The pages of *Demain* played host to a variety of views on the issue, ranging from support for a limited extension of the franchise to veterans and elites to the rejection of the 'old barbaric patriotism, father of the *Union Sacrée*', in favour of the revolutionary emancipation of the indigenous.[132] The subsequent support of a sizable majority on the Algerian left for the communists at the Congress of Tours did not, however, mean that socialists in Algeria wholeheartedly endorsed Leninist anti-imperialism. Many communist activists in Algeria believed that the specificity of Algerian colonialism would exempt them from the embrace of anti-colonial politics.[133] In the years that followed, as Comintern leaders moved to disabuse them of this belief and as the authorities brutally repressed the party, the grip of the communists on the shrinking left in the colony loosened and the socialists began to experience limited revival. The 'indigenous question' became a key dividing point between the different wings of the left, meaning that the kind of 'universal' rhetoric of class struggle grounded in the post-war 'moral economy' that had obscured such conflicts in 1919–20 was no longer possible. The indigenous contribution to the Great War continued to feature in the rhetoric of reform promoted by both the communists and the socialists, as we have seen in the Blum-Viollette debates in Chapter 2, but it was never the central prism through which either wing of the left understood or framed the 'indigenous question'.

Conclusion

For the left in Algeria, the post-war moment represented a unique opportunity. In what was particularly hostile territory for the ideas of universal socialism, the persistent sense that the working-class contribution to the war had not been sufficiently rewarded opened a new political space for

[132] J. Ranzet, 'Le Socialisme et la Question Indigène: Quelques Vérités', *Demain*, 18 September 1920 and P. Delapointe 'Le Socialisme et la Question Indigène', *Demain*, 16 October 1920.

[133] Drew, *We Are No Longer in France*, 29–32 and Sivan, *Communisme et nationalisme*, 17.

the left. Activists, whether in the Socialist Party, the trade union movement, or the pages of the left-wing press, recognized the potential rallying power of arguments grounded in the post-war 'moral economy' among the urban working classes in Algeria. They sought to prolong official wartime discourses centred on the 'equality of sacrifice' into the post-war moment, arguing that the capitalist system itself represented a breach of this essential principle. Their rhetoric spurred thousands of workers from different ethnic backgrounds out on to the streets on May Day 1919 and on to the picket lines during the 'syndicalist spring'. The left's attempt to broaden its support base in late 1919 saw this same political language adapted to appeal beyond the bounds of the industrial working classes in the form of the campaign *contre la vie chère*. Activists sought to convince both the working classes and the *petite bourgeoisie* that the left alone could be trusted to build a post-war economy and society that respected justice and equality, the principles upon which victory in the Great War had been secured. The evocation of the war and the new social morality it engendered had granted the left in Algeria an unprecedented level of public support.

However, both the message and the success it secured contained within them the seeds of the downfall of the Algerian left. Although the left as a whole was committed to the reconstruction of society on the basis of the 'equality of sacrifice', its activists did not share a common understanding of how this vision should be realized. The unity of the immediate post-war moment soon disintegrated, as the different factions of the left struggled to impose their model of a just post-war 'moral economy' on the movement. The left's limited success served to stir up their adversaries in the colony, thus initiating a spiral of radicalization that would lead to the unsuccessful revolutionary strikes of early 1920. Whereas previous calls for a just post-war moral order had either been simply dismissed or appeased by granting minor concessions, the attempt of the left in the colony to mobilize for the end of the capitalist system in May 1920 would be brutally crushed. Appeals in favour of the forced imposition of the just post-war order through revolutionary syndicalism could not compete with the mobilization of the administration and large swathes of civil society in defence of the status quo.

The fact that the opponents of the labour movement also framed their actions in terms of the legacy of the Great War undermined any attempt by the left to monopolize the symbolic capital of the wartime sacrifice. From the outset, the mainstream conservative press had stressed the need for a perpetuation of the *Union Sacrée*, directly contradicting the left's call for the post-war reordering of society. Throughout the 'syndicalist spring' and the subsequent campaign *contre la vie chère* these two positions were debated, with no conclusive winner. However, the events of 1920 would change this. If the left's call for a perpetuation of the 'equality of sacrifice' had resonated with a significant proportion of the wider public for much of 1919, the right's defence of the 'fraternity of arms' became dominant in the revolutionary context of 1920. The veterans of the Great War were put front and centre stage in the subsequent campaign, bestowing their unique political capital on the campaign to crush the left. The notion, promoted by the right, that the social order, and with it the colonial order, was under threat successfully mobilized thousands across the colony.

In the post-war moment, the left struggled to reconcile its commitment to the 'equality of sacrifice' with its ambiguous attitude to the indigenous population. The left's mobilization of European and indigenous side by side under the guise of the class struggle incorporated indigenous workers into the labour movement while simultaneously erasing their specificity and failing to address the particular issues that faced them. While the labour movement never brought its declared egalitarianism to its logical conclusion by endorsing legal equality for the indigenous, it did provide a structure and a language through which working-class indigenous Algerians could stake their claim for compensation. In the dying days of the war, the left in Algeria had expressed the desire to transform 'the fraternity of arms' between European and indigenous into a form of 'social fraternity' and 'political fraternity', an ambiguous formula that is more notable for what it did not mean, total equality, than what it did.[134] Throughout the post-war moment, this ambiguity would ensure the left could avoid division over this most contentious of questions for a largely European movement operating in the context of a settler colonial society. Nonetheless, the call to replicate the equality of the trenches in any facet of post-war society opened the door to a fundamental challenge to European hegemony. While such a challenge did not emerge from within the left in the immediate post-war period, the possibility that it might do so fuelled internal division and strengthened external opposition. These would eventually lead to the movement's collapse in the colony. The left's deliberately vague attitude to where the indigenous fit in both its rhetoric and in its vision of a just post-war society pointed to the pitfalls of using the language of the Great War for any cross-community organization in colonial Algeria.

[134] Mama, 'Politique et Réformes Indigènes', *Le Droit du Peuple Nord-Africain*, 17 March 1918.

For the left, the potential polysemy of the Great War made it an attractive but eventually unsustainable rhetorical strategy. The left's recourse to a language anchored in the Great War may have contributed to temporarily swelling its ranks but, in the end, its inability to control the multiple meanings that could be ascribed to this most versatile of framing strategies fuelled the tensions that would lead to its defeat. For its opponents, the left's attempts to monopolize the legitimacy to be garnered from the Great War proved relatively easy to challenge. The victory of the 'fraternity of arms' over the 'equality of sacrifice' in the immediate post-war moment secured the right's almost uncontested monopoly over the evocation of the Great War in social conflicts. In the years that followed, the emergent extreme right in the colony would capitalize on this as it sought to impose its own vision of Algeria's future.

4
Communal Contributions and Racial Hierarchies

On 1 June 1938, Augustin Ibazizen, a Kabyle lawyer, Catholic convert, and naturalized French citizen, addressed a local meeting of the extreme-right *Parti Social Français* in the city of Blida. Ibazizen, a decorated veteran of the Great War, called on the inhabitants of the colony, indigenous and European, to recreate the 'union sealed on the battlefield through the common spilling of blood' so that 'all the disparate races' of the empire could forge a common future and 'sing the Marseillaise in one voice'.[1] The evocation of the sacred memory of the Great War by a party official from a French extreme-right movement was standard practice. The fact that this official was an indigenous Algerian, albeit a naturalized French citizen, and his message was one of racial unity is perhaps more surprising. But, as this chapter will show, the extreme right in interwar Algeria developed a specific rhetoric around the Great War that was designed to legitimize its vision of a renewed empire. The experience of the Great War was mobilized not only by the various extreme-right movements to promote their alternative visions for Algeria but also by those who sought to contest the politics of racial exclusion. They struggled over the political meaning of the communal contribution to the Great War of the colony's three principal cultural groups or, in the vocabulary of the extreme right, 'races': the Jewish, the Muslim, and the European communities. The story of the extreme right in interwar Algeria shows once more that the Great War was a key rhetorical strategy for debating, delineating, defending, and defying the racial boundaries that underpinned the colonial project.

Algeria: Fertile Ground for the Extreme Right

Despite its rich history, the extreme right in Algeria has largely been absent from the existing historiography of both the interwar extreme right and

[1] Police Commissioner of Blida to the Prefect, 1 June 1938, ANOM/91/K/75.

politics in Algeria. The predominance of narratives focused on the rise of Algerian nationalism have obscured the significance of the extreme right.[2] The huge numbers of extreme-right activists in Algeria have not featured in the prominent theoretical debates around the existence of a 'French fascism'.[3] Those works that have studied Algeria's extreme right stress the colony's particular penchant for the politics of the radical right. Where Pascal Blanchard speaks of Algeria's 'fascist vocation',[4] Samuel Kalman asserts that 'Algerian settlers were in reality deeply xenophobic and anti-Semitic, openly favouring authoritarian government while rejecting republicanism altogether'.[5] While such broad assertions of the settlers' inevitable and unbreakable 'fascism' obscure the plurality of political life among the European community, there is an undeniable kernel of truth in their analysis.

The electoral victories and mass mobilization achieved by the extreme right in Algeria speak for themselves. Large sections of the European population in the interwar period did 'eschew the political left, centre and traditional right in equal measure', favouring in their place the local chapters of metropolitan movements or their Algerian homegrown counterparts.[6] In an effort to explain this Algerian exceptionalism, Samuel Kalman proposes a form of colonial 'brutalising thesis', arguing that from the very outset of French rule the racial violence that permeated the colonial state paved the way for an embrace of the extreme right in Algeria.[7] However, as he acknowledges, a commitment to political violence and racial hierarchy did not necessarily imply support for the replacement of the parliamentary regime with an authoritarian state.[8] The French Republican colonial state, far from being opposed to political violence and racial hierarchy, was actually predicated on them. When, in the interwar period, it seemed as though the colonial state might moderate its commitment to both racial hierarchy and the political violence necessary to uphold it, the extreme right offered the ideal alternative.

The persistent political potency of anti-Semitism in Algeria contributed to the expanded constituency for the extreme right. The mass naturalization of the children of European immigrants in 1889 created a whole new class

[2] Pascal Blanchard, 'La vocation fasciste de l'Algérie coloniale dans les années 1930', in *De L'Indochine à l'Algérie: la jeunesse en mouvements des deux côtés du miroir colonial, 1940–1962*, eds. Nicolas Bancel, Daniel Denis, and Youssef Fates (Paris: La Découverte, 2003): 177–94, 178.

[3] See Kevin Passmore, 'L'historiographie du "fascisme" en France', *French Historical Studies* 37, No. 3 (2014): 469–99.

[4] Blanchard. 'La vocation fasciste'.

[5] Kalman, *French Colonial Fascism*, 2.

[6] Ibid.

[7] Ibid., 10–1.

[8] Ibid., 11.

of voters who felt insecure in their 'Frenchness' and sought to assert their claim to membership of the nation over their Jewish neighbours. In the late 1890s, at the height of the Dreyfus Affair, this bitterness turned violent, with vicious anti-Semitic riots spreading across the colony.[9] This history of anti-Semitic violence in the colony created an auspicious environment for the growth of extreme-right movements. They could capitalize on the grievances of Europeans and, to a lesser extent, indigenous Muslims who felt that the Crémieux decree had unfairly granted rights and political power to an undeserving and potentially subversive population. Thus, the politics of exclusion of racial others was well established in Algeria prior to the arrival of the extreme right. In the interwar years, it would become the building block for new political movements that sought to strengthen the racially exclusionary settler polity. Their first target, the Jewish community, would embrace the memory of the Great War as a key weapon against the politics of prejudice.

'What if the Unknown Soldier Were a Jew?' Algeria's Jews and the Extreme Right

Although the Crémieux decree of 1870 had unilaterally granted full citizenship to Algeria's Jews, the community's integration into the national community was by no means secure by the time the Great War broke out. The electoral anti-Semitism of the turn of the century was the political expression of a deep-seated hostility to the Jewish community among sections of settler society. Within the Jewish community, the attempt to reconcile French citizenship with the continued practice of traditional religion also proved contentious. The fact that these debates took place in the context of a colonial society further complicated the dilemmas facing Algeria's Jews. As Joshua Cole has pointed out: 'Constant reminders of their former status as *indigènes* hobbled Algerian Jews with a set of temporal handicaps, a perceived inability to live authentically within the modern world'.[10] Service in the war, that most modern of experiences, could perhaps overcome this perception of backwardness, putting the citizenship of Algeria's Jews beyond question.

[9] Stora, *Algeria 1830–2000*, 10.

[10] Joshua Cole, 'Constantine before the Riots of August 1934: Civil Status Anti-Semitism, and the Politics of Assimilation in Interwar French Algeria', *Journal of North African Studies* 17, No. 5 (December 2012): 839–61, 842.

The service of 13,000 Algerians Jews, 2,800 of whom would pay the ultimate price, was a key moment in the community's history. The outbreak of war did not mark the end of anti-Semitism in Algeria. Indeed, the accounts of discrimination from Jewish Algerian soldiers during the war were so copious that the Consistory of Constantine officially called on the governor general to intervene.[11] Yet, this bigotry notwithstanding, the Great War marked a great advance for the Jewish community, both in the metropole and in Algeria. The spirit of the *Union Sacrée* saw an abandonment of open anti-Semitism among political elites and its exclusion from public discourse.[12] Even as long-standing an anti-Semite as Maurice Barrès endorsed the Jewish community's contribution to the war effort, including the Jews among *Les Diverses Familles Spirituelles de la France* (1917).[13] Jewish leaders used their community's contribution to the war to stress their co-religionists' unquestionable loyalty to the Republic, presenting participation in the war as the final step in the long quest for total emancipation and assimilation. Jews had proven their patriotism and thus had, it seemed, definitively sealed their position in the national community as fully fledged citizens.[14]

The spirit of racial and interfaith harmony that had characterized the language (if not the practice) of the years of the *Union Sacrée* began to falter once the immediate threat to the nation disappeared. While anti-Semitism made its way back into public and political discourse, Jewish participation in the war had fundamentally altered the form it took. Outside of the most radical fringes of the extreme right, the old-fashioned language of racial and religious hatred was replaced by what one rabbi called a 'socially acceptable anti-Semitism'.[15] In the immediate post-war period, the recent memories of Jewish soldiers falling in defence of the *Patrie* militated against the revival of the kind of national-populist anti-Semitism that had been so widespread since the Dreyfus Affair. Nonetheless, Jewish communities remained alert both to the danger posed by a potential resurgence of anti-Semitism and the role the evocation of the Jewish war record could play in offsetting this. In the metropole, a high-profile *Commission historique de recherche de documents sur les Israélites de France pendant la guerre* had been founded in September 1916 under the presidency of Emile Durkheim to gather evidence

[11] Ibid., 71. [12] Ibid., 68.

[13] Maurice Barrès, *Les Diverses Familles Spirituelles de la France* (Paris: Editeurs Emile-Paul Frères, 1917).

[14] Michel Winock, *La France et les Juifs: de 1789 à nos jours* (Paris: Seuil, 2004), 174.

[15] Ralph Schor, *L'Antisémitisme en France dans l'entre-deux-guerres* (Brussels, Editions Complexe, 2005; 1st Edition 1992), 11.

of 'how Frenchmen of Jewish origin behaved in the war'.[16] In 1920, the commission's secretary, Albert Manuel, published the result of this research as a book entitled *Les Israélites dans l'armée française, 1914–1918*, offering a detailed breakdown of Jewish casualties and the citations issued to Jewish soldiers during the war.[17] The community's participation in the war, now 'scientifically' established under the aegis of France's leading sociologist, could be mobilized against any future resurgence of anti-Semitism.

Across the Mediterranean, two prominent activists in the Jewish community, the lieutenant-aviator Léon Mayer and the doctor Henri Aboulker, drew on Algeria's previous experience of organized resistance to anti-Semitism to form the *Comité algérien d'études sociales* in 1915.[18] In a parallel effort to the work of Durkheim's commission, the committee gathered information about the participation of Algeria's Jews in the war, publishing the results in 1919 as the *Livre d'or du judaïsme algérien.*[19] Where Manuel's introduction to *Les Israélites dans l'Armée Française* never explicitly addressed the issue of anti-Semitism, opting instead to evoke Jewish service as a defence of the Zionist project,[20] the preface to the *Livre d'or* underlined the book's importance in the struggle against anti-Semitism. The book opened with a dedication to Léon Mayer. It claimed that the young airman, who had been shot down over Macedonia, had proposed publicizing the community's war record as the key weapon in the fight against what he considered the inevitable future resurgence of anti-Semitism. Mayer had supposedly called for Algeria's Jewish community 'to arm ourselves [*sic*] against our detractors and to prove by official and authentic documents the inanity' of the accusations of those 'who go as far as to question our patriotic sentiments'.[21] The book would embody the sacred bond that now existed between the nation and the Jews of Algeria, ensuring that their position within the national community would never again be called into question.[22] The committee's militant approach would soon prove justified.

[16] Philippe Landau, 'La communauté juive de France et la Grande Guerre', *Annales de démographie historique* 103 (2002): 91–106, 96.

[17] *Les Israélites dans l'Armée Française, 1914–1918* (Angers: Commission historique de recherche de documents sur les Israélites de France pendant la guerre, 1920).

[18] David Cohen, 'Les Circonstances de la Fondation du Comité Algérien d'Etudes Sociales ou la prise de conscience d'une élite intellectuelle juive face au phénomène antisémite en Algérie (1915–1921)', *Revue des études juives* 161, No. 1–2 (January–June 2002): 179–225.

[19] *Le Livre d'Or du Judaïsme Algerien* (Algiers: Publications du Comité d'Etudes Sociales, 1919).

[20] Albert Manuel, 'Avertissemen', in *Les Israélites dans l'Armée Française, 1914–1918*, ii.

[21] A.C., 'A Léon Mayer', in *Le Livre d'Or*, 5–6.

[22] 'Préface', in *Le Livre d'Or*, 10.

Within a year of the Armistice, Algeria witnessed an attempt to revive the colony's long-standing tradition of political anti-Semitism. In 1920–1, the city of Constantine, the most proportionately Jewish of Algeria's large cities, played host to a violent campaign by the anti-Semitic press that resulted in pitched street battles between European and Jewish youths.[23] The resurgence of popular anti-Semitism was exploited for commercial gain by the owners of a new bi-weekly publication, *La Tribune*, which, at its peak, reached a circulation of 6,000.[24] A key element of *La Tribune*'s attack on the Jewish community was the charge that they had not played their part in the Great War. In June 1921, the newspaper reported on a meeting held by its director, M. Amalfitano, in which he questioned the Jewish contribution to the war and attacked their trumpeting of Jewish service: 'Their rallying cry is "we fought in the war!" Did Frenchmen not also fight in the war? To hear them speak, you would think that they alone drove back the enemy.'[25] He further contended that the only way to secure the future of the *Patrie* for which so many Frenchmen fell was to reject Jews and their supposedly pernicious influence.[26] The Jews were portrayed as the agents of both anarchic disorder and international finance, in sharp contrast to the selfless heroes who had fallen to save France from such forces.

For those who rallied against this sudden upsurge of anti-Semitism, the war record of the Jewish community seemed the most powerful counter-argument. The fact that *La Tribune*'s campaign coincided with the first convoy of bodies repatriated from the battlefields, including some Jewish soldiers, was highlighted to great effect by the Jewish press and community leaders. In an article celebrating the imminent repatriation of the war dead, *La Verité*, the leading Jewish newspaper in Algeria, vilified those behind the anti-Semitic campaign as 'troublemakers', pleading that 'France remain united in peace as she was in war'.[27] This sentiment was echoed by a Jewish councillor in Constantine, who evoked the image of the arrival of the corpses of 'two soldiers who fell in defence of their country, a Catholic and a Jew' to plead for the perpetuation of the *Union Sacrée* and an end to any 'violence and hatred'.[28] The place offered by the colonial authorities to the Jewish community in the nascent culture of commemoration granted them a powerful counter-narrative with which to challenge the hatred promoted by *La Tribune* and its supporters.

[23] Cole, 'Constantine before the Riots', 840–1. [24] Ibid.
[25] 'Une Grande Réunion', *La Tribune*, 20 June 1921. [26] Ibid.
[27] 'Le Retour des Morts', *La Vérité*, 30 June 1921.
[28] Deliberations of the Municipal Council of Constantine, 16 June 1921, ANOM/93/B/3/528.

The resistance of the Jewish community was not, however, restricted to the rhetorical defence of the war dead. Following the participation of a group of Jewish athletes from Constantine in a ceremony at the Tomb of the Unknown Soldier in Paris, anti-Semites sacked the hall used by the gymnasts. In retaliation, a group of Jewish veterans descended on the printing house that published *La Tribune*, smashing the press.[29] Faced with the undeniable presence of Jewish veterans, *La Tribune* temporarily switched tack, asserting that the events at the printing house simply confirmed that Jewish veterans had, in fact, fought the war for the 'blue flag of Israel'[30] and now sought to 'threaten French citizens'.[31] When the visibility of Jewish veterans undermined attempts to obscure the Jewish communal contribution, *La Tribune* could easily reformulate its charge of treachery by claiming Jewish participation was born of self-interest not patriotism.

In the end, the anti-Semitic incidents of 1920–1 in Constantine petered out without causing major disruption to the administration of the city or its Jewish population. *La Tribune* failed to spark either the kind of persistent anti-Semitic campaigns the city had seen in the past or the deadly pogrom it would experience in the not so distant future. The traditional forces of political anti-Semitism in the city did not rally to *La Tribune*'s cause. Emile Morinaud, a key figure in the populist anti-Semitism of the turn of the century, had, by the early 1920s, built an electoral alliance with the city's Jewish community.[32] Furthermore, *La Tribune*'s campaign coincided with the drive by Morinaud and the European political elite to undo the wartime suspension of full disciplinary powers over the indigenous population. This measure to protect European hegemony would require Jewish support.[33] His official response expressed support for the Jewish community, asserting that 'such a campaign, coming after a war in which everyone did his fraternal and patriotic duty, could have no effect on the public'.[34] The Muslim community were all but absent from the public discourse around the campaign, as political anti-Semitism remained a strategy employed in a competition between rival electoral lobbies among the city's colonial citizens.[35] Finally, and perhaps most importantly, the persistence of the memory of the *Union*

[29] 'Une campagne antisémite provoque à Constantine de regrettables incidents', *Le Matin*, 16 June 1921.

[30] 'Le Courage Juif: Représailles Françaises', *La Tribune*, 26 June 1921.

[31] Cole, 'Constantine before the Riots', 843.

[32] Ibid., 843.

[33] Ibid.

[34] 'Une campagne antisémite', *Le Matin*, 16 June 1921.

[35] Cole, 'Constantine before the Riots', 844.

Sacrée and the Jewish sacrifice of the war, so clearly underlined in official commemorative culture, not only reinforced the resistance of the Jewish community but also militated against a resurgence of anti-Semitism in respectable political discourse.

As new political movements with no connection to the *Union Sacrée* began to emerge in post-war Algeria, anti-Semitism crept back into the language of mainstream politics. In Oran, the capital of the most demographically European of Algeria's departments, a local doctor and charismatic speaker Jules Molle founded the *Unions Latines*, a political grouping with one driving goal: 'to defend the predominance... of the citizens of the Latin race against the political machinations of the Jewish electoral bloc'.[36] Dr Molle's successful campaign for the mayoralty in 1925 embraced a virulent brand of electoral anti-Semitism.[37] Jews were portrayed as a 'caste apart' whose 'blind submission to their leaders' compromised the republican electoral system.[38] Against this bloc stood the new 'Algerian race' formed by the 'three Latin races of the Mediterranean basin', 'the men of French blood, Spanish blood and Italian blood'.[39] Dr Molle presented himself as the figure to unite this new race, with his mouthpiece, *Le Petit Oranais*, interspersing appeals to *latinité* with virulent denunciations of the Jews. This did not, however, represent a simple resurgence of the violent anti-Semitic politics of the turn of the century. Molle's supporters recognized that the long-term viability of their organization as a political force was dependant on their ability to conduct an anti-Semitic campaign within or just beyond the boundaries of Republican legality.[40] The Unions Latines (UL) avoided overtly violent actions against Jews, preferring '"legal" forms' of discrimination such as economic boycotts and a refusal to hire Jews for municipal jobs.[41] In Molle's Oran, the *Union Sacrée* seemed a distant memory.

The Jewish community's defence against the UL relied heavily on the evocation of the war. In February 1928, members of the Jewish community and their political allies formed the *Club civique oranais* with the aim of counteracting Molle's campaign.[42] The club supported those who pursued legal cases against Dr Molle for defamation while also seeking to convince

[36] Note on the Union Latine, 24 February 1931, ANOM/92//95.

[37] Sophie B. Roberts, 'Anti-Semitism and municipal government in interwar French colonial Algeria', *Journal of North African Studies* 17, No. 5 (December 2012): 821–37, 827–8.

[38] 'L'Union Latine, Notre Raison d'être', undated, ANOM/92//95.

[39] Ibid.

[40] Orion, 'A Propos d'un Départ', *Le Petit Oranais*, 20 May 1928.

[41] Kalman, *French Colonial Fascism*, 32.

[42] Note on the Club Civique d'Oran, undated, ANOM/92//95.

the governor general to ban the movement.[43] Molle's newspaper, *Le Petit Oranais*, by this stage bedecked with swastikas, launched a stinging attack on the club, denouncing the Jews as false republicans and asserting that they 'vote mechanically as one man'.[44] In its response, the *Club civique* defended the republican patriotism of the Jews by evoking the egalitarian experience of the war.[45] The article went on to evoke what would become one of the standard tropes of the campaign against anti-Semitism in interwar Algeria (and the metropole): 'If, by chance, during your future visit to Paris, you were to bow before the sacred slab of the Unknown Soldier who sleeps under the *Arc de Triomphe*, could you not, then, ask yourself the following question: What if the Unknown Soldier were a Jew?'[46] The Tomb of the Unknown Soldier embodied the universality of loss: the anonymity of the body interred underneath the Arc de Triomphe 'guaranteed the heroism of all'.[47] Thus, for a minority group such as the Algerian Jews, the possibility that one of their own could have been chosen to represent the fallen of the nation as a whole was a powerful symbol of their integration into the national community, a symbol that their opponents could not easily dismiss.

While the *Club civique* waged an intensely political campaign against the outburst of anti-Semitism in Oran, challenging their opponents in the courts and in the pages of the political press, the leaders of Algeria's Jewish community pursued a less aggressive strategy. They sought to emphasize the Jewish contribution to the Great War as the final phase of Jewish assimilation. The official leaders of Judaism in the colony successfully lobbied and fundraised for the construction of a monument to Algeria's Jewish war dead in the European cemetery in Algiers. The inauguration, on Armistice Day 1927, was attended by leading figures of both the Jewish community and the colonial authorities. The speech given by the chief rabbi of France, Israël Lévi, established a direct link of filiation between the Jews who fought in the war and preceding generations of Algerian Jews who had benefited from French rule:

> They were the grandchildren of those who, almost a century ago, were overjoyed to see the French flag bringing civilisation and freedom to this

[43] Kalman, *French Colonial Fascism*, 34–5.
[44] Roger Bonsens, 'Le Club Civique', *Le Petit Oranais*, 13 May 1928.
[45] The Club Civique Oranais to the Director of the Petit Oranais, 15 May 1928, ANOM/92//95.
[46] Ibid.
[47] Stéphane Audoin-Rouzeau and Annette Becker, *14–8: retrouver la Guerre* (Paris: Gallimard, 2000), 224.

> land; they were the sons of those who had the joy of receiving the title, so desired, of French citizen, they longed to prove to France that she was not wrong to presume that they would be grateful and were proud to seal the charter of their emancipation with their blood.[48]

The Great War was the zenith of this symbiotic relationship, a cataclysmic event that sealed the union between France and Algeria's Jewish community. Faced with a rising tide of anti-Semitism, the leaders of the Jewish community embraced the consensual commemorative culture of the Republic, seeking to mobilize the memory of the war to perpetuate the politics of the *Union Sacrée.*

Molle's unexpected death in 1931 coincided with a period of transformation for the extreme right in Algeria. A new style of politics was emerging alongside traditional forms of municipal populist anti-Semitism. The nebulous political groupings such as the UL that had been little more than a vehicle for the personal ambitions of local politicians, using anti-Semitism to mobilize supporters, now gave way to more organized and disciplined mass movements imported from the metropole. The rise of indigenous political movements in the wake of the 1930 centenary celebrations changed the dynamic of racial politics in Algeria, leading the extreme right to alternately, even simultaneously, court the indigenous population and call for a reinforcement of the repressive machinery of the colonial state.

These changes were paralleled in the Jewish community, where the institutional bodies (the *Consistoires*) and groups of local notables saw their monopoly on the struggle against anti-Semitism challenged.[49] In 1928, a group of young Jewish activists in Paris, dismayed at what they considered the passivity of official Judaism in the face of rising anti-Semitism, came together to form the *Ligue International Contre l'Antisémitisme* (LICA), an organization that sought to combat the political forces promoting hatred of the Jews.[50] It would play a key role in defending Algeria's Jews throughout the 1930s.

This blend of the old and the new in the politics of Algeria's extreme right would manifest itself most violently in the anti-Semitic riots that erupted in the city of Constantine in August 1934. In the late evening of 3 August, a

[48] *Inauguration au Cimetière Israélite de Saint-Eugène à Alger du Monument aux Morts de la Grande Guerre (1914–1918)* (Algiers: Association Consistoriale Israélite d'Alger, 1927), 23.
[49] Michel Abitbol, *Les Juifs d'Afrique du Nord sous Vichy* (Paris: Editions Maisonneuve, 1983), 48.
[50] Schor, *L'Antisémitisme*, 212.

drunken Jewish soldier got involved in a heated dispute with a group of Muslims who he had insulted as they carried out their ablutions in the washroom of the Sidi Lakhdar mosque. An angry mob gathered outside the soldier's house, throwing stones and shouting insults, with his Jewish neighbours, in return, raining down projectiles on the crowd. A rumour quickly spread that a stray bullet had severely, or possibly fatally, injured a young indigenous man.[51] In the days that followed, pitched battles raged across the city, often without any intervention by the police, leaving in their wake twenty-five dead from the Jewish community and three from the Muslim community.[52] The riots in Constantine were remarkable both for their ferocity and for the fact that it was the indigenous inhabitants of the city, and not the European population, who had perpetrated most of the violence against the Jewish population.[53] The distinct demography of Constantine as a majority Muslim city with a large Jewish population may go some way towards explaining this particularity.[54] However, the key to understanding the exceptional violence between the Jewish and Muslim communities lies in the transformation of politics in the years directly preceding the riots.

While Constantine had witnessed few incidents of violent anti-Semitism in the period 1930–2, 1933 saw a sharp increase in the city in the form of anti-Semitic political action that combined traditional Algerian populist anti-Jewish feeling with the strategies of mobilization of the new movements of the extreme right.[55] That year saw the arrival of Henri Lautier, an anti-Semite polemicist from the metropole whose newspaper, *L'Eclair Algérien*, would play a key role in stoking tension in the city. *L'Éclair* condemned the Jews, who, supposedly so absent in the trenches, were omnipresent in the organizations that distributed financial assistance to veterans. Their insignificant sacrifice had served only to entrench Jewish dominance of the corrupt political system, leaving the veteran community cowed and impotent.[56] Lautier further developed these allegations in his book *Le Ghetto*, with a whole section dedicated to '*Les Juifs et la Défense Nationale*' in which he claimed Algerian Jews had 'usurped the title of veteran' and 'had not died for France but rather they killed 1,700,000 Frenchmen in order to colonise

[51] Pierre Darmon, *L'Algérie des passions, 1870–1939* (Paris: Editions Perrin, 2012; 1st Edition 2009), 647.
[52] Cole, 'Constantine before the Riots', 839–40.
[53] Ibid., 840.
[54] Ibid., 840.
[55] Ibid., 849.
[56] Edition spéciale de *L'Eclair Algérien*, ANOM/91/1K/38.

us, to pillage us, to subjugate us'.[57] When Jewish and Christian youths from rival swimming clubs clashed in May 1933, a police report held Lautier responsible for the climate of conflict that had taken hold in the city.[58] The local police force, however, was not necessarily hostile to Lautier and his followers. Sympathy for anti-Semitism and the extreme right was a notable feature of local police forces across the colony.[59] The head of the city's police force described Lautier as 'intelligent, agreeable, and extremely well educated', claiming that his charge that the Jews had shirked their responsibilities during the war were based on 'serious and precise documentation'.[60] Constantine's Jews could not, it seemed, rely on the police to hold back the rising tide of anti-Semitism.

The city's Jewish community did not remain passive in the face of this fresh onslaught of anti-Semitism. Lautier's slanderous accusations were met with particular hostility by veterans, with one of their number approaching him in the nearby city of Souk-Ahras and punching the polemicist in the face.[61] Official Judaism in the city continued to rely on the somewhat unlikely alliance it had built with the former anti-Semite Emile Morinaud, who as city mayor and deputy for Constantine offered protection to his Jewish constituents.[62] Unfortunately, for the Jews of Constantine, the transformation of politics that Algeria had experienced in the early 1930s meant that the old logics of municipal politics no longer applied. Not only were the local authorities, the police force, and the most powerful political leader, Morinaud, half-hearted in their opposition to the riots,[63] they also held little sway over the mobs attacking the Jewish quarter. Sections of the Muslim community that had remained indifferent to the anti-Semitic polemics of the early 1920s had a radically different reaction in 1934.

While there is little evidence that local Muslim political leaders stoked hate against the Jews, they did not actively discourage it.[64] The efforts of

[57] "Le Ghetto", Résumé de Publications en préparation d'Henri Lautier, undated, ANOM/91/1K/38.

[58] Departmental Security Report, Constantine, 30 May 1933, ANOM/GGA/9H/53.

[59] See Samuel Kalman, 'Avec une brutalité toute particulière: Fascist Sympathies, Racial Violence, and the Municipal Police and Gendarmerie in Oran, 1936–37', in *The French Right between the Wars: Political and Intellectual Movements from Conservatism to Fascism*, eds. Samuel Kalman and Seán Kennedy (Oxford: Bergham, 2014): 48–64.

[60] Constantine Police Commissioner to the Prefect, 11 September 1933, ANOM 91/1K/38.

[61] Police Commissioner of Souk-Ahras to the Director of General Security, 23 June 1934, ANOM/91/1K/38.

[62] Cole, 'Constantine before the Riots', 843.

[63] Abitbol, *Les Juifs d'Afrique du Nord*, 34.

[64] Cole, 'Constantine before the Riots', 848.

Muslim leaders including the charismatic Dr Bendjelloul, leader of the powerful local branch of the *Fédération des Elus Musulmans Algériens*, to secure the same rights as the Jewish community without renouncing their personal status led to tensions.[65] The growing hostility towards the Jews on the part of politicized Muslims in Algeria was also connected to the rising tensions between the Jewish and Muslim communities in mandate Palestine. Although Zionism attracted few recruits among Algeria's Jews, elements within the Muslim community, especially those with access to the Middle Eastern press, imbibed the growing hostility towards the global Jewish community.[66] The new mass movements of the extreme right were only too happy to fan the flames of hatred. They also acted as a source of political pressure on the uneasy coalition that underpinned Morinaud's truce with the Jewish population, leaving the Jews without important allies in their moment of need.[67] While the Constantine pogrom was the highpoint of anti-Jewish violence in interwar Algeria, political anti-Semitism had once more established itself as a force to be reckoned with; one that the extreme right hoped would transcend both class and racial boundaries.

For the LICA, the Great War remained the best weapon in the struggle against anti-Semitism. In the wake of the riots, the front page of *Le droit de vivre*, the LICA's newspaper, bore a striking juxtaposition of two images under the title 'Jewish blood has been spilled in France'. The image on the left, entitled 'August 1914', showed a column of foreign Jews marching through Paris on their way to, as the caption puts it, 'volunteer and die for France'. Its mirror image on the right showed a scene of devastation beneath the title 'August 1934'. The caption informed the reader that 'in Constantine, Jews die because of the authorities'.[68] The heroic selflessness of the foreign Jewish volunteers who, though free of any legal responsibility to enrol had rushed to defend France, was harshly contrasted here with the failure of the authorities in Constantine to meet their legal obligation to defend the citizens of the city's Jewish community.

Le Droit de vivre's response gave particular importance to the recently formed LICA veterans' association,[69] which, as LICA president Bernard

[65] Ibid., 850.

[66] Charles-Robert Ageron, 'Une émeute anti-juive à Constantine (août 1934)', *Revue de l'Occident musulman et de la Méditerranée* 13–14 (1973): 23–40, 38.

[67] Cole, 'Constantine before the Riots', 846.

[68] 'Le sang juif a coulé en France', *Le droit de vivre*, August 1934.

[69] 'Appel aux Ligueurs anciens combattants et mobilisés de la guerre 1914–18', *Le droit de vivre*, 25 March 1934.

Lecache pointed out, was led by a Jewish war amputee from Algeria.[70] Writing on behalf of the veterans, J. Hadjadj declared that they 'could not remain indifferent when faced with the painful events in Constantine'. Turning once more to the notion of mutual obligation, he sardonically questioned the nature of the rights enjoyed by the Jewish veterans of Constantine: 'Algerian Jewish veterans for whom, like for all the others, the phrase "They have rights over us" was pronounced. What rights? The right, perhaps, to see their women and children the innocent victims of a pack of Arabs whipped up by our own followers of Hitler.'[71] The state's failure to meet its duties to the Jewish community could, according to Hadjadj, only be remedied by a purge within the local administration and 'the dissolution of the fascist leagues'.[72] The Jewish veterans were once more centre stage in the fight against anti-Semitism in Algeria.

Veterans were also central to the 'fascist league' that was the principal target of Hadjadj and the LICA. More than any other movement on the extreme right, the *Croix de Feu* (CdF) drew its strength, in terms both of rhetoric and of membership, from the generation that had participated in the war. This reliance on the war as the central reference point for political action complicated its attitude toward the Jewish community. In his 1934 treatise on the ideology of the CdF, the movement's founder Colonel François de La Rocque seemed to reject anti-Semitism and other forms of racial hatred by openly evoking the Great War. He asserted that 'the men of 1914–1918 would protest from the depths of their heroic tombs' were any government to 'exclude from the French community those who, having given their blood immediately became an essential part of it'.[73]

And yet, for all his denunciation of the politics of ethnic division, La Rocque's universalist message carried an important condition: 'their devotion alone counts, with the sole condition that this devotion is sincere, proven, and confirmed'.[74] Jews who embraced the nationalist vision promoted by the CdF were 'proper Frenchmen'; those who did not were fair game.

The CdF in Algeria found it particularly difficult to reconcile the paradox at the heart of La Rocque's attitude towards the Jews. Tensions constantly arose among the movement's cadres, who attempted to rein in the open anti-Semitism of local activists. A letter from the organization's leader in

70 Bernard Lecache, 'Nous accusons', *Le droit de vivre*, August 1934.
71 J. Hadjadj, 'Les Anciens Combattants de la LICA exigent…', *Le droit de vivre*, August 1934.
72 Ibid.
73 Colonel de la Rocque, *Service Public* (Paris: Éditions Bernard Grasset, 1934), 156–7.
74 Ibid.

Algeria, Commandant Debay, to the governor general acknowledged that 'a good number' of its members were 'inclined to be unsympathetic to the Jews', declaring that the left-wing politics of the Jews was to blame for this.[75] This victim-blaming aside, he asserted that the movement was committed to preventing 'comrades from making personal comments that could engage the responsibility of the movement'.[76] This was hardly a forceful condemnation of the ideology behind these comments, but it is indicative of a desire to distance the CdF from open anti-Semitism.

The notion that a 'good Jew' would be welcomed in the CdF was central to its rejection of allegations of anti-Semitism. In 1933, La Rocque had refuted claims of anti-Semitism by evoking the membership of the archetypal 'good Jew', the veteran who would testify 'that the issue of religion has never been raised in our association'.[77] Elsewhere, the CdF explicitly stated that religion or ethnicity was irrelevant; your war record alone determined your status as a good Frenchman.[78]

Key to this effort to use the war to counter claims of anti-Semitism was the CdF's commemorative service at Paris' Synagogue de la Victoire. In his 1933 letter to Lecache, La Rocque had declared that the CdF would participate every year in a ceremony in honour of the war dead at 'Notre-Dame, a Jewish temple, and a Protestant temple'.[79] When, in 1936, the grand rabbi of Paris and war veteran, Jacob Kaplan, announced that he would welcome the CdF into the synagogue, he provoked outrage, not least among Algeria's Jewish community. A series of as yet unclassed documents in the Archives of the *Consistoire Central* testify to an intense campaign by both the institutions of official Judaism and more openly political activist groups in Algeria against the presence of the CdF in the synagogue. On 11 June 1936, M.E. Yaffi, a representative of the LICA in Algiers, wrote to the president of the local *Consistoire* to express his dismay at the invitation extended to the CdF. He described the CdF as 'clearly anti-Semitic in North Africa', referring to its 'odious propaganda' and its predominant role in anti-Semitic violence, before calling on the *Consistoire* to send a formal protest to Paris.[80] The following day, the president of the Algiers *Consistoire*, M. Kanoui, sent

[75] Commandant Debay to the Governor General, 5 April 1936, ANOM/GGA/3CAB/47.

[76] Ibid.

[77] La Rocque quoted in Robert Soucy, *French Fascism: The Second Wave, 1933–1939* (New Haven, CT: Yale University Press, 1995), 154.

[78] Katz, 'Jews and Muslims in the Shadow of Marianne', 140.

[79] La Rocque quoted in Soucy, *French Fascism: The Second Wave*, 154.

[80] M. Yaffi, Secretary of the LICA to the President of the Algiers Consistory, 11 June 1936, Archives du Consistoire Central (ACC), Dossier Antisémitisme-Algérie (as yet unclassed).

a telegram of protest to the chief rabbi citing the 'constant and well-known anti-Semitic actions of the *Croix de Feu*'.[81] The chief rabbi's response bears testament to deep tensions within the Jewish community around the attitude towards the CdF. He suggested that the telegram had been motivated by the overzealous action of the LICA and defended CdF participation, pointing to the movement's official rejection of anti-Semitism and its attempts to crack down on anti-Jewish actions in Algeria.[82] M. Kanoui's response contained a whole list of charges against the CdF, including its endorsement of openly anti-Semitic candidates, and declared that their participation, 'under the pretext of homage to our dead, sullied our sacred space'.[83] While the pillars of institutional Judaism and the activists of the campaign against anti-Semitism in the metropole clashed over the CdF and its supposed commitment to the *Union Sacrée*, the Jews of Algeria now seemed united. This unity would be much needed in the dark days ahead.

The election of the Popular Front, a left-wing government under a Jewish prime minister who was proposing to reform colonial rule in Algeria, would lead to a dramatic increase in anti-Semitic activity in Algeria. The Algerian branch of the *Parti Social Français* (PSF), which had replaced the disbanded CdF following the Popular Front's *anti-ligue* legislation, proved less reticent than its predecessor organization to endorse political anti-Semitism.[84] Faced with fierce competition from rival movements of the extreme right, the party cadres seemed more willing to give activists free rein in Algeria and this invariably meant an upsurge in anti-Semitism.[85] The distinction between the 'good Jew', typically represented by the Jewish war dead whose death conveniently robbed them of the right to contest the PSF, and the 'bad Jew', whose hostility to the PSF bore testament to his inherent treachery, did not completely disappear from the new party's discourse. In the first issue of the PSF's North African newspaper, *La Flamme*, the group's leader in Constantine and deputy in the National Assembly, Stanislas Devaud, addressed what he called the 'irritating Jewish question' by asserting that the 'Dead of the Great War' proved that the 'Jews have a truly French soul'.[86]

[81] Telegram from the President of the Algiers Consistory to the Chief Rabbi, 12 June 1936, ACC Dossier Antisémitisme-Algérie.
[82] Chief Rabbi to the President of the Algiers Consistory, 15 June 1936, ACC Dossier Antisémitisme-Algérie.
[83] President of the Algiers Consistory to the Chief Rabbi, 15 June 1936, ACC Dossier Antisémitisme-Algérie.
[84] Kalman, *French Colonial Fascism*, 133.
[85] Ibid.
[86] Stanislas Devaud, 'Le PSF et les problèmes algériens', *La Flamme*, 15 January 1937.

So here it seemed as though 'loyal' Jews, particularly those who had fought in the war, were welcome in the ranks of the Algerian PSF. However, this message of tolerance was undermined by the increasing dominance in the party's discourse of a racial understanding of the Jew as irredeemably perfidious. Speaking at a meeting in Oran in April 1938, a PSF local representative M. Sarocchi claimed to reject racism but openly endorsed an intrinsically racialized conception of 'the Jew'. He asserted that the 'Jewish question' in North Africa was not one of 'religion or race' but rather 'a question of mentality and spirit'. The 'Jewish spirit', he affirmed, 'is marked by…idealism, pride, and anxiety, to which we must add the taste for revenge and the desire for power'. Above all else, the 'Jew is revolutionary by birth'.[87] Sarocchi had dispensed with the concept of the 'good Jew', suggesting that Jews were biologically incapable of loyalty. In October 1938, the Congress of the Constantine Federation of the PSF, under the stewardship of Devaud and in the presence of La Rocque, would officially come out in favour of the boycott of Jewish businesses in the city.[88] By the late 1930s, the PSF had endorsed the politics of anti-Semitism. Even the limited concessions it had made to the possibility of Jewish loyalty, centred on the communal contribution of the Jews to the Great War, were increasingly abandoned in favour of a racialized conception of the Jew. If the 'good Jew' had ever existed, he had died on the battlefields of northern France.

The PSF's major rival on the political scene, the *Parti Populaire Français* (PPF), had not initially endorsed anti-Semitism and counted some Jewish comrades from Jacques Doriot's days in the Communist Party among its most prominent members.[89] Nevertheless, the movement's leader in Algeria, Victor Arrighi, recognized that the party's earlier rejection of anti-Semitism alienated large swathes of the European population and moved to incorporate anti-Jewish policies into the party's platform by 1938.[90] The party's rhetoric rarely acknowledged Jewish participation in the Great War. In an address to the Second North African Congress of the PPF, on 12 November 1938, Arrighi spoke in glowing terms of the previous day's veterans' parade before calling for the revocation of the Crémieux Decree to save France from the 'permanent blackmail of this racist bloc'.[91] Unlike the CdF and its successor, the PSF, for whom the Great War would always be a central reference point,

[87] Police Commissioner of Oran to the Prefect, 23 April 1938, ANOM/92//70.
[88] 'Le Premier Congrès de la Fédération PSF de Constantine', *La Flamme*, 28 October 1938.
[89] Soucy, *French Fascism: The Second Wave*, 278.
[90] Kalman, *French Colonial Fascism*, 140.
[91] 'Rapport du 11 novembre 1938 devant le 2ème Congrès Nord-Africain', ANOM/91/1F/392.

the PPF largely avoided the problematic 'good Jew'/'bad Jew' dichotomy by simply obscuring Jewish participation in the war and all that it implied for nationalist politics.

In their efforts to refute these claims of Jewish treachery, politicians and activists in the colony turned constantly to the Great War. At an Algeria-wide level, it was once again the LICA and its political allies that led the charge against the anti-Semites. Alarmed at the rise of anti-Semitism among the Muslim population, stoked by the extreme right, the LICA and local Jewish elites sought to build alliances with Muslim leaders. In the wake of the Constantine riots, religious and secular leaders from both communities sought to foster dialogue and minimize conflict, notably through the foundation of groups such as *Le Comité d'Union Sémite Universelle* and the *Union des Croyants Monothéistes*.[92] While divisions over the Palestinian question proved an important obstacle to a Muslim-Jewish united front against the extreme right,[93] the shared experience of the Great War was seen as a potential point of convergence. This is clear in the discourse employed by LICA president Bernard Lecache on his tour of Algeria in March 1937. Throughout his visit, Lecache referred to the war as a moment of racial unity that proved, beyond doubt, the loyalty to France of Algeria's Jewish and Muslim populations. After all, he said, 'the shells and bullets, before penetrating our chests, did not ask what confession we were'.[94] At a joint meeting with the prominent *Association des 'Ulama Musulmans Algériens* (AUMA) leader Cheikh El-Okbi in the colony's capital, he attacked those who were scare-mongering about the unity of Jews, Muslims, and Europeans under the Popular Front as traitors to the memories of the war dead.[95]

Local activists across the colony echoed Lecache's vision of a renewed Union Sacrée as a progressive force of racial unity. In 1936, the *Comité algérien d'études sociales*, which had disbanded in 1921 as anti-Semitism in Algeria seemingly abated, was resurrected by a new generation of Jewish notables as the *Comité juif d'études sociales*. Once more, the war was to be its central weapon in the fight against anti-Semitism, 'the old and unjust

[92] Aomar Boum, 'Partners against Anti-Semitism: Muslims and Jews Respond to Nazism in French North African Colonies, 1936–1940', *Journal of North African Studies* 19, No. 4 (2014): 554–70, 563.

[93] Ibid., 566.

[94] Lecache, 'La Grande "Tournée" nord-Africaine de la LICA', *Le droit de vivre*, 17 March 1937.

[95] Lecache, 'Nous travaillons à la grandeur de l'Algérie Française et de la France', *Le droit de vivre*, 3 April, 1937.

prejudices against Jews'.[96] In Algiers, the local Popular Front deputy and LICA member Marcel Régis launched a stinging attack on anti-Semites, echoing a classic argument of the defenders of the Jews:

> Who is to say that the Great Unknown Soldier who sleeps under the sacred altar is not Jewish? The corpse was solemnly selected at Verdun, where North African battalions lost most of their troops. Let him sleep in peace, the Immortal Hero…what France wanted was never to know if he was named Paul, Mohammed, or Jacob.[97]

For Régis, the LICA, and the Jewish supporters of the Popular Front, the war embodied their vision of a racially united Algeria, sharing a common struggle for the republican values of liberty, equality, and fraternity. The fact that members of all Algeria's communities had fought and died together belied the racial divisions promoted by the extreme right and cast their attempts to row back on the citizenship of Jews as treacherous. By evoking the Jewish war dead, the opponents of the extreme right challenged their self-proclaimed monopoly on patriotism and undermined their claim to the heritage of the Great War.

But how successful was this attempt to mobilize the war against the anti-Semites? The actions of the Algerian Jewish community, whether through local committees, official institutions, or an activist organization like the LICA, did not halt the advance of extreme-right movements among large sections of the European population in the late 1930s. Their record in the 1920s is more mixed, with a degree of success in Constantine, in part due to the alliance with Morinaud, but a failure to destabilize Molle in Oran. The ardent defence of the war record of the Jews did push direct attacks on the Jewish communal contribution to the margins of extreme-right discourse by the end of the period. The principal actors on the extreme right avoided the kinds of numerical debates that had previously been favoured by anti-Semite polemicists. In many cases they avoided referring to the Jewish contribution to the war altogether. One could even argue that the Algerian Jewish community's constant reference to the war successfully challenged any attempt by the extreme right to monopolize the symbolic capital of the Great War. While, as we shall see, the war was a favoured reference in extreme-right attempts to win over the Muslim population, it was not

[96] 'Comité Juif d'études sociales: Déclaration fondamentale', *Bulletin de la Fédération des Sociétés Juives d'Algérie*, February 1937.
[97] 'Tract de la LICA: Guerre à la haine', 16 June 1938, ANOM/92/2541.

frequently employed when addressing the European population. The memory of the participation of the Jews, who had fought as citizens with the same status as their European compatriots, made any attempt to articulate an anti-Semitic vision of European supremacy in terms of the glory of the war extremely problematic.

Fraternity or Hierarchy in the Trenches: Muslims, the Great War, and the Extreme Right

The extreme right's principal issue with Algeria's Jewish population, their allegedly undeserved status as citizens, did not apply to the colony's indigenous Muslim community. Over the course of the interwar period, the attitude of Algeria's extreme right towards the indigenous evolved from a combination of indifference, occasional open hostility, and restrained paternalism towards a guarded attempt to woo this increasingly politicized constituency. The Muslim communal contribution to the Great War lay at the heart of extreme-right discourse around the indigenous population.

In the years immediately after the war, the colonial authorities' development of a commemorative culture that celebrated racial unity and reconciliation, even while reproducing European hegemony, made tribute to the Muslim fallen almost a prerequisite for political respectability in Algeria.[98] Nonetheless, as we have already seen in Chapter 2, certain opponents of the proposals for political reform in the wake of the war were happy to minimize the number of Algerian war dead and thus undermine their claim for new rights. Once the controversy surrounding political reform passed and the final project left European hegemony largely unthreatened, these polemics faded. In the language of the nascent extreme right in Algeria, the indigenous is mainly notable by his absence. In the Latinist tradition, the *Union Sacrée* had been portrayed as the coming together of the various European populations in Algeria under the French tricolour, actively excluding the Jews. The Muslim population stood completely outside it.[99] Coverage of commemorative ceremonies centred on disputes with the Jewish community and did not reference the indigenous.[100] In his speech at the inauguration of Oran's

98 Jansen, 'Une autre "Union Sacrée"?', 32–60.

99 'L'Union Sacrée en Algérie: Les Etrangers', *Le Petit Oranais*, 17 September 1920.

100 'Mauvaise Besogne', *Le Petit Oranais*, 15 May 1925 and 'A propos d'un incident survenu à l'issue de la cérémonie d'inauguration', *Le Petit Oranais*, 2 March 1925.

war memorial, Dr Molle only referred to the specific contribution of the indigenous to the war in passing, dedicating more time to his municipality's financial contribution to the monument.[101] The duties of public office bound Dr Molle and his equivalents elsewhere in Algeria to honour the indigenous war dead in the commemorative discourse promoted by the colonial authorities. Nevertheless, the indigenous contribution to the war never became a point of reference in their everyday language of politics.

The new movements of the extreme right in the 1930s would, in contrast, place the indigenous contribution to the Great War at the heart of their political discourse. In the context of a rapid process of politicization among the masses, these movements could not ignore the indigenous, seeking instead to co-opt them into their wider political vision of Algeria and her place in the empire. The Great War would be a key point of reference in this campaign, a discursive strategy that was met with varying degrees of hostility and enthusiasm among indigenous political actors.

The CdF was the first extreme-right movement to undertake a significant recruitment campaign among the indigenous population. In its early years, the CdF had targeted indigenous veterans, subjecting prospective members' morality and political opinions to close scrutiny and often accepting them only on recommendation from a former comrade-in-arms.[102] The Algiers branch participated in commemorative services at the *Grande Mosquée* and Muslim veterans were encouraged to express themselves at the group's meetings.[103] By early 1934, however, these efforts had met with little success and the colonial authorities estimated the indigenous membership across the colony at below 100.[104] The growing appeal of anti-Semitism to sections of the indigenous community and the rapid expansion of the CdF in the wake of the Constantine riots of August 1934 saw an intensification of indigenous recruitment. In 1935, the Paris leadership officially invited indigenous veterans to sign up to the movement, a policy that provoked mixed reactions among the European leadership of the organization at a local level in Algeria.[105] Certain indigenous members, most notably Augustin Ibazizen, rose to prominence within the organization, leading the recruitment drive. Ibazizen spoke of the need to recreate the unity of the dark days of the war, calling on European members to help educate his fellow Muslims to shun

[101] 'M. le Gouverneur Général en Oranie,' *Le Petit Oranais*, 26 May 1927.
[102] Note on the Croix de Feu among the Indigenous, undated, ANOM/GGA/3CAB/47.
[103] Kalman, *French Colonial Fascism*, 66.
[104] Note on the Croix de Feu among the indigenous, undated, ANOM/GGA/3CAB/47.
[105] Kalman, *French Colonial Fascism*, 67.

the revolutionary manoeuvres of the communists and nationalists.[106] This sort of paternalist discourse did not resonate with many indigenous, and despite the attempts to couple references to the Great War with political anti-Semitism and an increasing social activism on the part of the female members of the CdF, recruitment remained extremely limited, largely confined to veterans living in major urban centres.[107]

With the recruitment drive making little headway among the indigenous, the CdF sought to expand their influence through constructing alliances with indigenous political leaders. In 1935, the president of the Algiers federation of the CdF invited Mohamed Benhoura, an ally of the AUMA, the editor of *La Justice*, and a veteran of the Great War, to lead a new indigenous section.[108] Benhoura's newspaper was permeated with references to the Great War and the CdF seemed attractive to this ambitious activist. An article in *La Justice* spoke of the 'utility and importance of this project' as a means of renewing the unity of the French and the indigenous who had not hesitated 'to offer themselves up as a sacrifice when the *Patrie* was in danger'.[109] By the end of 1935, Benhoura's growing impatience with the movement was evident. In an article entitled 'Muslims and the *Croix de Feu*', he outlined what he perceived to be the common vision shared by the indigenous community and the CdF, rooted in a celebration of military culture and a reactionary anti-Semitism, and lamented that their alliance was only held back by the CdF's refusal to embrace equality for indigenous subjects.[110] He would eventually endorse the Popular Front, despite his reactionary tendencies, asserting that only 'the socialo-communists' had included indigenous demands in their programme.[111]

Other prominent indigenous political figures who initially had been receptive to alliances with the CdF would follow the same path towards rupture as Benhoura. Dr Bendjelloul built a temporary alliance with the CdF at a local level that benefited both sides electorally in the short term.[112] Again, once the Popular Front government laid out its concrete proposals for reform and the CdF rejected them outright, he renounced any alliance with

[106] Special Report from the Orléansville Police, 27 January 1936, ANOM/GGA/3CAB/47.

[107] Note on the Croix de Feu among the indigenous, undated, ANOM/GGA/3CAB/47.

[108] Kalman, *French Colonial Fascism*, 68.

[109] 'Création d'une section musulmane de Croix de Feu et Briscards à Alger', *La Justice*, 1 January 1935.

[110] 'Musulmans et Croix de Feu', *La Justice*, 19 December 1935.

[111] 'L'indigène devant les élections législatives', *La Justice*, 25 April 1936.

[112] Kalman, *French Colonial Fascism*, 68.

a force he now considered opposed to indigenous reform.[113] For Samuel Kalman, the key to understanding the indigenous reformers' flirtation with the CdF lies in the reforming potential that was implied in the rhetoric of the fraternity of the trenches, a central element of the movement's discourse from 1932 on.[114] There is a kernel of truth in this analysis. However, we might also suggest that skilled political operators like Bendjelloul and Benhoura had much to gain from a potential alliance and were willing to use the CdF's seeming commitment to a *Union Sacrée* to window-dress what was essentially a marriage of convenience. Either way, the CdF had established a model for recruiting indigenous members, combining the unifying and reconciliatory language of the Great War with the partisan polemics of anti-Semitism and anti-communism and practical assistance in the form of social aid. This model, which left European hegemony firmly intact, would be replicated and expanded on by other extreme-right movements in the years that followed.

The CdF's successor movement, the PSF, intensified efforts to recruit indigenous members. On a tour of North Africa in the summer of 1937, La Rocque addressed the indigenous using the smattering of Arabic he had learned as a colonial officer in the southern Oranais and Morocco. He asserted that the PSF was 'the friend of the Muslims' and sought to 'recreate the fraternity that marked the war'.[115] The PSF anchored its rejection of the Blum-Viollette in its commitment to the indigenous community's contribution to the war. The project's failure to extend citizenship to all veterans became a central point of attack for the opponents of the Popular Front, including the PSF. The PSF's rival project envisaged the naturalization of all veterans once they renounced the personal status, a requirement that had proven historically toxic to the vast majority of indigenous Algerians. The cause of indigenous veterans was increasingly promoted by the organization as a means of attacking the Popular Front's failure to bring material and moral relief to the most loyal indigenous Algerians.[116] While the PSF cloaked the extremely limited extension of political rights contained in its counter-project in the language of the Great War, what it really sought was a return to the unity of the war, when indigenous Algerians fought in the trenches for France, not on the streets of Algeria for the Popular Front and even the nationalists. This nostalgic vision of a peaceful and strictly hierarchical

[113] Ibid., 69. [114] Ibid. [115] *La Flamme*, 1 July 1937.

[116] Special Departmental Police Report, Constantine, 23 October 1938, ANOM ALG 93/B/3/635.

colonial society was promoted by the party's newspaper *La Flamme*, most notably in an article for Armistice Day in 1938 entitled 'Under the Sign of the Blood Spilled in Common: Christians and Muslims of Algeria, Understand Each Other'. It celebrated the 'mixing of blood' of Algeria's European and Muslim communities 'for the same sacred cause', calling for the reestablishment of this fraternity 'under the sign of the Croix de Feu' and its commitment to the motto 'All souls are equal'.[117] For the PSF and its predecessor, the CdF, the souls of the fallen were equal, but not the rights of the living.

In contrast to the PSF, the PPF placed imperial policy at the centre of its political programme, asserting that the renewal of France would come from the strength of her 'Empire of 100 million Frenchmen'.[118] Its vision of the empire granted more political representation to the indigenous while leaving European hegemony intact.[119] It is hardly surprising, then, that the PPF campaign to rally indigenous actors to its cause proved much more vigorous and ultimately more successful, with the PPF the only extreme-right party to secure a significant indigenous membership (circa 20 percent).[120] The movement's leader, Jacques Doriot, had extensive experience of North Africa and of strategies of appealing to indigenous communities from his days as the Communist Party's expert on colonial issues. His role in supporting Abd-el-Krim's uprising in Morocco was highlighted to indigenous audiences to demonstrate his sympathy to the indigenous cause,[121] much to the scorn of the PSF.[122] The party produced bilingual propaganda in Arabic and French.[123] A number of high-profile figures from the indigenous community were recruited at an early stage and would subsequently lead efforts to expand the party's base among the indigenous community. Their campaign would make much use of the memory of the Great War.

Conservative veterans were among the most important of the small number of indigenous Algerians who rallied to the PPF. The most prominent was Dr Djilali Bentami, a member of a prominent family of indigenous notables, who had studied medicine in the metropole before going on to

[117] 'Sous le signe du sang versé en commun: chrétiens et musulmans d'Algérie, comprenez-vous', *La Flamme*, 11 November 1938.

[118] Philippe Machefer, *Ligues et fascisme en France 1919–1939* (Paris: Presses Universitaires de France, 1974), 28.

[119] Kalman, *French Colonial Fascism*, 138.

[120] Blanchard, 'La vocation fasciste', 190.

[121] Head of Departmental Security to the Prefect, 22 October 1936, ANOM/92//84.

[122] Blanchard, 'La vocation fasciste', 187.

[123] PPF poster reproduced in Police Commissioner of Batna to the Sous-Préfet, 23 January 1937, ANOM/93/B/3/635.

serve in the Great War. Elected to the municipal council of Mostaganem in 1935, he had initially allied himself with the CdF and used his position as president of the city's *Association des Anciens Combattants Musulmans* to promote a conservative vision of indigenous reform in veteran circles.[124] He explained his support for the PPF by evoking the service of the indigenous 'loyal collaborators' to prove that indigenous Algerians 'prefer to remain subjects under the folds of the tricolour flag than free citizens under the German or Russian boot'.[125] Bentami and other indigenous figures[126] combined the standard claim of the French extreme right that the sacrifice of the war dead was best honoured by fighting the forces of subversion that threatened the *Patrie* with an insistence that this struggle should be complemented by reforms rewarding the past and guaranteeing the future loyalty of the indigenous masses.

This line was echoed by senior figures of the party from the European community. Doriot asserted that attempts by the communists to drive the indigenous away from France would fail, evoking the 'sacred links' forged between Muslims and the French during the war. He even embraced the central universalist trope of French commemorative culture, suggesting to his Muslim audience that 'the Unknown Solider…is perhaps one of yours'.[127] The party's counter-project, unlike that of the PSF, proposed extending the franchise to the whole of the adult male indigenous population. The leader of the Oran PPF, Gaston Vidal declared that the war sacrifice granted 'rights' to the 'indigenous masses', rights which the Blum-Viollette Project had restricted to the elites.[128] However, while the PPF outstripped its PSF rival in both its propaganda in favour of reform for the indigenous and its engagement on the ground with the indigenous community, the same nostalgic yearning for the *Union Sacrée* as a moment of national unity that respected racial hierarchy lurked behind its rhetoric. In a speech evoking the Muslim contribution to the war, Victor Arrighi declared that what was lacking above all else in Algeria was a leader, one who could inspire both love and discipline in the indigenous population: 'When there was a chief, the Muslims loved us. When there is no one left to rule us but a coalition of Jews and

[124] Blanchard, 'La vocation fasciste', 189.

[125] 'L'immense majorité des maires d'Oranie adhèrent publiquement au Rassemblement national', *Oran Matin*, 2 July 1936.

[126] Larbi-Aribi, 'Appel à mes pauvres frères musulmans', *L'Oranie Populaire*, 15 May 1937.

[127] 'Jacques Doriot à Oran', *Oran Matin*, 30 November 1936.

[128] Police Commissioner of Oran to the Prefect, 2 February 1937, ANOM/92//84.

incompetent politicians, they hate us.'[129] While the PPF acknowledged the necessity of reform, it believed that what was most imperative in Algeria was a restoration of authority. The renewal of the fraternity of the trenches would require a restoration of a military-style discipline predicated on the racial hierarchy of the colonial state.

For all their talk of political reform and representation for the indigenous community, the colonial policies of these extreme-right movements sought a regime grounded in an 'intimate hierarchy', a kind of paternalist authoritarianism where indigenous development would take place under the strict stewardship of French citizens.[130] The experience of the Great War, in which indigenous troops had fought alongside but subordinate to European troops, embodied the kind of loyal and subservient collaboration that defined the imperial vision of movements such as the CdF, PSF, and the PPF. Where supporters of radical reform for the indigenous framed the war as a moment of republican equality giving rise to citizenship rights, their opponents on the extreme right saw the war as a moment of unity and discipline, in which collaboration across racial lines did not compromise the colonial hierarchy. This nostalgic vision of an Algeria united racially behind a strong militaristic imperial regime held little appeal for most of Algeria's indigenous community. With the exception of a limited number of reactionary *évolués* and certain groups of veterans, even those who shared elements of the extreme-right agenda and were susceptible to propaganda citing the war were eventually driven away by the refusal to contemplate any form of equality in political rights. Indeed, when the extreme right eventually came to power in Algeria, any extension of political rights to the indigenous slipped off the agenda, with an authoritarian paternalism steeped in references to the communal contribution to wars past and present dominating the Vichy colonial state's indigenous policy. Once more, the glory of the fallen would be mobilized to avoid the equality of the living and to safeguard the primacy of the European community.

Settlers and Soldiers: Algeria's Europeans, the Great War, and the Extreme Right

For the extreme right in Algeria, the non-Jewish European community always constituted both their principal support base and the dominant force

[129] *Le Pionnier*, 19 May 1938. [130] Sanos, *Aesthetics of Hate*, 223.

in their vision of Algeria, past, present, and future. In the metropole, the experience of the war was a key point of reference for the extreme right in its appeals to the mass of French citizens. As we have already seen, it was also widely mobilized by these movements in their appeals to indigenous Algerians. Surely, then, it would lie at the heart of attempts to win over the Europeans.

In the immediate aftermath of the war, European political leaders celebrated the Great War as the moment that marked the total integration of the various European populations into the French nation.[131] Behind the notion of the unity of the European population, regardless of national origin, lay the imperative to present a united front to ensure continued European hegemony. The wartime *Union Sacrée*, understood as the unity of the European population in this narrative, would have to be maintained to fight attempts to radically reform the political structure of the colonial system.[132] Multi-racial solidarity was trumped by the need for an alliance to protect European superiority and this political reality directly shaped visions of Algeria's Great War.

The focus on the unity of Algeria's European community across boundaries of national origin would persist throughout the rest of the 1920s, shaping the attitude of the extreme-right municipalities in the latter half of the decade. In Dr Molle's Oran, the attempt to 'Latinize' the memory of the Great War proved particularly controversial. His *Unions Latines* movement placed the 'Latin' community at the heart of Algeria's war effort, asserting that 'the Latin elements of this country contributed more than any other and this alone is proof of their quality as good Frenchmen'.[133] This commitment to the celebration of a Latin vision of the Great War was visually communicated in the *Unions*' participation in commemorative ceremonies in the city, where the wreaths laid by the movement were often decorated with ribbons representing the Spanish and Italian flags.[134] At the inauguration of the city's monument to the victims of submarine attacks, a member of the audience denounced the movement's decision to lay a wreath decorated with the national colours of Italy and Spain. A Mr Darot claimed that Spanish neutrality was in part to blame for the sinking of a French ship, the Medjerda,

[131] Jean de St Genest, 'L'Union Sacrée en Algérie: Les Etrangers', *Le Petit Oranais*, 17 September 1920.

[132] Charles Collomb, 'France d'abord', *L'évolution nord-africaine*, 3 April 1919.

[133] 'L'Apéritif d'Honneur de la Salle Paixhans', *Le Petit Oranais*, 17 November 1930.

[134] 'A propos d'un incident survenu à l'issue de la cérémonie d'inauguration', *Le Petit Oranais*, 2 March 1925 and 'Mauvaise Besogne', *Le Petit Oranais*, 15 May 1925.

and thus it was unacceptable that the Spanish national colours appear in the ceremony. The UL's reply stressed the Latin character of Algeria's war sacrifice, while condemning Darot and his associates for their links with the treacherous Jews.[135] Where the memory of European unity had been mobilized in the early 1920s against the threat of indigenous reform, in the Oran of the late 1920s it was against the imagined power of the Jews that Latin solidarity was evoked.

However, as we have seen, the Jewish community fought back against any attempt to diminish their claim to the legitimacy of the war. Their campaign undoubtedly served to complicate the municipality's effort to monopolize the memory of the Great War. Instead, Dr Molle and his supporters opted to anchor their legitimacy in a historical narrative that was more suited to their exclusionary philosophy of *latinité*, largely avoiding the potential pitfalls of the transcommunal narrative of the war. It was to the glory of ancient Rome and her dominance in North Africa, not the heroism of the trenches, that Molle et al. turned for historical legitimation of their project.[136] While it was difficult to assimilate the Jews to the Germans, who they had undeniably helped to defeat, comparing them to the hordes of Barbarians that toppled Rome made perfect sense for the proponents of *latinité*.[137] Moreover, the kind of populist authoritarianism favoured by Dr Molle and his followers sat much more comfortably with the political model of the Roman Empire than it did with the potentially emancipatory French Republic and its citizen armies.

The emergence of the CdF in the early 1930s in Algeria saw a new attempt by an extreme-right movement to employ the sacrifice of the war as a key element of their political language. It is hardly surprising that a group whose origins lay in the veterans' movement and whose initial support came from ex-combatants would constantly refer to the war. Nevertheless, as Samuel Kalman has convincingly demonstrated, for a movement of the extreme right to be successful among Algeria's European population, it had to adapt its political discourse and practice to the local environment.[138] For the CdF and its successor the PSF, this would mean Algerianizing its evocation of the Great War. The movement's leaders in the colony placed the war squarely

[135] 'A propos d'un incident survenu', *Le Petit Oranais*, 2 March 1925.

[136] 'L'Apéritif d'honneur de la Section d'Union et de Défense Latine de Gambetta', *Le Petit Oranais*, 9 February 1925.

[137] 'L'Apéritif d'honneur de la section d'Union Latine de Saint-Antoine', *Le Petit Oranais*, 20 April 1925.

[138] Kalman, *French Colonial Fascism*, 13.

within a wider narrative of French history that incorporated, even prioritized, the conquest of Algeria.[139] Speaking at CdF's first major mass meeting in Algeria in June 1935, the group's leader in North Africa, the commandant Debay, stressed the continuity between the soldiers of the conquest, the settlers, and the Europeans who had fought in the trenches:

> To serve! That is your watchword, the watchword of the French of Algeria for the last one hundred years... It is what the soldiers of Charles X did in this land, then the settlers and the civil servants. Then, the soldiers of Africa at Charleroi, the Croix de Feu today.[140]

The settler contribution to the Great War was, he argued, the latest in a long story of heroic sacrifice by Algeria's European community.

In the years that followed, with increasing competition on the extreme right and the expansion of the PSF far beyond veteran circles, the Great War would fade as a central point of reference. La Rocque would continue to evoke the Great War, but local leaders began to favour a historical narrative in which the *poilu* was rivalled, even overshadowed, by the *colon*. In Oran, the local PSF representative Marcel Gatuing, himself a decorated veteran with significant injuries from the war, continued to reference the war and to address the veterans as an interest group,[141] but also increasingly evoked the conquest, both military and agricultural. When Gatuing introduced La Rocque to a large crowd in Oran in 1937, he spoke of Algeria as 'this land made by the blood of our ancestors'.[142] *La Flamme*, the PSF newspaper in North Africa, was particularly vocal in its praise of the pioneer *colons*, 'men of diverse national origins who had fertilised the land with their labour'.[143] In March 1939, the newspaper published an article advocating the elevation of the *colon* in commemorative culture, arguing that 'alongside the soldier, the settler has his place at the foot of the cenotaphs.[144] In this narrative, the *colon*'s struggle to tame the inhospitable land of Algeria and make of it the prosperous colony that France so treasured was at the very least as worthy of official praise as the heroism of the frontline soldiers of the Great War.

[139] 'Dans les plis de nos fanions', *Bulletin de liaison du Mouvement Croix de Feu en Algérie*, 15 February 1936.

[140] 'Quinze mille Algériens ont acclamé la France et le colonel de La Rocque', *La Dépêche Algérienne*, 11 June 1935.

[141] Local Commissioner to the Prefect of Oran, 15 March 1938 and Police Commissioner of Oran to the Prefect, 24 December 1938 both from ANOM/92//70.

[142] 'Une Mer Humaine: 25000 à Oran', *La Flamme*, 1 July 1937.

[143] 'France', *La Flamme*, 30 September 1938.

[144] 'A côté du soldat le colon a sa place au pied des cénotaphes', *La Flamme*, 10 March 1939.

This discursive shift represented a concession by the PSF to the political culture of Algeria's European community, so deeply tinged with *latinisme*. While the PSF would happily evoke the Great War in its addresses to the Muslims, a narrative focused on the glory of the *colon* alone, and not the colony's racial others, was essential to extend its support base beyond veterans and into the European community at large.

In the political discourse of the PSF's principal rival, the PPF, the glory of the *colon* had always predominated over any fleeting evocation of the *poilu*. Speaking at a PPF meeting one month after the party's foundation in Algeria, a local activist set the tone for the party's discourse in the colony. Paying tribute to the labour of 'those who spilled their blood and sweat to make Algeria prosper', he argued that, to follow in the footsteps of their glorious ancestors, the French of Algeria would have to serve the PPF's campaign to secure the future of France and the empire.[145] The dominance of the *colon* in the party's symbolic discourse is most evident in the contrast between the PPF's North African newspaper, *Le Pionnier*, and that of the CdF/PSF, *La Flamme*. The CdF/PSF newspaper clearly pointed to the memory of the Great War with its reproduction in the masthead of the eternal flame that marked the Tomb of the Unknown Soldier (Figure 4.1). In contrast, the PPF paper's recurring image of farmers toiling the fields of Algeria flanked by an Arab sitting under a palm tree and a growing industrial city played to the notion of the *colon* as the essence of Algeria (Figure 4.2).

Victor Arrighi, the party's leader in North Africa, constantly reinforced this narrative. At a meeting in February 1937, Arrighi contrasted the cosmopolitan Jew and his obsession with money with the heroic *colon* who had built Algeria with his blood and sweat.[146] The party had neither the symbolic capital nor the political desire to rival the CdF/PSF when it came to evoking the Great War. Rather, it hoped that the myths surrounding the *colons*, which sat comfortably with the party's anti-Semitism and celebration of empire, would prove an effective means of mobilizing the European community.

From this analysis, it is clear that the Great War lost out in the extreme right's narrative of the European community's history to other historical points of reference that proved less potentially problematic. The celebration of ancient Rome and the pioneering *colons* did not carry with them the

[145] Police Commissioner of Philippeville to the Prefect of Constantine, 25 December 1936, ANOM/93/B/327.

[146] 'Sabiani, Arrighi, Vidal exaltent l'idéal du PPF', *Le Petit Oranais*, 22 February 1937.

Figure 4.1. Masthead of *La Flamme*
Source: La Flamme, 18 September 1937

Figure 4.2. Masthead of *Le Pionnier*
Source: Le Pionnier, 11 November 1937

same troublesome political baggage as the Great War. These narratives excluded Jews and effaced Muslims from Algeria's history, allowing movements of the extreme right to assert European hegemony in a way the Great War could never do.

Conclusion

The history of the evocation of the Great War by Algeria's extreme right speaks to three of the central themes of this book. Firstly, it highlights the potential polysemy of the war as a point of reference, not only between the discourse of different political movements, but even within the discourse of a single movement. The various movements of the extreme right not only offered rival (if often closely aligned) visions of the Great War to potential constituents outside the party, but they also offered distinct visions of the war to the 'racial' constituencies within their movements. Furthermore, the war would also be mobilized by the opponents of these movements, most effectively in the case of Algeria's Jewish community, whose interpretations of the same historical event had radically different political implications than those promoted by the extreme right. The sheer variety of experience that defined the Great War made it a common language between political foes.

Secondly, the story of the interwar extreme right in Algeria in general, its evocation of the Great War in particular, bears testament to the difficulties faced by political movements that attempted to apply metropolitan discourses directly to the colony. Even a symbolic reference point as supposedly universal as the sacrifice of the Great War was charged with potential meanings that complicated its use in Algeria. The heightened anti-Semitism of Algerian political discourse, the numerical strength of the Jewish community, and the dominance of a colonial system that granted extremely limited rights to the majority indigenous population all conspired to make a direct application of the 'veteran mystique' of the metropolitan extreme right untenable in Algeria. Instead, the narrative of the Great War would have to be adapted, even abandoned, to fit with the political realities of the colonial context.

Finally, the story of the place of the Great War in the language of the extreme right testifies to the different levels of agency of those actors who made up the multi-ethnic patchwork that was colonial Algeria. In this chapter, I have particularly underlined the capacity of the Jewish community, marginalized by the ubiquitous anti-Semitism but protected by their citizenship, to contest the narrative of the extreme right in the public space. It is not beyond reason to suggest that their intervention was key to undermining the attempts of extreme-right movements to mobilize the war in defence of their agenda. The indigenous community also played a role in shaping the extreme right's public discourse, whether acting within the organizations, in short-lived alliances with them, or in open opposition to them. Extreme-right discourse in the 1930s may well have mobilized a conservative and racially hierarchical vision of the Great War in its appeals to Muslims, but at least it acknowledged their place in Algeria, past, present, and future. Members of the European community demonstrated an impressive capacity to impose both their agenda and their language on the political movements of the extreme right, ensuring that Algerian political culture always trumped that of the metropole.

In the debates surrounding the extreme right's vision of an Algeria based on a strict racial hierarchy, the evocation of the Great War played an important if often contradictory role. It was employed as a justification for such radically opposed policies as total equality and racial segregation. The

Great War could be all things to all men. And yet, as Bakhtin underlined 'not all words for just anyone submit equally easily to... appropriation.'[147] This chapter has shown that the Great War could also be quickly dispensed with as a framing strategy when it either compromised a movement's potential popularity or seemed to favour the argument of political opponents. Thus, the place of the Great War in the language of claims-making of the extreme right in interwar Algeria varied widely depending on the constituency being targeted and on the resistance encountered.

Veterans from both the indigenous and European communities were a particularly important potential constituency for the extreme right in the colony. As we have seen in Chapter 3, they had been crucial in the defeat of the left in the immediate post-war period. However, like their metropolitan comrades,[148] veterans in Algeria never embraced extreme-right politics *en masse*. Rather, the majority remained focused on imposing their primacy on the democratic republican order, a task that would, as we shall now see, prove extremely difficult in the colonial context. Their leaders, like so many other political actors in interwar Algeria, would struggle to reconcile their rhetoric with the realities of practising politics in a colonial society.

147 Bakhtin, *Discourse in the Novel*, 294.

148 Antoine Prost, *Les anciens combattants et la société française 1914–1939 Volume 1. Histoire, Volume 2. Sociologie. Volume 3. Mentalités et Idéologies* (Paris: Presses de Sciences Po, 1977).

5

'They Have Rights over Us'

Algeria's Veteran Activists

On 20 November 1917, the newly appointed prime minister Georges Clemenceau declared solemnly to the National Assembly: 'Those Frenchmen we were forced to throw into the heat of the battle, they have rights over us'.[1] The struggle to establish exactly what these rights were and who ought to enjoy them was one of the defining features of the interwar period in metropolitan France and across the belligerent countries. In Algeria, this task was further complicated by the context of a colonial society faced with the rise of mass politics. There it would prove even more difficult to reconcile rhetoric with reality. This chapter traces the attempt to secure pride of place for the veteran in the post-war colonial order by analysing the development and discourse of Algeria's veterans' movement. Its central focus will be on the moderate and cross-community *Amicale des Mutilés et Anciens Combattants du Département d'Alger*, exploring how it sought to reconcile the quest for the primacy of the veteran with the existing primacy of the European inherent to the colonial system. The discursive strategies employed by the movement to frame its claims and their unintended consequences would play a key role in shaping this struggle.

Although post-World War I veterans' movements are the subject of extensive historical research in Europe,[2] their presence in colonial historiography is relatively limited. In the cases of the British and German Empires, the history of the colonial veteran has largely been subsumed into wider histories of colonial military service and/or narratives of post-war

[1] 'Intervention de M. Georges Clemenceau, président du Conseil des ministres, ministre de la guerre pour une déclaration du Gouvernement, à l'occasion de son investiture', *Annales de la Chambre des Députés*, 20 November 1917.

[2] Angel Alcalde, *War Veterans and Fascism in Interwar Europe* (Cambridge: Cambridge University Press, 2017), Deborah Cohen, *The War Come Home: Disabled Veterans in Britain and Germany, 1914–1939* (Berkeley, CA: University of California Press, 2001), Prost, *Les anciens combattants*, and Benjamin Ziemann, *Contested Commemorations: Republican War Veterans and Weimar Political Culture* (Cambridge: Cambridge University Press, 2013).

nationalism.[3] Scholars of French colonial history have more enthusiastically embraced the study of the veteran but their focus has mainly been confined to one colony: French West Africa.[4] West African veterans have proved a far more popular topic of research than their equivalents elsewhere in the colonies, a reflection, perhaps, of the endurance of the *tirailleurs sénégalais* as a trope in French colonial culture.[5] In North African historiography, the historical memory of veterans in Morocco[6] and the role of veterans in the nascent nationalist movement in Tunisia have received some scholarly attention.[7] Algeria's veterans, European and indigenous, have been overlooked as has the role of veterans' movements as intermediaries between ex-servicemen and the colonial state. Their story offers new insight into the post-war renegotiation of the social contract between the colonial state and those citizens and subjects who had fought to defend it.

Algeria's Veterans Emerging from the Great War

In the preceding chapters, we saw the transformative effect Algeria's participation in the Great War had on the language of high politics in the colony. Although individual veterans from both the European and indigenous communities played prominent roles in the debates surrounding issues of colonial and social reform, the war's great transformation for them was primarily personal. The ex-combatant, more than any other member of society, had a deep personal understanding of the social contract they had forged with the state through their participation in the war. While veterans'

[3] See for example Aravind Ganachari, 'First World War: Purchasing Indian Loyalties: Imperial Policy of Recruitment and 'Rewards', *Economic and Political Weekly* 40, No. 8 (February 2005): 779–88, Moyd, *Violent Intermediaries*, and Smith, *Jamaican Volunteers in the First World War*. A notable exception is the extensive work on the post-war settlement of white colonial veterans in the British Dominions. See Kent Fedorowich, *Unfit for Heroes: Reconstruction and Soldier Settlement in the Empire between the Wars* (Manchester: Manchester University Press, 1995).

[4] Echenberg, *Colonial Conscripts* and Joe Lunn, *Memoirs of the Maelstrom: A Senegalese Oral History of the First World War* (Oxford: James Currey 1999).

[5] See Eric Deroo, 'Dying: The Call of the Empire (1913–1918)', in *Colonial Culture in France since the Revolution*, eds. Pascal Blanchard, Sandrine Lemaire, Nicolas Bancel, and Dominic Thomas (Bloomington, IN: Indiana University Press, 2014), 132–9.

[6] Driss Maghraoui, 'The "Grande Guerre Sainte": Moroccan Colonial Troops and Workers in the First World War', *Journal of North African Studies* 9, No. 1 (Spring 2004): 1–21 and 'Moroccan Colonial Soldiers: Between Selective Memory and Collective Memory', *Arab Studies Quarterly* 2, No. 2 (Spring, 1998): 21–41.

[7] Thomas DeGeorges, 'A Bitter Homecoming: Tunisian Veterans of the First and Second World Wars' (PhD diss. Harvard University, 2006), 50–93.

expectations of compensation from the state varied widely, dependent on their political and legal status, their social class, and their experiences of the war, they shared a collective sense that their service entitled them to priority in post-war society. For the most politically aware, and in Algeria of the early 1920s this largely, but not solely, meant European veterans, the best means of achieving this primacy would be to organize collectively.

Collective action among European veterans dated back to April 1915, when the first association of the war wounded in Algeria, the *Amicale des Mutilés du Département d'Alger*, was founded in the colony's capital.[8] Although the *Amicale* was by no means the only movement established to represent the war wounded and, later, veterans of the Great War, its relatively large membership placed it at the centre of political action for the war generation. Its membership constantly expanded over the course of the interwar period (Figure 5.1).

Furthermore, the *Amicale*'s central position within the various umbrella organizations that united veterans at a local and regional level gave it a disproportionate weight in veteran policy in Algeria. The *Fédération Départementale d'Alger*, founded in 1932, would be dominated by figures from the *Amicale* throughout its existence. By 1940, under the presidency of Joseph Kerdavid, long-time head of the *Amicale* in the interwar period, its membership reached 15,648.[9] Similarly, the *Interfédération Nord-Africaine des Victimes de la Guerre et Anciens Combattants*, founded in 1923 and counting

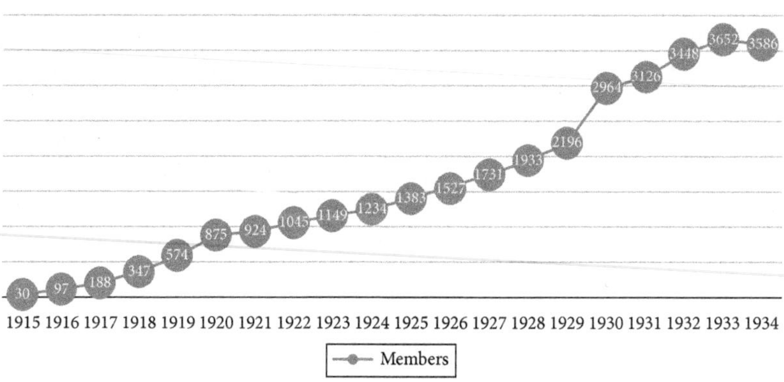

Figure 5.1. Membership of the *Amicale* as reported in *La Tranchée*, 2nd Fortnight, February 1935

[8] Departmental Security Note, Algiers, 26 June 1939, ANOM/91/1K/701.
[9] Departmental Security Report, Algiers, 31 May 1940, ANOM/91/1K701.

over 50,000 members by 1938, would serve to extend the *Amicale*'s policy influence far beyond the borders of the department of Algiers.[10] The *Amicale* was affiliated to the *Union Fédérale des Associations Françaises d'Anciens Combattants*, a national umbrella group of solidly republican and left-of-centre politics.[11] The moderate political orientation of the *Amicale* had the dual effect of creating close links with the administration while also forcing the organization's leaders to build consensus within its ranks concerning controversial issues, particularly those surrounding the legal and political status of indigenous veterans. In this regard, the contrast with two other prominent veterans' movements in Algeria is telling.

The *Amicale*'s first competitor came in the form of a newspaper, *Le Mutilé de l'Algérie*, founded in 1916. The newspaper's founder and editor-in-chief Joseph Ascione, a key figure in the movement against the left in the immediate post-war period, would go on, in 1923, to found his own organization, the *Association Générale des Victimes de la Guerre du Département d'Alger*.[12] The membership of this movement never reached the levels enjoyed by the *Amicale*. Affiliated to the other principal national federation, the *Union Nationale des Combattants*, the organization was extremely conservative with a dubious commitment to republican legality. Over the course of the interwar period, it increasingly allied itself with the extreme right, particularly the *Croix de Feu*,[13] and Ascione became a *persona non-grata* for the administration.[14] At the other end of the political spectrum stood the Algerian branch of the communist-leaning *Association Républicaine des Anciens Combattants* (ARAC), which, as we have seen in Chapter 3, was active in the colony as early as 1919.[15] The ARAC, which pursued the anti-imperialist agenda of the French Communist Party, had a significantly smaller membership than the other two organizations.[16] It conceived of veterans' campaigns as just one plank of a wider struggle against capitalism. The political radicalsim of both the ARAC and Ascione's extreme-right veterans meant that the internal contradictions in these organizations' discourse could be readily

[10] Departmental Security Report, Algiers, 31 May 1940, dossier 16C, ANOM/91/4I/54.

[11] See Millington, *From Victory to Vichy*.

[12] Departmental Security Report, Algiers, 31 May 1940, ANOM/91/1K/701.

[13] See for example 'Manifestation du 11 novembre des Croix de Feu et des Briscards de la Section de Médéa', *Le Mutilé de l'Algérie*, 24 December 1933.

[14] Prefect of Algiers to the Minister of the Airforce, 4 October 1938, ANOM/91/1K/701.

[15] Lerouge, 'L'Association Républicaine des Anciens Combattants', *La Lutte Sociale*, 8–14 October 1919.

[16] Membership in 1939 stood at 792, Prefect of Algiers to the Governor General, 3 July 1939, ANOM/91/1K/701.

ignored and the kind of complex attempts to build consensus, which defined the *Amicale*, were avoided. It is the *Amicale*'s moderation that makes it so interesting for the historian: among the veterans' organizations, it alone attempted to grapple with the contradictions inherent in translating metropolitan strategies into a colonial context.

Although indigenous veterans failed to organize collectively in the aftermath of the Armistice, hardly surprising given the repressive and exclusionary nature of politics in the colony, this does not mean that they did not seek to mobilize their participation in the war in pursuit of economic, social, and even political goals. As Chapter 6 will demonstrate, indigenous veterans and their families often proved tenacious in their pursuit of their just reward. Furthermore, a series of governmental reports in the months and years following the Armistice bears testament to a fear on the part of the colonial authorities that the indigenous veteran, with his newfound sense of entitlement, could pose a threat to the established colonial order. A May 1919 report lamented the 'bitterness' of indigenous ex-combatants and factory workers who had returned from France, claiming that their demands for compensation 'outweigh their commitment to discipline' and lead them to actions that are 'regrettable, sometimes dangerous'.[17] Such concerns were echoed in the September 1919 report, which described the 'rebellious spirit' of returned indigenous veterans who increasingly contested the authority of local indigenous leaders and even colonial administrators.[18] These documents testify to the anxieties of the administration around the capacity for individual or even collective action among indigenous veterans that their near total absence from veteran activism in the early post-war years occludes.

Early Responses to Inequalities in Provision

The legal and institutional framework of provision developed by the French government in the immediate aftermath of the Great War altered in small but significant ways when it crossed the Mediterranean. The law of 31 March 1919, which ushered in a new pension regime, is an example of how discrepancies in provision would sow the seeds of discord further down the

[17] Rapport sur la situation politique et administrative des Indigènes, May 1919, ANOM/GGA/11H/46.

[18] Rapport sur la situation politique et administrative des Indigènes, September 1919, ANOM/GGA/11H/46.

line. The indigenous war wounded, the most visible reminder of the war, were assimilated almost fully into the privileged ranks of the war generation: it was difficult to dispute that the loss of an arm or an eye was no less incapacitating for an indigenous veteran than for his European counterpart. In this way, the wartime 'moral economy of sacrifice' could be upheld in public through the patronage of the state. However, when it came to the provision for the dependants of the dead and the establishment of a programme to reserve jobs for veterans, the particularity of indigenous culture and legal codes trumped universalism, a phenomenon discussed in detail in Chapter 6. Polygamy, it was argued, made the extension of equal pensions to indigenous widows intolerable while indigenous veterans were only offered reserved jobs deemed appropriate for their limited intellectual capacities.[19] Alongside this legislation which emerged directly from the Great War, stood a whole complex of pre-existing compensatory measures for serving and retired indigenous soldiers that rejected any form of financial parity between European and indigenous. The equality embodied in the pensions of the war wounded contrasted sharply with the inferior rates for the *pensions d'ancienneté* accorded to indigenous soldiers who had served for a minimum of fifteen years.[20] This discrepancy is indicative of the 'conflicting impulses' that shaped the colonial state's inconsistent policy around the compensation of the wartime service of indigenous Algerians.[21] Just as the indigenous of Algeria were legally French nationals but not citizens, so too the veterans, the dependants of the war dead, and, to a lesser extent, the war wounded were second-class rights-holders among Algeria's war generation.

In the years immediately following the Armistice, the *Amicale*, in line with mainstream metropolitan veterans' groups, focused on pressurizing the government into recognizing the primacy of the veteran. When specifically referring to the colonial context, the *Amicale*'s newspapers often evoked the notion of inequality, focusing not on the difference in conditions between indigenous and European veterans but rather on the disparity between European veterans in Algeria and their metropolitan equivalents. Time and again the papers denounced laws that applied only to the metropolitan veterans but not to their North African counterparts, focusing in particular on Article 64 of the 31 March 1919 Law, granting free healthcare to the war wounded. The *Amicale* articulated its opposition to this perceived injustice

[19] *La Tranchée*, 1st Fortnight, March 1933.

[20] For a description of the range of laws that governed these pensions see Pierre-Rodolphe Dareste de La Chevanne, *Traité de droit colonial, Tome I* (Paris, 1932), 606–7.

[21] Fogarty, *Race and War*, 272.

in terms that highlighted the discrepancy between the narrative of the French state, which declared Algeria to be an integral part of the republic, and the reality experienced by veterans. When the *Amicale*'s newspaper, *L'Algérie Mutilée*, protested the absurdity of the inapplicability of Article 64 in Algeria, the language it employed bore a striking similarity to that mobilized by indigenous political reformists from Emir Khaled to Ferhat Abbas: 'it is inconceivable that such a law is applicable in France and not in Algeria. Did we not return home sick or mutilated for the same cause? Can we not aspire to the same rights as our metropolitan comrades?'[22] These sentiments were echoed in an article from July 1923, provocatively titled 'Is Algeria Really an Extension of France?'[23] Here the kind of argument often privileged in colonial historians' analysis of organizations of indigenous reform, indigenous labour movements, or even early national liberation movements was employed by an organization for whom the existence of an Algeria outside of France was inconceivable. The hypocrisies and contradictions in French republican colonial discourse were never the sole preserve of those who sought to reform or even destroy the colonial system; they could also be mobilized by groups who were resolutely opposed to a fundamental change to the power structures of colonial rule.

The language of equality in the discourse of the *Amicale* did not only refer to the differences between veterans in Algeria and their metropolitan counterparts; it also challenged arbitrary distinctions made by the state in its provision for different categories of rights-holders. The refrain, shared across the veterans' movement, 'Equal pensions for equal injuries', featured strongly in the *Amicale*'s discourse in the early period of its existence.[24] The point of departure for the campaign to ensure equality in state provision of pensions was not some sweeping republican notion of *égalité* but rather the 'equality of sacrifice' so central to the wartime 'moral economy'. The veterans railed against the granting of pensions at the same rate to wartime administrators or factory workers, who 'sheltered from the bullets and shells, earned high salaries' while the troops 'bore the weight of death's shadow on their shoulders'.[25] This 'equality of sacrifice' was completely reconcilable with the two forms of primacy that the leaders of the *Amicale* thought should define their society: the as yet unattained primacy of the veteran and the already existing primacy of the European. The inequalities in the power relations inherent in the colonial system were so entrenched that it did not occur to the European leadership of this transcommunal organization that building

[22] *Le Cri des Mutilés*, 1–15 March 1922.
[23] *L'Algérie Mutilée*, 16–31 July 1923.
[24] *Le Cri des Mutilés*, July 1920.
[25] *Le Cri des Mutilés*, October 1920.

a discourse around 'equality' could potentially undermine the European monopoly on power. There was, for the European leadership of the *Amicale*, no contradiction between using the language of the 'equality of sacrifice' and support for a colonial regime predicated on inequality.

The concerns of the indigenous members of the *Amicale* weighed little on the minds of the organization's leadership throughout the 1920s. The organizational structure of the *Amicale* militated against the involvement of indigenous veterans. The statutes of the association declared that 'indigenous Algerians who served France during 1914–1918 are considered Frenchmen' and thus eligible for membership.[26] Unlike the European members, their 'Frenchness' was not recognized *a priori* but, rather, it was predicated on their participation in the war. Only indigenous *veterans* were Frenchmen. The number of seats that could be occupied by indigenous Algerians on the executive committee of the organization was limited to a maximum of a third of the total.[27] Such regulations reflected a much wider and almost automatic restriction, even exclusion, of the indigenous from the *Amicale*'s discourse. While a long campaign was waged about the inequalities instanced by Article 64 of the 1919 law, those inherent in Articles 73 and 74, which affected only the dependants of the indigenous war dead, were completely absent from the organization's newspapers in this period. Motions referring specifically to indigenous concerns were few and far between at the organization's congresses.[28] The indigenous veterans' near total absence from the concerns of the *Amicale*'s leadership was visually expressed by the organization's official logo in this period, which showed an injured European *zouave* (identifiable by his uniform) receiving assistance from a Red Cross nurse (Figure 5.2).

In this period, the priority of European veterans over their indigenous colleagues was occasionally openly stated as the official policy of the *Amicale*. It was evident in the organization's efforts to regenerate the settlement programme in Algeria, probably inspired by the veteran settlement policies in place in the British Dominions.[29] The *Amicale* and other North African veterans' associations, gathered in the Interfederal Congress in Tunis (January 1923), called for the government to prioritize veterans in its existing settlement programme, which excluded the indigenous population,

[26] Article 5.1, 'Statuts de l'Amicale', *Le Cri des Mutilés*, 1–15 June 1922.
[27] Article 7, Ibid.
[28] 'Vœux du Congrès des Victimes de Guerre Tunis, le 7 janvier', *L'Algérie Mutilée*, 16–31 January 1923 and *L'Algérie Mutilée*, 1–15 February 1923.
[29] See Fedorowich, *Unfit for Heroes*.

Figure 5.2. Brochure for a concert organized by the *Amicale des Mutilés du Département d'Alger*, 5 July 1917, ANOM/93/B/3/444

while suggesting the government might 'study the possibility of creating small plots for settlement by indigenous war-wounded and veterans'.[30] Such an approach is hardly surprising in light of the study of settlement policy composed by the *Amicale*'s president, Joseph Kerdavid, in autumn 1921.[31] Kerdavid, who would remain the dominant figure in the *Amicale* for the rest of the interwar period, presented a vision of the Algerian countryside that drew on the racialized meta-narratives of history deeply embedded in colonial culture. The heroic figure of the pioneer settler toiling in harsh conditions to render the soil productive and to civilize the land was contrasted with the violent and savage indigenous. The war had not only depleted the ranks of these brave settlers but also inversed racial and gender hierarchies by drawing the virile European men off the land and into the trenches, only to be replaced by women, children, and even the indigenous. The only solution was to reinforce European settlement with the best and bravest of the nation, the veterans.[32] Here the motifs of the fraternity of the trenches and Franco-indigenous brotherhood that were omnipresent in public, political, and memorial discourse in the immediate aftermath of the war were replaced with the more traditional tropes of Algeria's European community, in which civilization was constantly under threat from the barbarous indigenous.

Although the indigenous rights-holders were obscured as a collective within the *Amicale*, the individual indigenous veteran did occasionally feature in the organization's wider language of claims-making. In the late 1920s, the *Amicale*'s newspaper, by now renamed *La Tranchée*, periodically gave space to the concerns of indigenous veterans. These individual cases served a dual purpose: to condemn the government's failure to recognize the priority of the ex-combatant and to reassert the transcendent nature of the entitlement of the veteran. The case of Mohamed Akoun, a veteran working in the postal service, is illustrative. Unable to secure a loan to which his status as a veteran entitled him, Akoun addressed his complaint to a meeting of the *Amicale* in February 1929. President Kerdavid assured him that the rejection of his application was the result of bureaucratic incompetence before pledging to intervene on his behalf. He then used the opportunity to highlight the *Amicale*'s commitment to the 'equality of sacrifice':

> During the war, when it came to the defence of the Nation shared by the French and the indigenous, we never considered to which race the spilled

[30] 'Vœux du Congrès des Victimes de Guerre Tunis, le 7 janvier'.
[31] *Le Cri des Mutilés*, 16 September–15 October 1921. [32] Ibid.

> blood belonged. It is thus just and absolutely natural that the same lack of differentiation should continue today. Veterans should fraternise today as they did in the darkest hours of the war. The treatment applied to one group should be applied to the other, and all advantages should be accorded without distinction of race or religion.[33]

Kerdavid's address exemplifies the *Amicale*'s approach to indigenous issues in the latter half of the 1920s: a tokenistic acknowledgement of aspirations for equality coupled with the co-option of indigenous grievances to a wider campaign against government ineptitude. The parity of pensions established by the law of 1919 allowed the European-dominated movements to assert that they, like the law, recognized all war wounded as equal. Such a discursive strategy permitted these organizations to largely ignore the particular problems facing the indigenous war wounded, widowed, and orphaned by simply incorporating them into their wider defence of a supposedly universal but inherently European vision of the rights-holder.

The difficulties of dealing with a complex and arbitrary bureaucracy were often denounced in these organizations' newspapers, but again the added obstacles faced by the indigenous were rarely acknowledged. The indigenous exercised little to no influence over policy formation within the *Amicale*. When questioned about the lack of an indigenous presence on the organization's executive committee, Kerdavid asserted that those who had been appointed 'always showed no interest in their mandate and had to be removed'.[34] He drew no connection between their supposed disinterest and that of the *Amicale* in the fate of their comrades. Racial stereotypes continued to inform the attitude of the leadership towards the indigenous and the voice of the indigenous struggling with an unjust system could only be heard when it was reflective of a general injustice.

The exclusion of indigenous actors is all the more significant when we consider the way in which provision for veterans evolved throughout the interwar period. France, in contrast to Britain and Germany, accorded a primary role to veterans' associations within the new bodies charged with the organization of provision.[35] Veterans' groups themselves had begun to organize provision before the state moved to cater for the war wounded and other veterans.[36] Thus, when the state belatedly entered the

[33] *La Tranchée*, 1st Fortnight, February 1929.

[34] *La Tranchée*, 2nd Fortnight, April 1929.

[35] In Britain provision was largely left to private charities while in Weimar Germany the state monopolized provision, excluding civil society. See Cohen, *The War Come Home*.

[36] Prost, *Les anciens combattants*, II, 217.

field of provision, it was forced to integrate the pre-existing structures of the veterans' associations into the newly formed *Office National des Mutilés*.[37] Veterans' organizations were entitled to elect members to the boards of these organizations who then coordinated the state's networks of patronage for the veterans, war wounded, and dependants in the dead. While this system successfully integrated veterans into the management of their own provision in the metropole, in Algeria it further skewed patterns of provision in favour of European veterans and against the specific needs of indigenous veterans.

In the period from 1917 to 1930, indigenous claims were either ignored or subsumed into the wider demands of the veterans' movements. The fact that these movements mobilized a language predicated on notions such as the 'equality of sacrifice' did not significantly impede the perpetuation of European hegemony. In this first period, the occasional tokenistic acknowledgement of the rights of the dependants of the indigenous war dead, restricted in number and politically unimportant, in no way suggested a conflict within the discourse of the veterans' movements between the primacy of the European community and that of the *génération du feu*. However, as indigenous participation in mass politics increased significantly over the following decade and as post-war provision expanded dramatically, the essential ambiguity that characterized notions of universalism in the *Amicale*'s discourse would leave a space in which competing visions of who was entitled to which rights would be pitted against each other.

Indigenous Veterans and the Rise of Mass Politics, 1930–6

If 1930 was the year of the great victory of the veterans' movement in the metropole with the granting of a general retirement pension to veterans, in Algeria it would be remembered for the festivities of the centenary of the French invasion. For the veterans' organizations, the centenary, with its strong military flavour, presented an excellent opportunity to stake their claim to priority in the colony. Unsurprisingly, in a narrative focused on integrating the primacy of veterans into the celebration of the glorious achievements of French colonialism, the indigenous veteran was at best an ancillary figure. The visit of a delegation of veterans from Algeria to the Paris Municipal Council on 3 January 1930 was indicative of the wider

[37] Ibid.

tone surrounding the centenary. In his address to honour the occasion, the vice-president of the council began by highlighting how the representatives of the citizens of Paris had acknowledged the primacy of the veterans by offering them the first reception of the centenary year.[38] He then went on to draw a clear link between their service on the battlefields of France and their ancestors' service to the great civilizing mission of the *Patrie*, binding the pioneering settler and the heroic *poilu* together in the continuity of the eternal French nation.[39] Finally, he presented the role of the European soldiers during the war as 'the most appropriate interpreters' to ensure the 'liaison with the indigenous contingent' as a microcosm of the privileged position of the European community in the empire as *the* intermediary between the colonial power and its subjects.[40] In this romanticized presentation of the veteran as the colonial settler par excellence, the figure of the indigenous veteran all but disappeared.

Nevertheless, the leaders of the veterans' movement understood that, on the ground, the indigenous veteran, far from disappearing, was becoming ever more assertive. The extension in early 1930 of a limited pension, the *retraite combattante*, to all those who had served at least three months in active combat endowed the indigenous veteran with new financial and political capital. The legal privileges previously offered by the *Loi Jonnart* were abstract and all too easily ignored by colonial administrators on the ground. Pensions, however, were a concrete measure that both acknowledged and reinforced the special position of the indigenous veteran.[41] The fact that the *retraite* was to be equal for Europeans and indigenous veterans in the Maghreb (but not elsewhere in the empire)[42] further strengthened the claims of Algerian indigenous veterans to a wider and far-reaching equality.

In early March, just weeks before the adoption of the *retraite combattante*, Kerdavid addressed a meeting of veterans from both communities declaring that, on the occasion of the centenary of the French invasion, European veterans wanted to demonstrate their 'fraternal sentiments to their indigenous comrades who had loyally fought for France'. They vowed to help their indigenous brothers-in-arms achieve 'an ever-greater improvement of their lot'.[43] The concrete result of this commitment came in May of that same year when the National Interfederal Congress of the Veterans and War-Wounded met

[38] *La Tranchée*, 2nd Fortnight, February 1930. [39] Ibid. [40] Ibid.

[41] Mann, *Native Sons*, 98.

[42] Décret portant règlement d'administration publique pour l'application de la loi de finances du 16 avril 1930, 24 November 1930, *Journal Officiel*, 26 November 1930, 13080.

[43] *La Tranchée*, 1st Fortnight, March 1930.

for the only time outside of the metropole, in Oran, to mark the centenary. In a notable first, the congress adopted resolutions specifically concerning the indigenous community. A motion was approved condemning Article 74 of the 1919 law, which restricted pension rights for the dependants of the indigenous war dead.[44] The congress endorsed the equality of the dead through the provision of equal pensions for their dependants, a group limited in number and political influence.

The North African veterans' movement's commitment to the equality of the living was, however, much more meagre. The Oran Congress did not endorse the parity of pension rights for veterans, though the possibility was raised for some undefined point in the future.[45] Instead, both the *Amicale* and the congress denounced the failure to recognize the primacy of indigenous veterans within indigenous society. Motions were passed demanding priority for veterans in the indigenous posts of the civil service and for the implementation of the laws reserving café licences for veterans against other indigenous enjoying official patronage.[46] Throughout this period, the moderate veterans' associations, chief among them Kerdavid's *Amicale*, remained committed to the establishment of the equality of the dead without ever endorsing equality for all those who had served France. They favoured a form of what I call 'segregated primacy' in which indigenous veterans were prioritized within an indigenous society that remained subordinated to the European community, which, in turn, reserved a privileged place for the European veteran. This policy represented the concrete expression of Gregory Mann's 'idioms of mutual if uneven obligation',[47] as the European leadership of the veterans' movement sought to recompense their indigenous brothers-in-arms without challenging the existing colonial hierarchy.

This policy was a direct response to tensions within the movement around contentious issues of colonial reform. In the early 1930s, indigenous veterans began to assert their voices within the movement. In 1934, at the fourth quarter general assembly of the *Amicale*, a strong indigenous attendance insisted on special attention for their demands, with one of their number, Ali Hamdad, addressing the assembly. The response of President Kerdavid was telling. While vowing to 'energetically defend' all members in 'questions of a moral and material order', he stressed 'the delicate nature of claims concerning the status of the indigenous'.[48] Unwilling to support a political

[44] *Le Mutilé de l'Algérie*, 4 May 1930. [45] Ibid. [46] Ibid.
[47] Mann, *Native Sons*, 65.
[48] *La Tranchée*, 1st Fortnight, January 1935.

project that would be anathema to its European membership, the *Amicale* committed itself more wholly to addressing the other concerns of indigenous veterans. Wielding its significant influence in the umbrella organization, the *Interfédération Nord-Africaine*, it promoted the improvement of conditions for indigenous veterans no longer as a niche issue but rather as one of the central planks of the North African veterans' movement's common programme. For the first time, the movement pledged support for the equalization of pension rights for all veterans as well as for the dependants of the dead.[49] The commitment to financial equality was not replicated in the political sphere. Here the notion of 'segregated primacy' remained intact.

Although still dominated by the European community, the administrative bodies and newspaper columns of the organization gradually opened up to indigenous veterans. Tahar Aouidad, a schoolteacher, veteran, and naturalized French citizen married to a Frenchwoman, became the key expert for the *Amicale* on indigenous issues, serving in prominent positions on committees and writing combative articles in the newspapers. Another important figure, Nait Kaçi, an indigenous entrepreneur, addressed the third quarter general assembly of 1937 with an intervention that was indicative of the *Amicale*'s efforts to balance the potential support of indigenous members for the Blum-Viollette Project with the hostility of the European members. Rather than openly endorsing the Blum-Viollette Project, Nait Kaçi proposed a motion stating that 'whatever the solution adopted by the metropolitan government' to the thorny issue of indigenous political rights, veterans must be given 'a place of priority'. He contrasted the indigenous elites, who owed their position to the generosity of France and were 'debtors of France', with the veterans who defended her and her 'creditors' and thus 'should benefit from a particular recognition'.[50] Here a prominent indigenous member evoked the wartime 'moral economy of sacrifice' to assert the veterans' claim to priority in the indigenous sphere over both the educated elites and the favoured collaborators of the colonial system. Nait Kaçi and the broader leadership of the *Amicale* asserted that securing the primacy of the veteran was more important than ensuring the extension of civil and political rights to at least some members of the indigenous community. In such a schema, indigenous veterans suffered discrimination not because of the inherently prejudicial racial order established by the colonial state but rather because

[49] *La Tranchée*, 1st Fortnight, April 1936.

[50] *La Tranchée*, October 1937.

the patronage of the colonial state unjustly favoured less deserving sections of the indigenous population.

The Emergence of the Indigenous Veterans' Associations

The arrival on the scene of a new set of indigenous-only veterans' movements in the mid- to late 1930s made it increasingly difficult to avoid a serious engagement on the issue of political rights.[51] These associations were far from uniform in nature and political orientation. Some remained firmly within the orbit of the moderate European veterans' associations. The aims of the *Amicale des Anciens Combattants Musulmans du Département d'Alger*, founded in 1938 under the presidency of Tahar Aouidad, directly echoed those of its sister organization.[52] While these types of organizations reproduced much of the discourse of the moderate cross-community associations, they were not simply puppets of the European leadership but rather gave a powerful voice to indigenous veterans who believed concessions could be secured through moderation.

Some of the emergent indigenous veterans' associations explicitly sought to challenge the moderate cross-community organizations. The indigenous veterans of Oran were the vanguard of this contestatory movement. As early as 1929, a group of around eighty indigenous veterans organized a petition invoking their service in the war in defence of some form of parliamentary representation for their community.[53] The following year they founded the *Ligue des Anciens Combattants Musulmans de l'Oranie* (LACMO),[54] an organization that would play a key role in challenging the refusal of the cross-community veterans' organizations to endorse political rights for the indigenous. At its inaugural conference in September 1930, the league paralleled the public discourse of the indigenous reform movement by contrasting the triumphalism of that year's centenary celebrations with the reality of life for the indigenous community and especially its veterans. The executive committee called on the authorities to move beyond the

[51] Thomas DeGeorges notes a parallel process in Tunisia where a veteran with a complex relationship with Tunisian nationalism founded *L'Union Nord-Africaine des Anciens Combattants Musulmans Engagés dans la Guerre de 1914–1918*. DeGeorges, 'Bitter Homecoming', 86.

[52] Statuts de l'Amicale des Anciens Combattants Musulmans du Département d'Alger, 9 February 1938, ANOM/91/4I/183.

[53] Jansen, 'Une autre "Union Sacrée"', 55.

[54] Departmental Security Report, 31 January 1933, Archives de la Wilaya d'Oran (AWO), I/14/4063.

rhetoric of fraternity and embrace real reform for the veterans: 'Let the Centenary not disappoint the hopes which it inspires in us, let it consecrate the indissoluble union of the victors of the Great War and translate this fraternity into concrete measures in line with our aspirations!'[55] The body of the congress issued an even more radical cry for political reform. Addressing itself directly to the 'People of France', the congress painted an exaggerated vision of indigenous participation in the war, evoking the '250000 mobilised' and '150000 who did not come back and now sleep eternally far from the land of their childhood'. In light of this great sacrifice in defence of the 'ideal of liberty', the indigenous troops had believed that they would finally be freed from the measures of exception in force in the colony. The reality of their post-war experience in Algeria was bitterly disappointing. They 'remained subject to the regime' and it seemed as though their 'wartime injuries had only served to hasten their death'.[56]

The only way to end this injustice that 'seemed incompatible with their sacrifice and with the essence of republican principles' was to grant indigenous veterans full citizenship rights.[57]

The league's leadership was aware that such a dramatic rupture with the pre-existing politics of veterans' movements in Algeria would prove controversial and sought to rebuff allegations of nationalism, declaring their commitment to 'the most basic justice that would be granting equal rights to those who have had equal duties'.[58] They denounced the post-war order in the colony, where racial hegemony was prized over wartime service. The congress posed a rhetorical challenge to the people of France, asserting that 'the sacrifice of one's life for the Patrie is the most beautiful act that a citizen worthy of this title can fulfil' and asking if 'we the veterans, have we not fulfilled this?' Surely, the people of France, 'the apostles of liberty and equality', could not tolerate a post-war order in which 'Algerians, long considered good enough for the trenches, are treated worse than citizen deserters, rehabilitated traitors, worse than the enemies of yesterday?'[59] Although the league's political agenda represented a challenge to the colonial authorities and the cross-community veterans' organizations, in the early years its audience was extremely limited. There is little chance that its 'Appeal to the People of France' found a public outside the Muslim quarters of the city of

[55] 'Centenaire de la Conquête de l'Algérie: La Ligue des Anciens Combattants Musulmans de l'Oranie, Congrès 14–15 septembre 1930', AWO, I/14/4063.

[56] 'Appel des Anciens Combattants Indigènes au Peuple de France, Congrès 14–15 septembre 1930', AWO, I/14/4063.

[57] Ibid. [58] Ibid. [59] Ibid.

Oran. Furthermore, for all the radicalism of their rhetoric, the LACMO's demands did not stray from the mainstream of moderate movements of indigenous reform in the colony. Oran's indigenous veterans sought not to break with the empire but rather to strengthen their own position within it.

While the veterans of Oran sought to organize collectively on a local basis, the indigenous reform newspapers began to feature articles calling for an Algeria-wide indigenous veterans' movement. In July 1934, an article appeared in *La Défense*, a newspaper close to the *Association des 'Ulama Musulmans Algériens* (AUMA),[60] expressing the discontent of indigenous veterans with the wider political situation in Algeria. The author, identified as a 'volunteer soldier and war amputee', combined metropolitan veteran discourses with the language of the movements of indigenous political reform. He began by attacking the 'Arabophobes' who had minimized the contribution of the indigenous troops to the French war effort, before offering his own inflated vision of this contribution. Turning to the question of colonial reform, he then argued that the 'fact that the indigenous Algerian has been subject to conscription and fulfilled his military duties gives him an incontestable moral right, in the absence of legal recognition, to consider himself a Frenchman'.[61] The use of the *impôt du sang* by this indigenous veteran as a justification for a distinctly political argument places him firmly within the claims-making tradition of indigenous movements for reform from the Young Algerians of the pre-war period to his contemporaries among the elites of the *Fédération des Elus Musulmans Algériens* (FEMA). In fact, he openly identified himself with the growing demand for reform among the indigenous population, approving of the efforts of indigenous activists to highlight their participation in the Great War. If the political justification for his claims owes much to the rhetoric of indigenous movements, his intervention in the political arena was legitimized by comparison with the metropolitan veterans' movements. Just as the 'war generation' in the metropole were preparing to 'descend into the Forum and impose on the country a policy of renewal', so too must the indigenous veterans, he argued, join the campaign to ensure 'the equality of all' in the colonies.[62] This intersection between the language of claims-making of the veterans' movements, transplanted from the metropolitan to the colonial setting, and the political

[60] The editor of *La Défense* Lamine Lamoudi served as secretary general of the AUMA 1931–5 and was later an active member of the *Congrès Musulman*. Benjamin Stora, *Dictionnaire Biographique de Militants Nationalistes Algériens* (Paris: L'harmattan, 1985), 348.

[61] 'Les Anciens Combattants Indigènes et la Politique Algérienne', *La Défense*, 13 July 1934.

[62] Ibid.

claims of the indigenous movements of reform would define the rhetoric of the indigenous veterans' movement's forays into the political sphere.

The following year the indigenous press played host to several voices from the new indigenous veterans' associations, pointing to a willingness on the part of indigenous veterans to engage in collective action of a specifically political nature. In April of that year, *La Défense* published a letter to the minister of the interior from the LACMO that combined the traditional demands of the veterans' movements, both colonial and metropolitan, with the claims of the indigenous political movements, simultaneously evoking the priority of the veteran and the *impôt du sang*.[63] The most striking contribution was to come, however, in November of that year from the *Ligue des combattants et victimes de guerre indigènes d'Algérie*, a group based in the town of Fort-National (Larbaâ Nath Iraten) in Kabylia. This article, which appeared in both *La Défense* and the FEMA-affiliated newspaper *L'Entente Franco-Musulmane*, quite pointedly asserted the right of the indigenous veterans' associations to engage in political campaigns while also implicitly attacking the restricted programme of the cross-community veterans' associations:

> In offering themselves as a sacrifice for the territorial integrity of the nation, the indigenous soldiers had the right to count on, once peace arrived, a real era of fraternity and honesty, compatible with the evolution of Muslim Algeria. People are shocked that our action is not limited to scrounging for decorations, grants, café licences or other favours of minimal importance and that we have the pretention to aim further and higher than certain immediate claims.[64]

The article not only trumpeted the veterans' refusal to restrict their agenda to 'veteran issues' alone but also called on the cross-community veterans' groups to acknowledge the necessity of a new settlement for the whole of the indigenous population. The author regarded the granting of rights to ex-combatants as just one step towards the wider emancipation of the whole of indigenous society, considering the 'veteran question' to be 'ephemeral' while 'that of the social order is eternal'.[65] The veterans had a moral responsibility to build a just post-war order for all the indigenous.

[63] 'Appel Des Anciens Combattants indigènes d'Algérie à M. le Ministre de l'Intérieur', *La Défense*, 5 and 12 April 1935.

[64] 'Ligue des combattants et victimes de guerre indigènes d'Algérie', *La Défense*, 29 November 1935 and *L'Entente Franco-Musulmane*, 28 November 1935.

[65] Ligue des combattants et victimes de guerre indigènes d'Algérie', *La Défense*, 29 November 1935.

In the advent of the election of the Popular Front, the more radical indigenous veterans' movements became part of the wider coalition of civil society and political organizations supporting the Blum-Viollette Project. The *Congrès Musulman* included the veterans as a special interest group represented on its committees[66] and ensured the presence of a veteran, the war amputee and vice-president of the *Association des Anciens Combattants Musulmans du Département de Constantine*, Bakir Benkalaya, in its delegation to the Popular Front government.[67] At a local level, indigenous veteran movements became increasingly vocal in the debate surrounding political reform. The example of the *Cercle des Anciens Combattants Musulmans* in the town of Batna is illustrative. Founded in late 1936,[68] the organization immediately dedicated itself to political action, sending telegrams in January 1937 to both Blum and Viollette expressing its 'profound gratitude' for the project and denouncing the campaign against it.[69] Months later a meeting of around 100 indigenous members, addressed by Benkalaya, called for reform not only in those areas traditionally targeted by veterans' associations (pensions, reserved jobs, etc.) but also in the social (indigenous housing) and political fields.[70] Directly referring to the Blum-Viollette Project, Benkalaya followed a well-worn strategy of both the metropolitan veterans' organizations and indigenous reform movements by contrasting the promises and rhetoric of wartime leaders with the practice of the post-war administration.[71] The parallel between the language deployed by the veterans' associations and that of indigenous reform leaders was no coincidence. In many cases, they had become inseparable allies.

Just as indigenous veterans echoed the words of indigenous political leaders, so too were these same leaders influenced by the rhetoric of the veterans' movement. The presence of articles from the indigenous veterans' movements in the indigenous press, particularly the AUMA-affiliated *La Défense* and to a lesser extent the FEMA-affiliated *L'Entente Franco-Musulmane*, exposed activists in these organizations to the language of claims-making of the veterans' movement. The cause of the veteran was integrated into the programme of the indigenous movements while the participation of veterans in

[66] Report from the Administrator of the Commune Mixte de Collo, 12 June 1938 and Police Commissioner of Souk Arras, 2 June 1936, ANOM/93/B/3/278.

[67] Report of the Effect of the Plum-Viollette Proposal on the Indigenous in the Department of Constantine, 20 January 1937, ANOM/91/2I/39.

[68] Police Commissioner of Batna to the Prefect, 23 March 1937, ANOM/91/2I/39.

[69] Police Commissioner of Batna to the Sous-Préfet, 11 January 1937, ANOM/91/2I/39.

[70] Police Commissioner of Batna to the Sous-Préfet, 20 April 1937, ANOM/91/2I/39.

[71] Ibid.

organizations such as the *Congrès Musulman* lent force to the assertion of the loyalty of the indigenous community to France. Occasionally, political leaders would directly evoke the language of the veterans' movement to legitimize their wider programme, with, for example, Ferhat Abbas citing the words of the metropolitan veteran leader Colonel Pichot to call the government to action on the Blum-Viollette Project: 'the time for generous declarations with no results has passed. Now, there is only time for action.'[72] The tropes of the veterans' movement had been incorporated into the political language of the movements of indigenous reform.

For the nationalists of Messali Hadj's *Parti du Peuple Algérien* (PPA), the indigenous veterans' movement's endorsement of the Blum-Viollette Project ruled out the possibility of any direct political alliance. Nonetheless, the PPA did engage with the cause of the veteran, attacking in harsh terms both the agenda of the cross-community organizations and the attempts of the authorities to undermine the political claims of indigenous veterans. It mocked the Algerian press's 'discovery of a sudden affection and concern for Muslim veterans' that centred on minor financial injustices and contrasted this with their constant attacks on indigenous political activists who struggled for the rights for which indigenous Algerians had fought and died in the Great War: 'Amidst the pamphlets and the appeals for repression and the hateful proclamations of the elected officials, we find every so often a few protests about the withdrawal of a café licence or a hunting licence. As if it were for such trifles that Muslims fought in 1914!'[73] Even a movement whose principal aim was the separation of Algeria from France, a political goal that sat uneasily with the indigenous veterans' movements' constant proclamations of loyalty to France, saw that political capital could be garnered by evoking the cause of the veterans.

The indigenous veterans' movement used their position in the umbrella organizations of the veterans' associations in North Africa to advance their cause. It was in his capacity as a member of the *Fédération Départementale* that Abdallah Nourreddine Bendjelloul (usually referred to simply as Nourreddine), leader of the LACMO, succeeded in pushing his organization's radical political agenda through the *Amicale*'s own newspaper. In January 1937, *La Tranchée* published a letter from Nourreddine that reproduced, almost verbatim, the 'Appeal to the People of France' issued by the league several years earlier.[74] Nourreddine would prove particularly adept

[72] *L'Entente Franco-Musulmane*, 20 April 1939.
[73] *El Ouma*, 1 April 1938.
[74] *La Tranchée*, 1st Fortnight, January 1937.

at manipulating and adapting the pre-existing structures and language of the veterans' movement in Algeria in an openly political campaign on behalf of the indigenous population. This challenge would have practical implications for the *Amicale*'s efforts to impose its policy on the umbrella organizations, which had long served as a proxy for Kerdavid and the group's leaders to control the wider veterans' movement. The authorities, both military and civil, that had hitherto happily devolved the social control of indigenous veterans to the moderate veterans' associations, grew increasingly alarmed at the perceived radicalization of indigenous veterans. Something would have to be done.

The Intervention of the 'Colonial-Military Complex'

Somewhat fortuitously for the authorities, and perhaps suspiciously so, the Algerian-born hero of the Balkan Front, Maréchal Louis Franchet d'Espèrey, stepped into the breach. By 1933, the Maréchal and other senior figures associated with both the colonial regime and the military had begun to discuss the possibility of a semi-official body to coordinate provision for indigenous veterans.[75] In 1934, the Council of Ministers was informed of the plan and with its approval secured, the *Amitiés Africaines* was officially founded the following year.[76] While not legally a state organization, the *Amitiés* relied on state funding in the form of subventions offered by government departments and local authorities.[77] At a time when indigenous political agitation was on the rise and the cross-community veterans' movements were struggling to reconcile their commitment to the primacy of the veteran with the colonial commitment to the primacy of the European, the *Amitiés* allowed the military and colonial authorities to exercise more direct social control over the veterans. From its conception, the *Amitiés* had two quite distinct goals. In public, the Maréchal described its mission as: 'giving life and force to the Franco-Indigenous military family and tying to our victories and our national destiny all those indigenous who have served our flag or fought at our side across the world'.[78] Echoing official commemorative culture, the *Amitiés* asserted that its aim was the perpetuation of the

[75] General Assembly of the Amitiés Africaines, 4 May 1938, ANOM/119APOM/2.
[76] Executive Committee of the Amitiés Africaines, 12 April 1935, ANOM/119APOM/1.
[77] Ibid.
[78] Marshall Franchet d'Espèrey to General Nogues, 11 April 1935, ANOM/91/1K/62.

sacred bond formed between the indigenous and France on the battlefields of the Great War and beyond. An internal document from 1935 eschewed the flowery language of unity, offering a much more pragmatic justification for the foundation of the organization. The organization's 'goal' was 'to ensure internal peace in North Africa' by 'protecting soldiers and veterans from the damaging propaganda' and ensuring 'that the defence of their interests will not be left to dubious groups or agitators'. It would also prepare them for any future mobilization and seek to minimize the 'material and moral' difficulties occasioned by military service.[79] In *realpolitik* terms, the *Amitiés* was intended to cater for the needs of indigenous veterans in a politically sound environment. Security concerns were as much a driving force behind the project as any commitment to the welfare of the 'Franco-indigenous family'.

Cooperation between the authorities and the *Amitiés* was extremely close from the beginning. The military assigned staff members to work on social projects for the *Amitiés* as early as 1936.[80] On the ground, the *Amitiés* set about building a network of *dar-el-askri* (pl. *diar*), an indigenous equivalent of the *maisons du combattant* or soldiers' centres run by the veterans' associations across France. Here indigenous veterans could gather socially, safe from the malign influence of agitators. While direct control of the *dar* rested with the local committee of the *Amitiés*, its activities were organized 'following the directives and the instructions it receives from the military authorities'.[81] Furthermore, the *diar* were to be 'put at the disposition of the military commander who provides both the management and the technical organisation'.[82] While the local committees included indigenous dignitaries, it was in reality the military, working in tandem with the local civil authorities and the senior *Amitiés* officials, that dictated policy at all levels of the organization. The services previously provided by veterans' associations, such as assistance with dealing with the state bureaucracy and spreading awareness of entitlements, were co-opted by the *Amitiés* and stripped of any potentially disruptive political agenda. The civil authorities even sought to prioritize the *Amitiés* by granting the organization a legally defined advisory role in the allocation of reserved jobs for indigenous veterans in 1938.[83]

[79] Committee of the Amitiés Africaines, 9 May 1935, ANOM/91/1K/62.
[80] General Laure, Commander of the Algiers Division to General Odry, President of the local Amitiés Africaines, 2 December 1936, ANOM/91/1K/62.
[81] Executive Committee, 22 December 1936, ANOM/119/APOM/1.
[82] Ibid.
[83] Executive Committee, 16 June 1938, ANOM/119/APOM/1.

Alongside these activities traditional to the veterans' movements, the *Amitiés* also sought to provide basic social services to indigenous veterans. By 1939, there were forty-eight local committees in place across North Africa,[84] largely focused on the operation of the *diar-el-askri*. The *dar-el-askri* served as a doctor's clinic where veterans and their families could receive medical care, a policy designed not only with a view to maintaining the loyalty of the veteran but also in line with the wider agenda of social hygiene practised in both metropole and colony. Furthermore, the *dar* sought to alleviate the food shortages that were chronic among both the rural and urban poor, providing food to veterans and their families and thus countering the highly emotive and effective image of the decorated veteran beggar, a leitmotif of the propaganda of indigenous movements of reform. In April 1937, the *Amitiés* claimed to be serving almost 20,000 meals and providing medical care to 500 veterans and/or their dependants every day.[85] This 'social action' was carried out in collaboration with, but subordinate to, 'official services' provide by the state and/or the army.[86] Armand Guillon, Franchet d'Espèrey's successor at the head of the association and a former resident-general in Tunisia, is clear in his assessment of the goals of this social intervention:

> The veteran takes the place to which he is entitled in Muslim society. His pension gives him a certain standard of living. His prestige, enhanced by his decorations, grows. He takes his place in the local assemblies, his advice is taken on board, his influence extends and supports that of France.[87]

Here we see the *Amitiés Africaines* co-opting another central plank of the programme and practice of the cross-community veterans' associations: 'segregated primacy'. The indigenous veteran was to be granted a place of priority within the indigenous sphere from which he could guarantee that the interests of the authorities were supported. His enhanced prestige would secure his election to the limited representative bodies of the indigenous community, and thus ensure that these institutions remain dominated by the acolytes of the colonial regime. However, the master plan of the *Amitiés Africaines*, like so many of the developmental projects that would follow in years to come, failed to acknowledge both the capacity of actors in the

[84] Armand Guillon, 'Une oeuvre du Maréchal Franchet d'Espèrey: les Amitiés Africaines', *Cahiers Charles de Foucauld* 41 (1956): 95–103, 98.

[85] General Assembly of the Amitiés Africaines, 20 April 1937, ANOM/119/APOM/2.

[86] Guillon, 'Une oeuvre du Maréchal Franchet d'Espèrey', 101.

[87] Ibid.

indigenous community for political action and the increasing indivisibility of social, economic, and political claims.

Despite the rapid expansion of the *Amitiés Africaines* in the four years following its foundation, the organization had not reached sufficient strength to challenge the predominance of transcommunal veterans' associations in catering for indigenous veterans. The organization's heyday was to come in the wake of the Second World War, with its expanded network of 177 *diar-el-askri* catering to some 330,000 veterans by 1953.[88] Nevertheless, the foundation of the *Amitiés*, with the support of the French government, shows the extent to which the *Amicale* and its sister organizations were perceived as having lost control of the indigenous veterans. The paternalistic ethos of the *Amitiés* fundamentally misunderstood the nature of the political action being undertaken by the indigenous veterans. Economic and social concessions were supposed to quell unrest in the ranks of the indigenous veterans and convert them into a loyal clientele base for the regime. Yet, as the activism of indigenous veterans, both within the cross-community associations and in the new indigenous-led organizations, had shown, the key demands of indigenous veterans were not purely related to patronage but also centred on issues of equality. Indigenous veteran leaders' conception of equality extended beyond pension rights to their right to participate in the shaping and application of policy, both within the veterans' movement and within the wider political system. The hierarchical structure of the *Amitiés* excluded indigenous veterans from decision-making, indeed often sacrificing them to the economic needs of the colonial system as evidenced by the controversial recruitment of veterans as labourers for private enterprise in the metropole.[89] While indigenous veterans did partake of the services offered by the *Amitiés*, often in large numbers, this does not mean that they willingly adopted the role the *Amitiés* hoped to assign to them, as a loyal pillar of the regime. The continued existence of the indigenous veterans' groups, many of whom were vocal in their demand for the extension of citizenship rights, is testament to the failure of the *Amitiés* to monopolize the indigenous veteran. The notion of 'segregated primacy', long promoted by the cross-community veterans' associations, was enforced as official policy through the *Amitiés*, becoming in practice what it had always been in theory: a (largely unsuccessful) attempt to buy off the indigenous veterans.

[88] Ibid., 100.

[89] See Report for 1937, General Assembly, 4 May 1938, ANOM/119/APOM/2.

Challenging European Hegemony within the Veterans' Movement

The gradual usurpation of the veterans' associations' role by the *Amitiés Africaines* was largely overshadowed within the moderate veterans' movement by the increasing assertiveness of radical indigenous veterans' groups. The indigenous veterans were now central players in the umbrella organizations that sought to federate veterans across North Africa. Furthermore, indigenous members within the cross-community organizations moved to impose a more pro-reform agenda. By 1939, the proportion of indigenous members within the *Amicale* stood at somewhere between one quarter and one fifth, as seen in Figure 5.3. The knock-on effects of the new weight of indigenous veterans in veteran politics in the colony could be seen in the image the cross-community *Interfédération* sought to present to the public. The contrast with the one-time emblem of the *Interfédération*'s most important member, the *Amicale*, is striking. Where once the figure of the wounded *zouave* was accompanied by a European Red Cross nurse, now the European soldier stood alongside his indigenous comrade-in-arms (Figure 5.4). However, the leaders of the indigenous veterans' movements would not be content with a simple acknowledgement of their presence: they wanted radical change.

In March 1937, Nourreddine and the LACMO organized a congress in Oran, drawing together the indigenous veterans' movements of North Africa. Delegates from across Algeria spoke out against government neglect

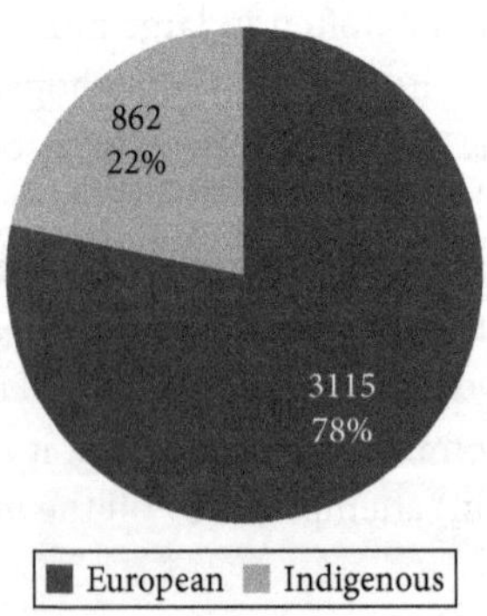

Figure 5.3. The ethnic composition of the *Amicale* membership in 1939
Source: Prefect of Algiers to the Governor General, 3 July 1939, ANOM/91/1K/701

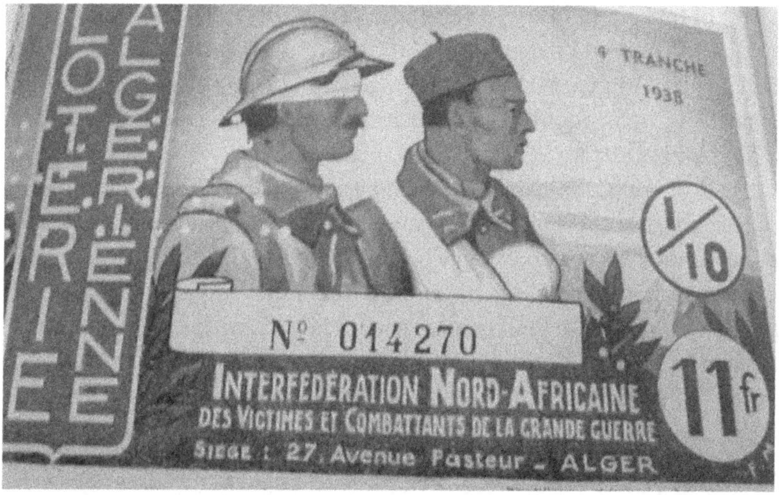

Figure 5.4. Lottery ticket of the *Interfédération Nord-Africaine des Anciens Combattants*, 1938

Source: Interfédération Nord-Africaine des Victimes de la Guerre et Anciens Combattants, Le XVI Congrès Interfédéral d'Alger, 16 et 17 avril 1938 (Algier: Imprimerie Imbert, 1938)

and demanded full support for the Blum-Viollette Project.[90] Later that year at the Interfederal Congress in Casablanca, Algeria's indigenous veterans presented a united front, blocking an attempt by the *Amicale* to impose its policy on the Blum-Viollette Project. The indigenous veterans wanted an unambiguous endorsement of the scheme, asserting that the *Amicale*'s non-committal stance put 'obstacles' in the way of a project they very much supported.[91] At the following year's Interfederal Congress in Algiers, the question of indigenous rights would once more prove extremely problematic. Tasked by the congress with reporting on the indigenous question, Tahar Aouidad was harshly critical of government neglect of indigenous veterans, comparing the fate of their claims to the fable of the Rock of Sisyphus.[92] In an attempt to rally wider support for the realization of indigenous demands, he framed the campaign in terms of national security, pointing both to the

[90] Departmental Security Report, 24 March 1937, AWO I/14/4063.
[91] *La Tranchée*, October 1937.
[92] Tahar Aouidad, 'Les Victimes de la Guerre et Anciens Combattants Indigènes Musulmans Nord-Africains', in *Interfédération Nord-Africaine des Victimes de la Guerre et Anciens Combattants, Le XVI Congrès*, 71–81.

threat of foreign influence in North Africa and the necessity of indigenous troops for national defence.[93] This rhetoric notwithstanding, Aouidad remained committed to the moderate agenda of the *Amicale*, stopping short of any endorsement of the Blum-Viollette Project and presenting a motion calling for priority for veterans in any reform plans.

The leaders of the more radical indigenous veterans' movements were not willing to rubberstamp this extension of the *Amicale*'s longstanding policy to the *Interfédération* as a whole. Once more, Nourreddine challenged the cautious agenda dictated by the cross-community organizations, declaring himself willing to temporarily renounce his claim to citizenship rights to support the provisions of Blum-Viollette, a statement that provoked agitation in the audience.[94] His colleague from Constantine, Bakir Benkalaya, called for a motion of support for the government and the rejection of Aouidad's proposition.[95] According to the official report of the congress, 'an extensive discussion' ensued.[96] Speaking on behalf of the cross-community organizations, Kerdavid articulated his rejection of the endorsement of the Blum-Viollette Project in terms of the primacy of the veteran:

> I take the responsibility here of demanding priority for indigenous veterans. If we have thought of demanding electoral rights for our comrades, it is because we believe, we veterans who fought alongside them in the war, that even those who live in the most distant hovels—even if these are the most ignorant—have the right to priority over those possessing a higher level of education. The indigenous veteran has spilled his blood for France, with us, for us, he is French…All others should be served after him.[97]

Kerdavid acknowledged that without the intervention of the indigenous veterans' organizations, the cross-community groups 'would never have thought of dealing with the question of electoral rights for the indigenous'.[98] While his rejection of Blum-Viollette had long been couched in terms of the primacy of the veteran, Kerdavid admitted that it was 'the most diverse political opinions' of the group's members that meant it 'cannot get behind one project or another'.[99] Unwilling and, perhaps, unable to rally the majority of his members to support a project that was roundly rejected by most of the European-led political movements in Algeria, Kerdavid and the *Amicale* pushed for the adoption of a motion calling for priority to be given to veterans in any reform of the political status of the indigenous. In the end, the motion was approved, with the official congress booklet reporting 'the

[93] Ibid., 71–2. [94] Ibid., 77. [95] Ibid., 78. [96] Ibid.
[97] Ibid. [98] Ibid. [99] Ibid., 79.

motion was adopted unanimously except for three votes'.[100] The *Amicale* had imposed its agenda on the *Interfédération* but had not succeeded in convincing the indigenous naysayers.

The following year, the Congress of the Interfédération Nord-Africaine, meeting in Tunis, offered another opportunity for the *Amicale* to promote its agenda. Aouidad presented an extensive set of resolutions detailing the reforms necessary to ensure indigenous veterans enjoyed all their rights and endorsing pension equality.[101] The report highlighted the ammunition that existing inequalities and abuses gave to 'agitators', stoking fears of the rising tide of nationalism.[102] The congress fully supported this element of Aouidad's programme. On the issue of civil and political rights, in a preliminary report in preparation for the congress Aouidad had proposed a motion that echoed, word for word, the position outlined the previous year. The absence of this motion or any specific comments regarding the political status of the indigenous in the congress' final report suggests that the *Amicale*'s efforts to impose its approach on this issue were stymied, presumably by the indigenous veteran leadership.[103]

Interestingly, two almost identical versions of Aouidad's final report exist in the archives: the official booklet of the congress[104] and a pamphlet issued under the same title as the section containing the report in the booklet.[105] The sole difference is the following passage, excluded from the official booklet but present in the pamphlet:

> The old formula of 'lesser needs' seems to perpetually postpone the improvement of the situation of the majority of the indigenous. It is true also that the Colonies only attract attention when their demands become tumultuous or urgent because of an external threat. Then, speeches are given, promises are made, great hopes are born that soon give way to great disappointments.[106]

While we can only speculate as to the explanation for this discrepancy, it seems reasonable to suggest that the censorship of the most virulent of Aouidad's criticism exposes the extent to which the still overwhelmingly

[100] Ibid.

[101] Les Revendications matérielles des anciens combattants et victimes de guerre indigènes par T. Aouidad in the Official Booklet of the 18th Congrès Interfédéral, Tunis, 25–6 March 1939, ANOM/91/1K/701.

[102] Ibid.

[103] Ibid.

[104] Ibid.

[105] Les Revendications matérielles des anciens combattants et victimes de guerre indigènes par T. Aouidad from 18th Congrès Interfédéral, Tunis, 25–6 March 1939, ANOM/91/4I/183.

[106] Ibid.

European leadership of the veterans' movements was sensitive to radical critiques of its attitude towards the 'indigenous question'. This discomfort reflects an awareness on the part of the leadership that its pre-eminence among organized veterans in Algeria was no longer guaranteed. Likewise, it was clear that the ambiguity of its attitude towards political reform was fast becoming untenable. Once a means of maintaining unity through avoiding conflicts over political reform, the idea of 'segregated primacy' had been fundamentally undermined by the failure to ensure priority for the indigenous veteran in his own sphere. Moreover, the rise of mass indigenous politics, feeding off and contributing to a growing sense that injustice was inherent to the colonial system, challenged the separation between political rights and social and economic rights. It now seemed contradictory to campaign for equal pension rights but not equal political rights. Not only was 'segregated primacy' unrealized after a decade of (often half-hearted) campaigning, it was now increasingly undesired by a population whose expectations had grown at a faster pace than the reform agenda within the veterans' movements.

The parallels between the *Amicale*'s indigenous policy and that of some of the principal actors discussed in earlier chapters of this book is striking. The most obvious convergence can be seen in the policy of the *Amicale* and that of the extreme right movements explored in Chapter 4. The *Amicale*'s transition from an almost total effacement of the indigenous toward a paternalism that embraced enhanced economic, social, and limited political rights for indigenous veterans almost directly mirrors the evolution of the extreme right over the interwar period. However, the dilemmas faced by the *Amicale* in dealing with this 'indigenous question' resonate beyond the extreme right and its rhetoric aimed at war veterans. The struggles faced by the left in the immediate post-war period over indigenous policy also seem to resonate with the *Amicale*'s policy in the 1930s. Indeed, a direct comparison can be drawn between the post-war left's vision of 'social and economic fraternity', the extreme right's 'fraternity of arms', and the *Amicale*'s 'segregated primacy', with each representing an attempt by European political leaders to counter demands for political reform with a combination of economic and social concessions and an imagined 'intimate hierarchy'.[107]

These policies left little room for the agency of indigenous actors. For Nourreddine Abdellah Bendjelloul of the LACMO, his political activism, both on the local scene in Oran and within the wider veterans' movement, proved

[107] Sanos, *Aesthetics of Hate*, 223.

too much for the colonial authorities. His implacable enemy, M. Oger, the head of the local veterans' office, had long supported his removal, claiming that the LACMO, once 'rid of Nourreddine', would 'enjoy universal sympathy and could take on the form of a real veterans' association'.[108] In this, he was supported by the prefect of the *département* of Oran.[109] In 1939, the authorities moved against Nourreddine, arresting him for fraud arising from alleged financial irregularities in the operation of the LACMO. He and his organization were expelled from the *Interfédération* and his reign over the most radical of the indigenous veterans' associations was brought to an end.[110] Months later, the courts would dismiss the case against Nourreddine for lack of evidence, but his control over Oran's indigenous veterans had been fundamentally undermined.[111] Never again would a radical indigenous veterans' organization emerge in Algeria to challenge European hegemony in both the wider veterans' movement and in colonial society at large.[112]

The case of Nourreddine Abdallah Bendjelloul is illustrative of both the potential and the limitations of political action framed in terms of participation of the Great War in colonial Algeria. His story shows that indigenous veterans in Algeria, contrary to the prevailing wisdom in the existing historiography, did in fact 'organize into particularly effective or disruptive groupings'.[113] Rick Fogarty is right to point out that they did not represent a 'violent challenge to the postwar political order',[114] but they did pose a sufficient threat to provoke an intervention by the colonial state and military to ensure that these 'unruly clients' did not morph into something altogether more dangerous.[115] Although their failure to secure political rights has largely obscured their successful campaigns for financial and social rights, perhaps their greatest achievement lies in their wresting back of control of their own representation from the European leadership of the cross-community organizations. Participation in the Great War was their ticket into the 'world of contact', with all its possibilities and constraints. They

[108] Report of the Secretary General of the Departmental Office of Veterans (Oran) on the Activities of the LACMO, 5 February 1938, ANOM/92/2541.

[109] Prefect of Oran to the Governor General, undated, ANOM/92/2541.

[110] Police Commissioner to the Prefect of Oran, 18 November 1939, ANOM/92/2541.

[111] Centre Départemental d'Information d'Oran, Bulletin des Renseignements, 2082, 24 April 1940, AWO, I/14/4063.

[112] For a detailed account of veterans in Algeria from 1940 to 1962 see Samuel André-Bercovici, 'Les anciens combattants dans l'Algérie coloniale: Les associations d'anciens combattants et l'Algérie française' (Master 2 Thesis, Université Paris 1- Panthéon-Sorbonne, 2014).

[113] Richard S. Fogarty and David Killingray, 'Demobilization in British and French Africa at the End of the First World War', *Journal of Contemporary History* 50, No. 1 (2015): 100–23, 116.

[114] Ibid., 117. [115] Mann, *Native Sons*, 63.

used the contradictions inherent in the discourse around wartime service promoted by both the cross-community veterans' movement and the French colonial authorities to push for the financial, social, and political empowerment of indigenous veterans. When their radicalism was perceived as a threat to European hegemony, both within the veterans' movement and in society generally, the colonial authorities moved to stifle opposition. In the most extreme case, that of Nourreddine, the European leadership of the cross-community veterans seemed only too happy to facilitate his expulsion from the veterans' movement. His war record and use of a rhetorical strategy that valorized loyalty to France could not insulate him from the reality of politics in a colonial sphere where racial hierarchy trumped all other concerns. Although the language of the Great War facilitated the negotiation of the relationship between subjects, citizens, and administrators in the colony, it could not change the fundamental rules governing politics, and indeed everyday life, in the colony.

Conclusion

If the focus in this chapter has been on conflict and contradiction, this has been at the expense of a broader analysis of the *Amicale*'s success in influencing public policy in Algeria and in attracting members from both communities. As a moderate veterans' movement, it offered guidance to those confronting an elaborate bureaucracy while also providing a non-overtly political forum for veterans to vent their frustration in relative freedom. Nevertheless, the study of the rhetoric of the *Amicale* offers an insight into the complex and plural meanings of the Great War in the language of politics in interwar Algeria. It exposes the dilemmas facing 'moderate', supposedly apolitical, movements attempting to employ metropolitan strategies to frame demands in a colonial context. In particular, it demonstrates that the potential polysemy of the Great War as a legitimizing discourse could serve to both subsume subaltern demands and elevate them into a radical critique of the existing colonial order. If the story of the *Amicale* cannot and should not be reduced to the contradictions that underlay its discourse, neither can it be understood without an analysis of the role the 'tensions of Empire' inherent in its language played in shaping its policy. Chief among these was the ambiguity inherent in the concept of 'primacy'.

Undoubtedly, the notion of primacy was far from uncontested within veterans' movements in the metropole: the war wounded often asserted their entitlement over veterans while political and ideological disputes undermined the universality of claims for the primacy of the *génération du feu*. These clashes notwithstanding, the fundamental concept of primacy remained much the same: the veteran should be first among equals; he should have priority above all others. How, then, could a moderate organization apply this logic to a colonial context? Who could countenance an indigenous veteran being treated on equal terms with a European veteran, particularly if this would grant him primacy over non-combatant Europeans? The *Amicale* initially chose to ignore the indigenous veteran, excluding him and other indigenous rights-holders from its discourse in the years immediately following its foundation. Subsequently, the organization attempted to subsume the claims of the indigenous, paying lip service to equality and half-heartedly pursuing his primacy in the indigenous sphere. The rise of mass politics in the wake of the centenary rendered this policy unsustainable; a solution would have to be found to meet some of the demands of the indigenous veterans without challenging the colonial status quo. In the period 1930–6, the *Amicale* began to develop the policy of 'segregated primacy', campaigning to end abuses, to promote priority for indigenous veterans in the indigenous sphere, and to establish parity of pensions for the dependants of the dead while remaining mostly silent on possible reforms towards equality, financial and political, for the living. Finally, faced with the challenge of the Blum-Viollette Project and the rise of the indigenous veterans' organization, the *Amicale* embraced the equalization of pension rights and redoubled its efforts to promote 'segregated primacy' in the political sphere. Even its non-committal stance on the expansion of citizenship was dressed in the language of primacy, holding that reform projects would only be legitimate if they respected the pre-eminence of the veteran.

While the veterans' movement had a particularly powerful claim to the legitimacy of the Great War, framing their demands in terms of their wartime service was not without its risks. The movement's evolution over the course of the interwar period illustrates how the European leadership failed to grasp the revolutionary potential of the egalitarian message that they were promoting. If the shared experience of the Great War initially brought veterans from both communities together in a common organization driven by the demand for recompense, differing opinions over how compensation should be doled out within the bounds of the colonial system would eventually drive large sections of them apart. The rhetoric of the *Amicale*, firmly embedded in notions of the 'moral economy of sacrifice' and 'mutual obligation', could not escape the shadow of the wider meta-narratives that shaped political language in colonial Algeria. The movement's tacit endorsement of the image of the pioneer settler, and its inevitable counterpart, the ignorant and savage indigenous, undermined its proclaimed commitment to a 'colour-blind' vision of veterans' rights. Its internal structures reproduced the restrictions and discriminations of the wider colonial system in Algeria, meaning that for most of the interwar period, the indigenous were absent not only from the *Amicale*'s discourse but also from its leadership. The organization's construction of a discourse that denounced inequalities between the metropole and Algeria, a common thread in European-dominated political organizations, legitimized forms of political contestation that questioned the nature of the relationship between France and Algeria.

Above all, however, it was the *Amicale*'s failed attempt to adapt the egalitarian discourse constructed by the metropolitan movements to a colonial setting that would spell trouble for the European leadership. By providing indigenous veterans with a legitimizing language predicated on notions of equality, the cross-community veterans' movement sowed the seeds of its own downfall. Whether indigenous veterans chose to employ this framing strategy internally, within the forums of the cross-community organizations, or externally, in new indigenous-dominated veterans' organizations, the European leadership could no longer ignore wholesale the claims of their indigenous comrades. The concept of 'segregated primacy', both as an aspiration of the *Amicale* and a practice of the *Amitiés*, fundamentally misunderstood the central demand of the indigenous veteran: that his voice should count, both within the veterans' movement and within wider Algerian society. The provision of social services, the campaign for pension equality, and the calls for the priority of indigenous veterans in the state sector were by no means unimportant advances made on behalf on the indigenous veteran community. However, they left intact the very hierarchy that indigenous veterans increasingly sought to challenge. Unlike their European counterparts, indigenous veterans could not shape the services and privileges to which their status as veterans entitled them because they exercised no direct influence over the authorities who provided them. Indigenous veterans came to realize that the only way to safeguard their interests was by securing real political power, both within the veterans' movement and within wider society. Reference to the war not only helped them recognize this salient fact of life in the colony but it also empowered them to fight against it.

Nevertheless, membership of a veterans' association was just one facet of the veteran experience. Indeed, in most belligerent countries, the majority of veterans did not join any form of collective organization. Even in France, where veterans' associations were at their strongest, an estimated one in two veterans remained unaffiliated.[116] It is probable that this figure was much higher for the indigenous veterans in Algeria. They would largely be left to their own devices when it came to the complicated task of claiming their post-war entitlements. Despite the many obstacles placed in their way, their persistence in pursuing their claims would, as we shall now see, put pressure on the colonial authorities to account for the gaps between rhetoric and reality in veteran policy.

[116] The figure for Britain was as low as 20 percent. John Horne, 'The Living', *Cambridge History of the First World War, Vol. 3: Civil Society*, ed. Jay Winter (Cambridge: Cambridge: Cambridge University Press, 2014): 592–617, 502.

6

Pensions, Posts, and Petitions

In December 1921, Zoueb Ben el Kamba, a veteran from the town of Biskra, wrote to the governor general denouncing the administration's failure to compensate him for his participation in the Great War. As the intellectual and political elites in Algiers rallied around Emir Khaled to call for political reform, a veteran 400 kilometres away in the foothills of the Aurès Mountains offered his own critique of the colonial administration: 'I am a poor unfortunate, I have no work, I look to you and to Merciful God, I had spilled my blood for France and hope now she will not let me die of hunger'.[1] This chapter examines the case of Zoueb Ben el Kamba and so many other indigenous actors who, often far from political power centres, mobilized their visions of the 'moral economy of sacrifice' to claim their 'just reward' from the colonial state. Their correspondence with the colonial and pension authorities testifies to a striking capacity to navigate a complex and often hostile bureaucracy as they sought to transform the colonial state's generous rhetoric into reality.

The story of indigenous rights-holders contributes to our wider understanding of the interaction between the expanding modern state, in this case an oppressive, racially hierarchical colonial state, and the population it governed. Their correspondence with the colonial administration, often mediated through intermediaries, paints a complex picture of the encounter between officialdom and the swathes of the indigenous population that seem to have been simultaneously subject to and beyond the reach of its control. The case of these indigenous rights-holders lies at the intersection of two intertwined concepts that underpin the modern state: legibility and eligibility. Here I draw inspiration from the work of the anthropologist, James Scott. Scott has highlighted the importance of the imposition of a form of 'legibility' for the expansion of the modern state.[2] In the face of the

[1] Zoueb Ben El Kamba to the Governor General, 4 December 1921, ANOM/GGA/3H/19.

[2] James Scott, *Weapons of the Weak: Everyday Forms of Peasant Resistance* (New Haven, CT: Yale University Press, 1985) and James Scott, *Seeing like a State: How Certain Schemes to Improve the Human Condition Have Failed* (New Haven, CT: Yale University Press, 1998).

encroachment of the state, Scott argues that the agrarian masses expressed their resistance through a combination of 'irony, petty acts of noncompliance, foot dragging, and dissimulation'.[3] In the polarized colonial state, he asserts, such resistance was embodied in 'wilful and massive noncompliance' on the part of the colonized.[4] Fred Cooper has nuanced the application of Scott's theory to colonial Africa, stressing the 'complexity of engagement of Africans with imported institutions and constructs'.[5] The evidence presented in this chapter backs up Cooper's vision of a complex colonial encounter. While it is true that large numbers of indigenous rights-holders (how many is impossible to quantify) did not vindicate their rights by engaging with the colonial state, it is also undeniable that a significant proportion did seek to do so, optimizing their eligibility by making themselves legible to the colonial state. The fact that rights-holders engaged in the long, complex, and potentially expensive process of assembling the myriad of documents required by the French colonial state demonstrates their understanding that legibility was a precondition to eligibility, even if their conception of both often differed from that of the colonial administrators who adjudicated their cases. Thus, the process of post-war claims-making became a means by which the 'world of contact' was expanded and reshaped.

Legislating for 'Mutual Obligation'

In the immediate aftermath of the war, French society, like all the belligerent societies, debated how the post-war order could best reflect the wartime 'moral economy of sacrifice'. We have already seen how these debates often centred on divisive and deeply ideological issues connected to colonial and social reform. However, it was the practical question of how the state would cater for and compensate those who had fought to defend France that was the most pressing for the legions of veterans, war wounded, widows, and orphans across the empire. As explained in Chapter 5, the first major piece of legislation that emerged in the aftermath of the Great War seemed to guarantee a form of financial equality for the indigenous of North Africa. The Law of 31 March 1919 sought to provide for the significant number of war wounded, widows, and orphans left in the wake of the

[3] Scott, *Weapons of the Weak*, 350. [4] Ibid., 298.

[5] Frederick Cooper, 'Conflict and Connection: Rethinking Colonial African History', *American Historical Review* 99, No. 5 (December, 1994): 1516–45, 1534.

horrors of the war.[6] When the project was presented before the *Assemblée Nationale*, the deputies Marius Moutet and Henri Doizy, long-time supporters of colonial reform, evoked the republican concept of the *impôt de sang* to justify the law's extension to indigenous populations in the colonies where conscription was enforced.[7] Their proposal was challenged in the senate by Dominique Delahaye, a Catholic monarchist. Delahaye asserted that the amendment, by singling out colonies in which conscription was in operation, would unjustly privilege one group of colonial subjects over another. Furthermore, he turned to a classic argument of those who sought to limit the rights of colonial subjects, asserting that the indigenous lifestyle required less financial resources than that of the European and, thus, it would be 'immoral to provide for the indigenous beyond their needs'.[8] Delahaye's amendment proposed that the rate for pensions granted to indigenous rights-holders should be set at exactly half the rate enjoyed by French citizens.[9] A lively debate ensued in which the president of the Commission on Pensions asserted that administrators from North Africa were anxious that the indigenous population be granted the financial compensation promised during the war.[10] In the end, the text presented by the government and endorsed by the assembly as Article 73 of the law seemed to embrace financial equality for North Africa: 'The rates fixed for the pensions of French soldiers are applicable to the indigenous troops of Algeria and the colonies or protectorates where recruitment has been carried out by means of conscription'.[11] Nevertheless, by adopting this amendment, the assembly rejected the sweeping egalitarianism advocated by Moutet and Doizy, opting instead for a nominal equality of rates, which masked a wider inequality of conditions.

This inequality was most blatant in Article 74, which regulated the provision for the dependants of the war dead. Once again, a nominal equality was maintained, with the same sum of money supposedly granted to the widow of an indigenous soldier as was conferred on her European equivalent. Nonetheless, whereas this sum was reserved exclusively for the use of the European widow, the indigenous widow had to share her pension with the other dependants of the war dead. The distribution of the pension among

[6] See Charles Valentino, *La Loi Lugol sur les Pensions Militaires aux Infirmes, Veuves, Orphelins et Ascendants (Loi du 31 mars 1919)* (Paris: Edition de la Revue Interalliée, 1920), 37–8.

[7] Charles-Louis Valentino, *Les Pensions aux indigènes des colonies et à leur ayants cause: textes et commentaires* (Paris: Berger-Levrault, 1925), 2–5.

[8] Valentino, *La Loi Lugol*, 497. [9] Ibid. [10] Ibid., 498.

[11] Article 73, *Journal Officiel*, 2 April 1919, 3389.

the dependants would be decided by 'the local authority, inspired by indigenous custom'.[12] The prospect of compensating the dependants of a polygamous indigenous soldier was cited to justify this discrimination. But, as Charles-Louis Valentino, a director at the Pensions Ministry pointed out, the wording of Article 74 applied this provision to all 'Muslim' families in North Africa, not just the small minority who engaged in polygamy.[13] The use of polygamy to prevent the extension of equality to the families of the indigenous war dead was by no means an isolated phenomenon. The history of post-war provision across the empire is marked by the evocation of the cultural particularisms of indigenous populations by colonial administrators in order to minimize the financial burden that would fall on colonial authorities.[14] However, as we shall see, indigenous intermediaries, working within the colonial system, would play an important role in disregarding the colonial authorities' vision of how indigenous familial pensions should be distributed.

While polygamy was mobilized to legitimize the limitation of widows' rights, some of the other restrictions in post-war provision for indigenous rights-holders seem to have had no specific justification. Indigenous widows in Algeria automatically lost their entitlement to a pension when they remarried, unlike French citizen widows, who had only to renounce part of their benefits following their remarriage.[15] In North Africa, the age at which indigenous war orphans lost their entitlement to a pension was set at eighteen, while the orphans of French citizens enjoyed a pension until the age of twenty-one. Similarly, female indigenous orphans who married lost their right to a pension, a provision that did not apply to European orphans.[16] These injustices, which seem relatively minor but had a serious impact on indigenous rights-holders, attracted little to no attention in the National Assembly. Once more, colonial administrators mobilized their understandings of indigenous family structure to minimize the potential financial strain that compensating indigenous rights-holders would represent.

Indigenous rights-holders were also affected by the failure of legislators to clarify the applicability of aspects of the pension law to North Africa. The principal controversy to emerge from this lack of legislative clarity centred on the applicability of the '*majorations*' or pension supplements accorded to the war wounded for each of their children. As Article 73 had extended

[12] Article 74, Ibid. [13] Valentino, *Les Pensions aux indigènes*, 9.

[14] See Dónal Hassett, '*Pupilles de l'Empire*: Debating the Provision for Child Victims of the Great War in the French Empire', in *French Historical Studies* 39, No. 2 (April 2016): 315–45.

[15] Valentino, *Les Pensions aux indigènes*, 25. [16] Ibid.

equality of rates but not of conditions to the indigenous war wounded, it seemed they were precluded from enjoying the benefits of the *majorations*. This was the impression given by a top military pensions official in Algeria to the governor general.[17] And yet this interpretation was not shared by all administrators, with the minister of the interior defending the applicability of the law to indigenous rights-holders.[18] While confusion reigned among administrators, indigenous rights-holders would consistently challenge this discrimination.

The other principal plank of post-war provision, the reserved jobs scheme, was particularly compromised by a blend of cultural particularism and administrative inadequacy. The vast majority of positions reserved for indigenous rights-holders were in the unskilled category, with posts such as road mender, railway labourer, and, above all, café operator, considered, as the *Amicale* would later put it, 'suited to the physical and intellectual aptitudes' of indigenous veterans.[19] While undoubtedly this was the product of a mind-set that saw the indigenous as ignorant and less capable, it also reflected the failure of the colonial state to educate its subjects, even those who served in its armies. Positions in the two skilled categories, as various forms of administrative assistants, required an ability to read, write, and speak French[20] at a time when illiteracy rates among military recruits were between 75 and 85 percent.[21] In any case, posts in the skilled categories were few and far between; in interwar Algeria, licences to operate a *café maure* were the principal means of realizing the *emplois réservés* programme. Once more, the system that developed to regulate the distribution of these licences proved wholly inadequate, leaving indigenous rights-holders struggling to optimize the reward they could reap from the state while attempting to minimize the state's interference in their lives.

The legislation of post-war provision reflected a wider lack of understanding of the difficulties that would face both administrators and indigenous claimants in Algeria. While the legislative framework was adjusted to recognize the 'cultural particularity' of indigenous Algerian families (and thus, minimize the state's duties), the administrative and infrastructural inadequacies of the colonial bureaucracy in Algeria were barely taken into

[17] Quartermaster General Levy to the Governor General, 26 July 1922, ANOM/GGA/3H/19.
[18] Minister of the Interior to the Governor General, 11 July 1922, ANOM/GGA/3H/19.
[19] *La Tranchée*, 1st Fortnight, March 1933.
[20] 'Emplois Réservés aux Indigènes d'Algérie', *Bulletin officiel du Ministère de la Guerre, Edition Méthodique* (Paris: Charles-Lavauzelle, 1917), 8 and 44–61.
[21] Recham, *Les musulmans algériens*, 49.

account. Indigenous claimants were required to provide the administration with a wide range of documents to justify their applications. What was already a complex task for citizen-veterans in the metropole would become a struggle for subject-veterans in the colonies, with Gregory Mann asserting that, in French West Africa, 'becoming a veteran could itself be a full-time occupation'.[22] Securing the documentation necessary to pursue a claim was a time-consuming and potentially expensive process. This was compounded by the colonial state's own administrative shortcomings, with an underresourced and ill-equipped bureaucracy struggling to render the colony's indigenous population legible. Nevertheless, certain indigenous rights-holders managed to negotiate this complicated process, maximizing their legibility to the colonial state and thus enhancing their eligibility for pensions.

Breaking through the Bureaucracy: Applying for a Pension

On 12 March 1925, the career soldier and veteran of the Great War Cheikh ben Koudier ben El Ala passed away, leaving behind three orphans and a young widow. Over the four months that followed, the soldier's widow and brother set about securing the documentation necessary for a pension application. Their dossier, submitted on 28 July of that same year, consisted of a total of thirty-two documents. Alongside the pension application form, birth, death, and marriage certificates, it also included certificates of non-remarriage, certificates of 'collective life', and proof of guardianship.[23] Despite this thorough paper trail, their application had still not been processed by early 1926, leading the deceased's brother to write to the minister of pensions to request a speedy resolution to avert 'the crises of poverty' that would affect the orphans and fully 'compensate them for the services given by their father'.[24] His request went unanswered. Undaunted by the slow-moving and unresponsive bureaucracy, the claimants secured an intervention on their behalf by the local deputy (and long-time opponent of indigenous reform) Pierre Roux-Freissineng, who was assured by the minister of pensions that their application would soon be granted.[25] A definitive pension

[22] Mann, *Native Sons*, 102.

[23] Summary of Application, Mme Oumelkheir, 28 July 1925, SHD/GR/13/YF/7150.

[24] Cheikh Ould Mohammed Boutarem to the Minister of Pensions, 2 March 1926, SHD/GR/13/YF/7150.

[25] Minister of Pensions to Deputy Roux-Freissineng, 26 December 1927, SHD/GR/13/YF/7150.

was subsequently granted, though this did not mean the family's trials with the colonial bureaucracy were finished. The subsequent remarriage of the widow required a redistribution of the pension, as did the marriage of one of the orphans. Over the course of the two decades that followed the death of Cheikh ben Koudier ben El Ala, his family had significant, if intermittent, contact with the pensions authorities, amassing a thick file of documents that testified to their existence as subject- and rights-holders in the colonial state. For this family, claiming their rights turned into a long, complicated, and, presumably, expensive process, but one they would follow through to the very end. They, and many other indigenous rights-holders, would, despite the many obstacles placed in their way, display an impressive capacity to vindicate their post-war rights.

The first, and perhaps greatest, obstacle that faced potential claimants was the struggle to gather the documents necessary to make an application for a pension or a reserved job. As the dossier of indigenous veteran pension claims recently compiled by the *Service Historique de la Défense* shows, the vast majority of claimants born in Algeria before 1893 had no birth certificate, as the colonial state had not yet compiled a civil register for indigenous subjects.[26] Instead, they had to apply for a document that estimated their age at the date at which the civil register had been opened in their territory. The situation for widows and orphans was particularly complex as they, unlike the men who had served in the army, had had little prior interaction with the administration and, thus, often had few or even no official papers. The birth of children in indigenous families in rural areas was not always reported to the authorities and birth certificates would have to be produced in these cases years after the event for a successful pension application.[27] Furthermore, the range of documents required for an application for a widow's and/or orphan's pension was extensive and went far beyond the already problematic requirement for birth certificates. The only specific reference in the Law of 1919 to the potential bureaucratic difficulties facing indigenous claimants covered the absence of a marriage certificate. Pensions authorities would recognize an act of marriage signed by a judge from the local Islamic court (*qadi*).[28] The onus was placed on the indigenous rights-holder to fill any other documentary lacunae themselves.

[26] See the Sous-série SHD/GR/13/YF, 'Pensions des troupes coloniales et des troupes indigènes 1850–1950', SHD.

[27] See for example Non-Inscription Certificate from the Commune Mixte de Cassaigne, 21 February 1941, SHD/GR/13/YF/7213.

[28] Article 74, *Journal Officiel*, 2 April 1919, 3389.

More often than not, indigenous veterans and other rights-holders were illiterate and would have to engage the services of translators and/or public scribes in order to vindicate their rights. This would, as we shall see, have important implications for the shape that their correspondence with the authorities took. Initially, however, it was the cost and hardship involved that was most significant for claimants. Writing in 1917, governor general Lutaud attributed the low numbers of indigenous applying for pensions during the war to a combination of ignorance of the law, delays, and costs of translation and local corruption.[29] In 1919, the new governor general, Jean-Baptiste Abel, clarified that there was no legal entitlement to free translations for claimants, affirming that local officials and military translators would share the burden together as volunteers.[30] The combination of these administrative obstacles and a whole myriad of other difficulties militated against indigenous veterans and rights-holders who sought to claim their due. By March 1921 for the 26,000 indigenous killed or missing during the war, the families of only 12,000 had established pension claims.[31] And yet, over the course of the interwar period significant numbers of claimants did undertake the arduous and costly process of vindicating their rights.

While the collection and submission of a whole range of documents to the state can be understood as an effort to achieve eligibility through legibility, the path to legibility was not without its bumps. If, as James Scott claims, the assignation of second names was a key component of the creation of the legible subject,[32] the case of the indigenous veteran bears testament to the challenges facing the colonial state. During the war, both the military and civil authorities had struggled to deal with the difficulties posed by the transliteration of indigenous names, often resulting in the failure to notify families when soldiers were killed.[33] In one particularly touching letter, an indigenous mother wrote to the authorities in June 1921 to ask if they 'could please do the necessary to find out if my son is dead, alive or a prisoner'.[34] The issue of the transliteration of indigenous names would once more complicate the claims pursued by indigenous rights-holders in the post-war period. Frequently, the documents presented by claimants carried many different versions of the same name. This would require the production of an

[29] Governor General to the Prefects and Commanders of the Military Territories, 21 March 1917, ANOM/GGA/3H/19.

[30] Governor General to the Minister of the Interior, 20 December 1919, ANOM/GGA/3H/19.

[31] Meynier, *L'Algérie Révélée*, 550.

[32] Scott, *Seeing like a State*, 2.

[33] See Peggy Bette, 'Veuves françaises de la Première guerre mondiale: statuts, itinéraires, combats' (PhD diss., Université Lumière Lyon, 2012), 78.

[34] Widow Rabes Hallouz to the Governor General, 8 June 1921, ANOM/GGA/3H/19.

acte d'individualité, a document that would list the variations in name and declare that they all referred to the one claimant.[35] This was not always sufficient to dispel the confusion among those administering pensions. In one case, a pension was issued to a veteran under a name that was completely different to his official name on the civil register and was only changed when he himself notified the authorities.[36] In another, a pension was granted to a veteran under his deceased brother's name and at a rate in line with his brother's much shorter service.[37] Indeed, the constant confusion that seemed to reign throughout the bureaucracy dealing with pensions applications indicates just how little knowledge the colonial authorities had about their subject populations.

When it came to assessing the changing conditions and entitlements of rights-holders, the authorities were largely grasping in the dark. Charles-Louis Valentino acknowledged that it was 'practically difficult' for the French state to assess when a widow had remarried.[38] This ignorance meant that indigenous widows could enter a new religious marriage without automatically losing their entitlements. When such an arrangement was discovered in the case of the widow of Mohammed Nedder in the *commune mixte* of Zemmora the local pension authorities simply decided that the widow should be considered remarried, even though no legally recognized marriage had taken place. The *Commission Locale de Répartition des Pensions*, which met a year and a half after Nedder's death, ruled that the pension was only valid until 30 September 1940, the date on which she supposedly remarried.[39] The local administrator of the *commune mixte* disputed the existence of a new marriage, asserting that her new situation should be considered a form of *concubinage* that did not impact her rights under pension legislation.[40] The case continued to puzzle the authorities in Paris as late as 1946, with the Ministry of Finance writing to the Ministry of Veterans seeking further clarification.[41] Whether such a clarification was ever forthcoming is not revealed in Nedder's file. What is clear, however,

[35] See the case of the veteran Yala, Ahmed ould Slimane, whose *acte d'individualité* listed five alternative versions, alongside the 'correct' version of his name. SHD/GR/13/YF/7164.

[36] Saad Mohammed ben Ali to the Algiers Division Commander, 24 March 1939 and Report on the Cancelation of a Proportional Pension, SHD/GR/13/YF/7223.

[37] Report on the Revision of a Pension, 8 March 1940, SHD/GR/13/YF/10023.

[38] Valentino, *Les Pensions aux indigènes*, 25.

[39] Procès-Verbal de la Commission de Répartition des Pensions de la Commune Mixte de Zemmora (hereafter PVCRP), 26 June 1941, SHD/GR/13/YF/10704.

[40] Administrator of the Commune Mixte de Zemmora to the Head the Departmental Pension Office, Oran, 22 December 1941, SHD/GR/13/YF/10704.

[41] Minister for Finance to the Minister for Veterans, 2 March 1946, SHD/GR/13/YF/10704.

is that the colonial state was often incapable of and, perhaps, uninterested in, strictly controlling the personal information and, by extension, the personal lives of its subjects.

The case of the widow living in *concubinage* or in a secret remarriage shows that gaps in the state's knowledge could also prove beneficial to claimants. The bureaucracy charged with allocating pensions was ill equipped to prevent indigenous claimants from using the state's ignorance of their situation to claim benefits to which they were not entitled. Many indigenous claimants, whether unsure of their rights or completely aware of their ineligibility, proved reluctant to move to transform the temporary allocations they had been granted during the war into a definitive pension, subject to a greater degree of scrutiny.[42] The nature of the documentary evidence available to the historian, emanating almost solely from the archives of the colonial administration, makes it impossible to track and quantify the cases of successful fraud by indigenous claimants. Nevertheless, there was clearly great potential for the optimization of compensation beyond the boundaries set by the law, allowing indigenous claimants to exploit the weaknesses of the colonial state. Thus, the process of applying for a pension presented many challenges, but also some limited opportunities to indigenous claimants.

There is no doubt, given both the legislation governing pensions and the underlying structures of rule that defined colonial society, that the power relations between the indigenous claimant and the pension bureaucracy were weighted in favour of the latter. By ruling an application invalid for any number of reasons, a bureaucrat in the pensions administration could deny a family its only source of income. Conversely, by taking a less strict approach to the application of discriminatory provisions in the legislation or a more flexible attitude towards non-standard documentation, pension officials could ensure the financial survival of an indigenous rights-holder. While we have seen here how indigenous claimants could use the colonial bureaucracy's own shortcomings to ensure they secured some form of compensation from the state, the most popular and effective means of optimizing their benefits was to win the ear of a sympathetic official or person of power.

Winning Favour through Correspondence

The rich correspondence of indigenous claimants with the pension authorities offers a fascinating window into the complex act of petitioning the colonial

[42] Governor General to the Prefects, 21 March 1917, ANOM/GGA/3H/19.

state. From the very beginning of French colonial rule, members of the indigenous elite had used petitions to negotiate their position within the new political order.[43] In interwar Algeria, petitions may be most readily associated with demands for colonial reform of Emir Khaled and, later, the FEMA. However, the letters addressed by individual indigenous rights-holders to officials are more representative of the act of petitioning as a day-to-day reality in colonial society. They offer an important, albeit heavily mediated, insight into how rights-holders understood their entitlements and, crucially, what strategies they, or their intermediaries, believed would optimize their compensation. Moreover, they expose another, and often overlooked, facet of the much debated 'world of contact': the role of intermediaries such as local indigenous officials, interpreters, and public scribes. Above all, they show how indigenous rights-holders themselves mobilized the wartime notions of the 'moral economy of sacrifice' and 'mutual obligation' to frame their demands for compensation, with varying degrees of success.

Given the extremely low literacy rates, it is probable that the vast majority of correspondence was written by third parties, especially public scribes. This explains why the same file might contain a pension application form signed with a thumbprint or the phrase 'illiterate' and a long hand-written letter making an extensive case for the granting of a pension.[44] One of the most striking aspects of the correspondence of claimants with the pension authorities is the frequency with which indigenous widows commissioned and sent letters to further their cases. If illiteracy was extremely high among indigenous male claimants, it was almost universal among war widows. This made women particularly reliant on both third-party intermediaries and sympathetic colonial officials. The mediating role of these public scribes and other go-betweens is crucial to understanding the process that translated the plea of the indigenous rights-holder into language considered legible and eligible by the colonial administration.

The agency of such public scribes is, perhaps, most famously addressed in Natalie Zemon Davis' account of 'pardon tales' in sixteenth-century

[43] Nourredine Amara, 'Les nationalités d'Amina Hanim. Une pétition d'hérédité à la France (1896–1830)', in *La nationalité dans le monde arabe: Négocier les appartenances et le droit*, ed. M'hamed Oualdi (Aix-en-Provence: Presses Universitaires de Provence, 2015): 49–72.

[44] See for example Letter to Minister for Pensions, 2 November 1920, SHD/GR/13/YF/8594, Letter to the Minister for Pensions, 4 March 1931 SHD/GR/13/YF/7114 and Mohamed ben Rabah to the Doctor-in-Chief of the Oran Rehabilitation Centre, 17 July 1937, SHD/GR/13/YF/10662.

France, *Fiction in the Archives*.[45] Zemon Davis argues convincingly that, despite the mediation of the scribe, the narrative voice of the supplicant remains largely intact. The petition was the result of 'a collective effort' that reshaped, reformulated, but also reflected the supplicant's original intention.[46] In the colonial context, Bhavani Raman's account of petition-writing under the East India Company underlines its social function as *the* legitimate form of contestation of colonial injustices, or as she calls it 'proper dissent'.[47] Furthermore, she highlights the disciplinary nature of the form of the petition, with the strict rules that governed what constituted a legitimate petition acting to prescribe the boundaries of acceptable behaviour for the indigenous actor.[48] Contestation of the colonial authorities could only come through skilled mediators.[49] By the advent of the twentieth century, the role of the public scribe in the same area of India had evolved considerably. Francis Cody has shown how, in developmentalist and democratic India, the petition is used to school the claimant in how to behave as a proper citizen with the rights and responsibility that status entails, something that was obviously not the case in colonial Algeria.[50] Nevertheless, Cody's description of the scribe's role as effectively translating a claim not only from one language to another but also, crucially, from one register to another holds true in the Algerian case. Alongside their role as facilitators of legibility, public scribes also act as assessors of eligibility, filtering through the emotive grievances of the claimant to find the information deemed 'relevant' and worthy of compensation by the state.[51] In the process, they replace the supplicatory pleas of emotion with the rights-based discourse of the modern state. The contrast with Natalie Zemon Davis' early-modern scribes is clear. Whereas in the 'pardon tales' of the sixteenth century the supplicant's narrative survived mediation, in post-colonial India the scribe sacrifices the claimant's voice on the altar of relevance. As Cody puts it, 'in the struggle over relevance in discourse…the state wins because it has written the very rules of the game'.[52] In the case of interwar colonial Algeria, I argue, the role of the public scribe lay somewhere between these two extremes.

[45] Natalie Zemon Davis, *Fiction in the Archives: Pardon Tales and Their Tellers in Sixteenth-Century France* (Cambridge: Polity Press, 1987).

[46] Ibid., 111.

[47] Bhavani Raman, *Document Raj, Writing and Scribes in Early Colonial South India* (Chicago, IL: University of Chicago Press, 2012), 182.

[48] Ibid., 191. [49] Ibid., 171.

[50] Francis Cody, *The Light of Knowledge: Literacy Activism and the Politics of Writing in South India* (London: Cornell University Press, 2013).

[51] Ibid., 180–8. [52] Ibid., 184.

Given the substantial power exercised by the public scribes, it is hardly surprising that colonial regimes regarded them with suspicion.[53] In his report on the condition of the indigenous veteran in post-World War II Algeria Serge Barthélemy, a young *stagiaire* from the prestigious *Ecole Nationale d'Administration*, characterized public scribes as 'venal and incompetent intermediaries',[54] a view widely held in administrative circles. The *Amitiés Africaines*, from its foundation in 1935 until the end of French rule, sought to offer an alternative to public scribes, providing assistance to claimants in the network of *diar-el-askri*.[55] In the interwar period, however, the extremely limited reach of the *Amitiés* meant that, whether the colonial officials liked it or not, public scribes would be the principal mediators of pension applications. Colonial officials may have failed to appreciate the extent to which this mediation was beneficial to them, not only in its transformation of grievance tales into legible applications but also in its moderating effect on the discourse of the aggrieved. But if scribes and their clients largely avoided the language of confrontation, what then was their favoured framing strategy to optimize compensation from the colonial state?

Supplication and the Evocation of Sacrifice

Poverty was the dominant leitmotif evoked by indigenous claimants in their correspondence with colonial officials. Repeatedly throughout the interwar period, war widows, orphans, and veterans, writing in the vast majority of cases through the mediation of a public scribe, presented their cases in bleak terms in a bid to secure the sympathy of officials. They married calls for the intervention of the colonial state grounded in the wartime 'moral economy of sacrifice' to more general appeals that insisted on the immediate gravity of their situation. Where the veteran Mohammed ben Ramdane Brik informed the minister of pensions that he was 'poor and the head of a large family which are a heavy burden',[56] his former brother-in-arms Ali ben

[53] See Benjamin N. Lawrence, 'Petitioners, 'Bush Lawyers', and Letter Writers: Court Access in British-Occupied Lomé, 1914–1920', in *Intermediaries, Interpreters and Clerks: African Employees in the Making of Colonial Africa*, eds. Benjamin N. Lawrence, Emily Lynn Osborn, and Richard L. Roberts (Madison, WI: University of Wisconsin Press, 2006): 94–114 and Johnson, *The Emergence of Black Politics*, 133.

[54] Serge Barthélemy, 'Mémoire de Stage de l'École Nationale d'Administration: L'Ancien Combattant d'Algérie', 15 December 1953, ANOM/FM/81F/1679.

[55] Report on the Work of the Amitiés Africaines, 1 September 1936, ANOM/100APOM/711.

[56] Brik Mohammed ben Ramdane to the Minister for Pensions, 8 April 1922, SHD/GR/13/YF/7216.

Messaoud Bouaris spoke of his 'heart broken by the pain of the precarious situation' of his family in his letter to the local chief medical officer.[57] These pleas for intercession by powerful officials reflect an understanding of post-war provision rooted not primarily in rights but rather in clientelism or even charity. It also draws on the longer tradition of petitioning that stretched back into the pre-colonial and early-modern period[58] and reflected the experience of claimants with customary/Islamic courts, which showed a flexibility in 'closing breeches in social relations' over the 'imposition of clear norms and rules'.[59] In the arbitrary world of the colony, where rights-holders (and even colonial officials) were often unsure of the rules governing pensions, securing the sympathy of a powerful administrator could be the key to a successful application.

Widows in particular had recourse to a language of supplication grounded in their assigned gender role as dependants. Given the limits placed on the action of indigenous women by both the gender and ethnic restraints of the society in which they lived, the degree to which they engaged in the potentially expensive and complicated act of petitioning represents a striking example of their all too often ignored agency. Petitions were one of the only means available to indigenous women living under a colonial regime to challenge and shape the structures, both societal and political, that governed their lives.[60] While women used petitions to assert their claims in what was essentially a political act, they did so in a manner grounded in traditional gendered conceptions of society. Their petitions stressed how the death of a husband left them 'without resources' and pleaded with the state to offer some form of financial security. Throughout their petitions, the emphasis is placed on the risk of, as one widow put it, 'total destitution'[61] unless the state intervenes. This kind of gendered language that underlined the weakness and dependence of women, contradicted to a certain extent by their capacity to petition the authorities, had been key to the historical emergence of the widow's pension as a form of entitlement.[62] In cases where

[57] Bouaris Ali ben Messaoud to the Doctor-in-Chief of the Constantine Rehabilitation Centre, 5 June 1930, SHD/GR/13/YF/7172.

[58] Cody, *The Light of Knowledge*, 173.

[59] Allan Christelow, *Muslim Law Courts and the French Colonial State in Algeria* (Princeton, NJ: Princeton University Press, 1985), 5.

[60] Chima J. Korieh '"May It Please Your Honour": Letters of Petition as Historical Evidence in an African Colonial Context', *History in Africa* 37 (2010): 83–106.

[61] Kébaili Fatma bent Slimane to the Minister for Pensions, 20 June 1935, SHD/GR/13/YF/7096.

[62] Kirstin A. Collins, '"Petitions without Number": Widows' Petitions and the Early Nineteenth-Century Origins of Public Marriage-Based Entitlements', *Law and History Review* 31, No. 1 (2013): 1–60, 5, and 49.

widows had children, their role as mothers, stripped of the 'natural' head of the family, was also pushed to the foreground. Mme Kaced Kiltieuna simply informed the director of pension services 'I am an unfortunate mother of three... we no longer have any support',[63] while the widow Fatma bent Mohamed Tekir offered a detailed account of her predicament:

> Deceased on 03/06/1937, my husband was retired and war-wounded at the rate of 100% and leaves me with three children, all very young, none can work, I have the honour to ask you, the Minister for Pensions, that I desire to benefit from a pension for my three orphan children, as well as myself, a widowed mother, in order to live.[64]

For widows and their intermediaries, it was clear that stressing their dependence was the best strategy to win the favour of pensions officials that was so important to securing their financial future.

Despite these attempts by indigenous claimants to win over colonial officials, the bedrock of the post-war pension regime remained rights-based provision. While colonial officials did, on occasion, recommend that relief be extended to those without a legal entitlement to compensation[65] or to those who had not properly formulated their applications,[66] pensions were not granted to those not legally eligible for them. The sympathetic intervention of colonial officials was often key to overcoming the obstacles on the path to eligibility but could not in and of itself abolish the conditions of eligibility. Thus, the correspondence of claimants would have to complement the emotive language of supplication with a clear attempt to vindicate legal rights.

Indigenous Claimants Assert Their Rights

In their quest to achieve eligibility, claimants would combine maximum legibility with the language of 'mutual obligation'. Letters formed part of a wider documentary package, with claimants providing official certificates that backed up their claim to a legal entitlement to compensation. In most cases, this was reinforced within the letters themselves, where claimants

[63] Widow Kaced Kiltieuna to the Director of the Pensions Service, undated, SHD/GR/13/YF/7091.

[64] Fatma bent Mohamed Tekir to the Minister of Pensions, 4 October 1937, SHD/GR/13/YF/7094.

[65] Governor General to the Prefect of Constantine, 15 March 1922, ANOM/GGA/3H/19.

[66] Prefect of Constantine to the Governor General, 19 September 1922, ANOM/GGA 3H/19.

detailed their service or that of their departed loved one. Often, the letters went on to draw a direct connection between their service and the compensation owed to them by the state, in language not unlike that employed by indigenous political leaders. Most claimants showed an understanding of eligibility grounded in both their legal rights born of participation in the war and their moral right to assistance. When the veteran Omar ben Larbi Yahiaoui wrote to the minister of pensions in April 1924 requesting an increase in his pension, he justified his demand by simply stating: 'I come to you to ask you to please increase my pension, as a former soldier with 18 years' service'.[67] Yahiaoui had no legal right to demand an increase, but he felt his service gave him the moral right to do so. Writing after his death, Yahiaoui 's widow, Meriem bent Mohammed, would combine an insistence on her legal right to compensation with a gendered plea for moral and material assistance:

> My husband, named Omar Yahiaoui, a volunteer recruit for sixteen years in Médéa, he fought in the war of 1914 until the Armistice. I think that I have the right to the pension of my husband because I am a young unfortunate, a mother of six children of young age that my husband left me as orphans and who have no one to help them.[68]

Clearly, while indigenous claimants and their intermediaries thought the benevolence of the colonial authorities had a bearing on the success of their applications, they also understood that service in the war had conferred rights and they were not afraid to assert these rights.

The assertion of rights made by indigenous veterans in their correspondence with colonial officials would contribute to a reshaping of the pension law in their favour. As we have already seen, much confusion existed in Algeria as to whether the provision of the Law of 1919 covering increases in pensions per child born (*majorations*) applied to the indigenous population. Almost immediately after the law was adopted, individual veterans began to write to colonial officials to demand the payment of *majorations*. Often detailing their extensive service, numerous veterans asked why they were not receiving the *majorations* granted to their European comrades-in-arms.[69]

[67] Omar ben Larbi Yahiaoui to the Minister of Pensions, 30 April 1924, SHD/GR/13/YF/7139.

[68] Meriem bent Mohammed to the Quartermaster General of Algiers, 11 June 1941, SHD/GR/13/YF/7139.

[69] Mohand ben Arzeki Djebbar to the Minister for Pensions, 4 November 1920, SHD/GR/13/YF/7108, Benkaçi Mohammed ben Mohand to the Minister for Pensions, 16 October 1921, SHD/GR/13/YF/7224, and Boulafani to the Minister for Pensions, 16 July 1920, SHD/GR/13/YF/7101.

The volume of correspondence from indigenous veterans and their assertion of their right to the *majorations* forced the issue. The colonial authorities turned for guidance to the *Conseil d'Etat*, which ruled in favour of the indigenous veterans, arguing that while the text of the law did not suggest an entitlement to *majorations* for indigenous veterans, the law's spirit most certainly did.[70] Through their challenge to administrators and their assertion of rights, individual indigenous veterans and their mediators had brought this injustice to public attention, winning a significant victory.

Most correspondence focused, however, on critiquing the slow-moving and byzantine bureaucracy that governed pensions rather than calling for an end to legal forms of discrimination. Indigenous claimants used their own correspondence and interventions by third parties to inquire about the progress of their dossiers and even to criticize the constant delays that deprived them of their rights. Here once more the language of supplication was used interchangeably and often simultaneously with the assertion of a legal right to compensation. The veteran Brahim Benmara criticized the administration's delay in granting him his *majorations* by stressing his legal right to the payment, making no reference to his own financial situation.[71] In contrast, Mme Rali Reira, the grandmother and legal guardian of two war orphans, underlined their poverty in her enquiry about the progress of her pension application, made two years earlier, asking to be given the means to 'feed the children of my son'.[72] In September 1920, the veteran Ahmed Slimane wrote to the minister of pensions to denounce the fact that he had yet to receive the pension to which his service entitled him. After recounting his military record in detail, he complained that 'while almost all retired soldiers have received their pensions, increased for extra service and for children, I have received nothing'. Alongside this rights-based argument, rooted in a comparison with the treatment given to his peers, Slimane evoked the situation of poverty in which he, the head of a young family, found himself.[73] Thus, in their complaints, as elsewhere in their correspondence, indigenous claimants combined distinct strategies in their aim to secure a speedy and successful application for compensation.

It is difficult to assess to what extent these complaints, whether stressing rights or emphasizing financial precarity, were successful in speeding up

[70] Décret du Conseil d'Etat 24 march, 1923 cited in Valentino, *Les Pensions aux indigènes*, 6–8.
[71] Benmara Brahim to the Minister for Pensions, 27 May 1937, SHD/GR/13/YF/10694.
[72] Rali Reira to the Minister for Pensions, 25 February 1940, SHD/GR/13/YF/7119.
[73] Ahmed Slimane to the Minister of Pensions, 12 September 1920, SHD/GR/13/YF/10109.

individual applications. On occasion, they would lead an official to take a more proactive role in examining the claimant's application. The literate veteran Saïd Guerroui-Mérouani, writing to the minister of war without the mediation of a public scribe, denounced the delays that plagued his applications. He declared himself to be on his 'knees' pleading for a pension to compensate his 'zealous and devoted service to the adoptive Fatherland' so he would no longer have to 'beg for bread on the streets'.[74] His constant complaints resulted in an order from the undersecretary for administration that the requested payments be made.[75] Ali ben Messaoud Bouaris' letter to a local pension official led to a full report into his case that ensured he had received all monies due to him and resulted in an increase in the rate of his disability pension.[76] However, the response received by Brahim Benmara telling him to 'wait for the ministerial decision' was far more typical.[77] Whether correspondence from claimants or intermediaries acting on their behalf did much in concrete terms to further their cases is hard to establish. What is clear, nonetheless, is that claimants believed that correspondence with the authorities was the only means they could ensure attention was paid to their claim and could thus favour a positive outcome. They were willing to spend time, effort, and money on correspondence with no guarantee of achieving the desired result.

In those cases where applications did not achieve the desired result, some claimants went further than simple correspondence, opting to appeal in the courts system. Under legislation, claimants had the right to pursue an appeal to the Departmental Pensions Tribunal and subsequently to the Regional Pensions Court.[78] Of the 102 dossiers studied in Vincennes, fifteen resulted in a rejection of some form and of these ten were appealed. If this proportion seems startlingly high, it is possibly because files that simply contained a rejection and no further information may have not been preserved. Nonetheless, the fact that indigenous claimants were willing to pursue their claims in the court system is interesting in and of itself. Engaging in some form of legal action would normally require the employment of third

[74] Guerroui-Mérouani to the Minister of War, 12 May 1918 and Guerroui-Mérouani to the Minister of War, 27 March 1919, SHD/GR/13/YF/7133.

[75] Undersecretary for Administration to the Head of the 5th Squadron, 6 June 1919, SHD/GR/13/YF/7133.

[76] Bouaris Ali ben Messaoud to the Doctor-in-Chief of the Constantine Rehabilitation Centre, 5 June, 1930 and Departmental Pensions Office Report, Constantine, 16 September 1930, SHD/GR/13/YF/7172.

[77] Departmental Pensions Office to Mr Benmara, 25 February 1937, SHD/GR/13/YF/10694.

[78] For more details on the procedures involved see Valentino, *La Loi Lugol*, 550.

parties to prepare the case, meaning more money spent on public scribes and on legal advice. Given that the court was held in the departmental capital, it would also mean the expense and hardship of travel for those living outside the large cities. This explains the failure of certain litigants to follow through with their application for appeal[79] or to turn up when they secured an appeal hearing.[80] Claimants represented themselves before the court, arguing with the assistance of a court interpreter.[81] In these circumstances, it is hardly surprising that most appeals were based on a sense of grievance, with claimants failing to produce documentation that proved eligibility and thus giving no legal substance to their appeal. The ruling in the case of Boudina ben Ali Chikhi is exemplary in this regard. The widow was contesting the refusal to grant her a war widow's pension as the illness that killed her husband was not connected to his service.[82] When her case was unsuccessful before the Departmental Tribunal, she appealed to the Regional Court in Algiers. The court dismissed her application in the following terms: 'Given that the appellant has produced no new documents or other means susceptible to change the judgement of the first court and the motives for its decision; it is thus right and proper to confirm the decision of the court with the following ruling: Unfounded'.[83] None of the appeals pursued by the claimants whose dossiers I examined was successful. Courts were unmoved by arguments for a right to compensation grounded in tales of woe and poverty, and appellants were unable to provide the documentation necessary to prove eligibility. The belief of indigenous claimants that stressing their grievance and their precarity, a belief undoubtedly fuelled by the flexibility and consensus that underpinned the practice of Islamic law in the colony,[84] clashed directly with the 'rational' and rules-based justice of the French court system. The evocation of the 'moral economy of sacrifice' may have proved successful for some claimants in their correspondence with

[79] Dept. of the Seine Pensions Tribunal, 25 November 1938, SHD/GR/13/YF/7147 and the Office of Conflict-Resolution to the Department of Pension Liquidation, 22 February 1926, SHD/GR/13/YF/7077.

[80] Judgement of the Department Pensions Tribunal, Algiers, 27 March 1939, SHD/GR/13/YF/7096.

[81] Minutes of the Bailiff of the Departmental Pensions Tribunal, Constantine, 17 December 1941, SHD/GR/13/YF/7143 and Judgement of the Department Pensions Tribunal, 14 March 1938 SHD/GR/13/YF/12440.

[82] Argument of the Widow Chikhi Boudina ben Ali before the Departmental Pensions Tribunal, Algiers, 26 November 1935, SHD/GR/13/YF/7117.

[83] Minutes of the Bailiff of the Regional Pension Tribunal, Algiers, 21 January 1938, SHD/GR/13/YF/7117.

[84] Christelow, *Muslim Law Courts*, 4–8.

administrators, but it held no legal weight in their court actions. Thus, while the possibility of appeal not only existed but was also pursued by certain indigenous claimants, it did not seem to offer a real means of undoing perceived injustice.

Indigenous claimants may have shown an understanding of their right to compensation, but this understanding did not necessarily align with that of colonial administrators or the French court system. It is clear from their correspondence that the concept of a moral right predominated over that of a legal right dependent on specific conditions of eligibility. Here once more we can see an expression of Gregory Mann's 'idioms of mutual if uneven obligation' where different conceptions of what the state owed to those who served it lead to misunderstandings and disappointments. It also underlines the state's struggle to impose its formulation of bureaucratic justice even on those who sought to make themselves legible and eligible. Its rigid application of a supposedly rational form of justice clashed not only with pre-existing indigenous legal traditions but also with the arbitrary nature of much of what passed for governance in the colony. Indeed, the insistence on a normative rules-based adjudication of cases within the pension system contrasted sharply with the practice of those elements of the system that had been devolved to the local representatives of the colonial state and the colonial Muslim law courts. In these areas, a flexible approach to the law would often disregard the strict interpretations of those who directed the pensions administration, stressing moral imperatives over legal rights.

Distributing Pensions: Muslim Law and Moral Rights

Under the provisions of the Law of 31 March 1919, the dependants of a deceased soldier were to share one familial pension between them. The process of allocating the pension was devolved to local committees sitting as *Commissions de Répartition de Pensions* at a communal level. The commissions would include two indigenous members, the *qadi*, or Islamic judge, and the *caïd*, or local chief, who would ensure the division was realized in accordance with Islamic law. In larger settlements where the European population was bigger and the powers of local government more extensive (*communes de plein exercice*), the *caïd* could be replaced by an elected indigenous municipal councillor. One European representative would also sit on the commissions.[85] The decisions taken by these commissions belied the French state's commitment to a strictly rational system for the adjudication of pension claims, showing once more that the universal and equal application of the law, a supposedly essential republican principle, did not apply to the indigenous population of Algeria. The introduction of a discretionary element to the pension distribution system also meant that certain categories of rights-holders could benefit from the longstanding goal of traditional justice: 'closing breeches in social relations'.[86] Local administrators proved willing to prioritize the state's moral duty to compensate those who had served during the war over the claimant's duty to fulfil the requirements of eligibility.

According to the 'expert' advice offered to the pensions' administration, Islamic law was, like French law, codified, rational, and fixed and would thus give rise to a specific pattern of distribution of familial pensions. Marcel Morand, professor of Muslim law in Algiers and a key figure in the creation of indigenous legal codes in the colony, presented a detailed report to the Ministry of Pensions outlining that Islamic succession law would dictate the sharing out of the pension.[87] He set out a clear schema for each of the potential rights-holders, which he asserted was based on the Maliki School of Islamic Law, predominant in Algeria. Widows without children would receive one quarter of the pension, while those with children would receive one eighth. The father and mother of the deceased would each receive one sixth. The one eighth traditionally paid to the relevant state authority in Islamic succession law should be divided among the various rights-holders. Finally, the orphans should receive the remainder, with male orphans entitled to a share double that of female orphans.[88] The most striking aspect of this proposed distribution was the clear gender discrimination, both against female orphans and against the widow, whose claim on the pension of her husband was minimal. During the Great War, the governor general had rejected the direct application of 'Muslim' succession law, especially the inclusion of the deceased's parents in the distribution of pensions, arguing that it would exacerbate the 'already precarious situation' of the indigenous

[85] Note from the Governor General's Office on the Attribution of Pensions to Deceased Indigenous Soldiers, undated, ANOM ALG GGA/3H/19.
[86] Christelow, *Muslim Courts*, 5.
[87] For his detailed report see Valentino, *Les Pensions aux indigènes*, 17–23.
[88] Ibid., 18.

woman in Algeria.[89] In fact, the practice of local commissions varied widely, often diverging from the supposedly standard interpretation in ways that particularly benefitted women.

Early government consultations suggested that the interpretation of Islamic law offered by Morand was being followed. Four reports submitted in early 1921 by military administrators in the *Territoires du Sud* affirmed that their local commissions were distributing pensions strictly in line with this particular version of Islamic succession law.[90] As a result, war widows who were childless received only a quarter of their husband's pensions with the other three quarters going to her parents-in-law (half to the father and a quarter to the mother).[91] The parents of the deceased or 'ascendants' were benefitting widely from this distribution pattern. While the colonial state had proven reticent to alter the perceived injustice of a distribution that left widows without resources, the prospect that indigenous ascendants could potentially receive more money than their European equivalents was unacceptable. The authorities would have to act. The *Conseil d'Etat* issued a ruling on 9 May 1922 stating that 'in no case could indigenous ascendants receive more than the rates given to their metropolitan equivalents'.[92] Thus, the strict adherence to a particular version of Islamic law, which the colonial state refused to alter in order to assist widows, was completely discarded when it was found to challenge European supremacy.

In any case, many local commissions in the late 1920s and throughout the 1930s would move away from the strict interpretation of succession law, opting instead for a social approach to the distribution of pensions. Ascendants all but disappeared from their rulings, reflecting both the natural decrease in their number over time and the effects of the *Conseil d'Etat*'s ruling. Of the sixty-six dossiers from the *Service Historique de la Défense* that include the deliberations of a local *commission de repartition* in Algeria, only two granted an allocation to an ascendant, and in one of these cases the

[89] Governor General to the Minister of the Interior, 23 September 1916, ANOM/GGA/3H/19.

[90] Head of the Annexe of In Salah to the Governor General, 15 March 1921, Head of the Annexe of Marnia to the Commander of the Division of Oran, 24 February 1921,

Commanding Officer of the Circle of Touggourt to the Military Commander of the Territory, 11 March 1921 and Head of the Annexe of El Oued to the Commanding Officer of the Circle of Touggourt, 24 February 1921, ANOM/GGA/3H/19.

[91] Head of the Annexe of El Oued to the Commanding Officer of the Circle of Touggourt, 24 February 1921, ANOM/GGA/3H/19.

[92] Valentino, *Les Pensions aux indigènes*, 19.

ascendant was also the legal guardian of the orphans.[93] This meant that widows without children became the sole claimants on the familial pension. Of the nineteen widows who had no children in the sample, every single one received the whole pension, even in cases where there was a claim from ascendants.[94] These widows received the same amount as their European equivalents (though this equality only applied to war widow pensions and not the separate pensions for long service). Furthermore, the distribution patterns followed in cases where widows had children rarely complied with the models outlined by Morand. Only seven of the thirty-six commissions that dealt with widows with children assigned one eighth of the familial pension to the widows, the share they would supposedly receive under Islamic succession law.[95] A further five cases followed the general principles outlined by Morand, allotting widows an equal share to female orphans, half that allocated to their sons.[96] Elsewhere, local commissions opted for an equal distribution between orphans and widows in a total of four cases.[97] In the rest of the dossiers, twenty out of the thirty-six, widows were granted the largest portion by the local commission, with their share even reaching a proportion of seven eighths of the pension in three cases.[98] Thus, local commissions in their majority disregarded the narrow interpretation of Islamic succession law defended by the 'experts', opting instead for patterns of distribution that reflected the place of the widow as the head of the family and sought to compensate her accordingly.

The local commissions also proved reticent to discriminate between female and male orphans. According to Morand's theory, male orphans should receive exactly double the sum allocated to their sisters. Of the twenty-five

[93] PVCRP, 30 December 1938, SHD/GR/13/YF/7122 and PVCRP, 3 March 1939, SHD/GR/13/YF/7119.

[94] See PVCRP, 17 April 1941, SHD/GR/13/YF/7230.

[95] Pension for the Dependants of a Deceased Indigenous Career Soldier, 12 July 1948, SHD/GR/13/YF/10712, PVCRP, 6 January 1941, SHD/GR/13/YF/7214, PVCRP, 26 January 1932, SHD/GR/13/YF/10707, PVCRP, 27 November 1937, SHD/GR/13/YF/7128, PVCRP, 24 February 1939, SHD/GR/13/YF/7232, Liquidation of a Pension for an Indigenous North African Widow and Orphans, 24 June 1941, SHD/GR/13/YF/7045, and PVCRP, 30 December 1938, SHD/GR/13/YF/7122.

[96] PVCRP, 21 July 1941, SHD/GR/13/YF/7068, PVCRP, 26 December 1940, SHD/GR/13/YF/7213, PVCRP, 3 October 1939, SHD/GR/13/YF/7106, PVCRP, 17 April 1940, SHD/GR/13/YF/7044, and PVCRP, 22 June 1936, SHD/GR/13/YF/7077.

[97] Decree of the Prefect of Constantine, 30 September 1940, SHD/GR/13/YF/7143, PVCRP, 27 July 1940, SHD/GR/13/YF/7222, PVCRP, 3 June 1940, SHD/GR/13/YF/7130, and PVCRP, 1 June 1939, SHD/GR/13/YF/7099.

[98] PVCRP, 19 December 1939, SHD/GR/13/YF/7098, Pension for the Dependants of a Deceased Indigenous Career Soldier, 2 July 1948, SHD/GR/13/YF/10710, and PVCRP, 5 October 1942, SHD/GR/13/YF/7091.

cases in the dossiers studied where a pension was divided between orphans of different genders, only eleven followed this pattern. In the remaining fourteen cases, female orphans received a share equal to that granted to their brothers. Once more, many local commissions had prioritized their own understandings of the moral right to a pension over a strict legalistic approach. Their stress on the moral right underpinning pension distribution, coupled with a practical understanding of the functioning of family units that had lost their male head of household, made them more sympathetic to the plight of widows. Unlike the bureaucrats who ran the pensions administration, local commission members, both European and indigenous, looked beyond simple rules of eligibility, incorporating social and moral justifications into their rulings.

The story of the commissions not only underlines the role of local intermediaries in responding to the needs of indigenous rights-holders but it also demonstrates the lack of interest shown by the upper echelons of the colonial and pensions administrations in ensuring a just distribution of compensation for indigenous claimants. While individual voices within the colonial regime may have expressed concern about potential breaches of the 'moral economy of sacrifice', an intervention was only staged when European supremacy was put into question. Once responsibility for the distribution of the familial pension had been devolved to the local commissions, the pension administration largely washed its hands of this element of provision for indigenous rights-holders. A bureaucracy that proved so zealous in monitoring eligibility and ensuring respect for the law seemed totally unconcerned with the varied and arbitrary patterns of distribution followed by local commissions. Indeed, it is most significant that the administrators of a programme based on the fundamental principle of a universal and legal right to compensation showed little to no interest in how this compensation was divided up among indigenous rights-holders. As was often the case, universalism did not apply to the indigenous subjects of Algeria.

Posts, Petitions, and Preferential Treatment

When it came to the other principal system of post-war provision, the granting of reserved jobs, the notion of any form of universal right was completely undermined by the colonial state's failure to invest in the scheme. With little oversight from the metropole, the legal framework of the scheme was constantly disregarded and decisions were often made arbitrarily at a local level. While above we have seen the positive potential of local devolution, arbitrary decisions by colonial officers were, at very best, a double-edged sword. Where there was paternalism or even humanitarianism, there was also often favouritism and politically motivated discrimination. For these reasons and more, the reserved jobs scheme came to embody the serious shortcomings that defined the colonial state's efforts to compensate its indigenous subjects for their participation in the Great War.

The first piece of legislation to deal with the reservation of jobs for indigenous veterans of the Great War dates back to 11 January 1916. It established a list of appropriate jobs that were in the gift of the colonial state.[99] An instruction issued in March 1917 offered a detailed plan for the programme, outlining the eligibility requirements for claimants, the quantities and types of posts involved, and the administrative structure that would govern their distribution. Posts in the first category required candidates to be fully literate in French and in Arabic and to have 'notions of arithmetic'.[100] From the outset, the government acknowledged that very few such posts would be made available. A paltry twenty-five positions as '*adjoint indigène*'[101] were to be reserved while the availability for other jobs in this category was described as 'variable',[102] or 'rare'.[103] The second category, consisting of lower administrative positions, suffered from a similar dearth of available posts.[104] The vast majority of claimants, however, would fall into the third category, where positions offered included various forms of manual labour and the granting of licences to operate *cafés maures*. The military alone bore responsibility for assessing eligibility in the third category.[105] This left the bulk of the indigenous veterans, and those most likely to be illiterate and disinclined to challenge authority, at the mercy of local military officers and their arbitrary decisions.

As the legislation around the project developed over the interwar period, its scope and complexity increased. The Law of 30 January 1923 opened up the reserved jobs to other rights-holders such as widows and orphans, placing ever more pressure on the extremely limited number of posts available in Algeria.[106] A presidential decree in August 1930 facilitated the

[99] Decree Concerning Reserved Jobs for Indigenous Veterans in Algeria, 11 January 1916 in 'Emplois Réservés aux Indigènes d'Algérie', *Bulletin officiel du Ministère de la Guerre*, 5–6.

[100] 'Instructions for the Attribution of Reserved Jobs to Indigenous Veterans in Algeria', 30 March 1917, *Bulletin officiel du Ministère de la Guerre*, 8–9.

[101] Ibid., 58–9. [102] Ibid. [103] Ibid., 45. [104] Ibid., 17.

[105] Ibid., 21.

[106] Albert Legrand, *La législation sur les emplois réservés* (Paris: Librairie Générale de Droit et de Jurisprudence, 1941), 7.

programme's application in Algeria by specifying a clear process for the acceptance and rejection of offers of reserved jobs.[107] No financial support was offered to make the trip to wherever the post was available, although the law did evolve to allow candidates to turn down posts outside their region without losing their place on the panel for upcoming jobs.[108] This provision reflected an ongoing problem for the authorities, who, for lack of positions in large population centres, tried to coax applicants into accepting posts in distant regions of the colony. This policy, as we shall see, would prove a dramatic failure.

The 1930 decree also dealt with one of the most controversial aspects of the programme's application in Algeria: the role of colonial officials in assigning jobs. It specified that no position reserved for a veteran could be granted to a civil candidate as long as a military candidate was available.[109] All nominations required approval by the Ministry of Pensions whether they were 'exceptional' or routine nominations.[110] This reflected a well-founded concern on the part of the ministry that local officials were not respecting the rules in the colony and were granting positions to favoured local elites over indigenous rights-holders, thus breaching the law's commitment to respect the 'moral economy of sacrifice'. Nowhere was this truer than in the colonial authorities' assigning of café licences for the *cafés maures*.

The *café maure* had a historical heritage in Algeria that predated the arrival of the French. The number of cafés expanded greatly as Algerian society urbanized in the interwar period. Cafés were the centre for public life among the indigenous community, a place where discussion and debate flourished. Unsurprisingly, they attracted much interest from the authorities.[111] Placing veterans who had demonstrated their loyalty to France in charge of these cafés was seen as a doubly beneficial policy as it would help the colonial state meet its responsibility to compensate indigenous rights-holders while also keeping the cafés out of the orbit of potential agitators.[112] Thus, rather than simply vindicating the right of a veteran to a position, the granting of a café licence was also a political act that sought, not

[107] Presidential Decree, 24 August 1930, 'Emplois Civils Réservés aux Indigènes de l'Afrique du Nord', *Bulletin officiel du Ministère de la Guerre, Edition Méthodique* (Paris: Charles-Lavauzelle, 1931), 14.

[108] Article 12, Ibid., 8.

[109] Article 52, Ibid., 15.

[110] Article 53, Ibid., 15–16.

[111] Omar Carlier, 'Le café maure. Sociabilité masculine et effervescence citoyenne (Algérie 17e–18e)', in *Annales. Economies, sociétés, civilisations* 4 (1990): 975–1004, 988, 995.

[112] Minister for War to the Prime Minister, the Minister for the Interior, the Office of Algerian Affairs, 22 February 1936, ANOM/FM/81F/1686.

always with success, to mobilize the retired soldier in a form of non-military defence of the colonial order.

Throughout the interwar period, indigenous veterans, whether collectively or individually, constantly condemned the colonial authorities' alleged failure to give them priority of access to licences. The cross-community organization the *Amicale* was persistent in its calls for an end to local favouritism in the distribution of licences[113] while the ever active *Ligue des Anciens Combattants Musulmans de l'Oranie* (LACMO) in Oran protested vocally against arbitrary patterns of patronage.[114] Writing in 1929 to the prefect of Constantine, the veteran Lauri ben Ahmed Lakdari criticized his local authority for granting positions to those who had been 'sheltered from the dangers of the war'.[115] His former comrade-in-arms Saïd Mahia wrote to the minister of pensions in August 1939 alleging that officials in the *commune mixte* of Maillot had given a 'helping hand' to local indigenous leaders to ensure their families received café licences.[116] A powerful sense that the moral (not to mention legal) duty to provide posts to indigenous rights-holders was being sacrificed to shore up an increasingly contested colonial regime took hold not only among rights-holders themselves but also among some colonial administrators.[117]

The negative effects of the politicization of provision for indigenous claimants were compounded by the extreme inadequacy of the system set up to provide and distribute *emplois réservés* and café licences. The scheme's most dramatic failure lay in its inability to provide anywhere near enough jobs to meet demand. In contrast to pensions, which were funded centrally by the French state, the reserved jobs scheme fell within the remit of the colony's own budget.[118] A 1936 report exposed the scarcity of posts for indigenous veterans. It claimed that the number of reserved jobs provided to indigenous claimants over the preceding five years averaged less than 100 a year. Even in those years where they did exceed 100, 1935 and 1936, the percentage of posts made available compared to the total number of

[113] Kerdavid, 'Les revendications Nord-Africaines', *La Tranchée*, 1st Fortnight, April 1936 and 'Victimes de Guerre Indigènes', *La Tranchée*, 1st Fortnight, June 1937.

[114] Vœux de Protestation de Tous les Délégués du Département d'Oran de la Ligue des Anciens Combattants Musulmans, 21 September 1936, ANOM/FM/81F/1686.

[115] Lakdari Lauri Ben Ahmed to the Prefect of Constantine, 30 January 1929, ANOM/93/B/3/193.

[116] Said Mahia to the Minister of Pensions, 29 August 1939, ANOM GG/3H/20.

[117] Governor General to the Minister of the Interior, 26 October 1934, ANOM/FM/81F/1686.

[118] See Article 1 of the Presidential Decree, 24 August 1930, 'Emplois Civils Réservés aux Indigènes de l'Afrique du Nord', *Bulletin officiel du Ministère de la Guerre*, 5.

claimants on the waiting lists stood at 5.65 and 4.08 percent, respectively.[119] This dramatic shortage had serious implications both for the operation of the scheme and for the thousands of veterans who hoped to benefit from it. It also made it even more galling for veterans when posts were gifted to local allies of the colonial regime.

To ease the massive backlog of applications colonial officials granted posts and café licences to veterans in regions far from their homes, particularly in the desert regions of the south. This too proved disastrous, with veterans often illegally subletting their cafés to locals or simply abandoning their posts to return home. Veterans, who had been languishing on waiting lists for long periods, would often accept a licence in a distant region and then seek a transfer to their home region, a complex process that involved expensive travel to and from their café and writing many letters in the hope of finding a sympathetic ear within the administration. The case of the veteran El Oukal Ben Chaa Ben Henni is illustrative in this regard. In 1933, after twelve years on the waiting list, he was finally assigned a café licence in the town of Laghouat, some 400 kilometres away from his home in Oran.[120] Travelling to Laghouat, he established a sublet agreement before an Islamic judge with a third party who would run the café on his behalf. When this was discovered by the authorities, he was given one month to regularize his situation. He never returned to Laghouat and on 24 October 1934 his licence was revoked.[121] El Oukal did not, however, renounce his claim to a café licence. First, he contacted the LACMO, which unsuccessfully appealed the decision on his behalf.[122] He then wrote to the prefect of Oran, claiming that illness had prevented him from taking up his post and asserting that he believed that the legal approval of the *qadi* had been sufficient to justify the transfer of the licence to a third party.[123] The prefect proved sympathetic and wrote to the governor general's office asking that El Oukal's case be re-examined as he was a father of five of 'good behaviour and morality'.[124] The administrator charged with distributing the café licences replied that

[119] Note from the 'Direction de l'Infanterie' on Indigenous North African Troops, 9 November 1936, Annexe Emplois Résérvés, 3, SHD/GR/9/N/122.

[120] Note from the Director of Indigenous Affairs and Military Personnel to the Secretary General of the Government, 6 June 1939, ANOM/GGA/3H/20.

[121] Colonel Bertschi, Military Commander of the Territory of Ghardaïa to the Governor General, 8 April 1935, ANOM/GGA/3H/20.

[122] Note from the Director of Indigenous Affairs and Military Personnel to the Secretary General of the Government, 6 June 1939, ANOM/GGA/3H/20.

[123] El Soukal Benchaa to the Prefect, undated, ANOM/GGA/3H/20.

[124] Prefect of Oran to the Governor General, 27 February 1936, ANOM/GGA/3H/20.

there were no vacancies available in Oran.[125] El Oukal secured further interventions on his behalf not only by the LACMO[126] but also by the *Interfédération*[127] and the local conservative deputy René Enjalbert.[128] Eventually, the governor general decreed on 20 June 1939 that El Oukal's licence be transferred to Oran, though even then it is not clear if this ruling had an immediate effect.[129] El Oukal, a veteran who, being based in a large city, had access to and made use of several different channels through which he could pursue his claim, still only enjoyed the benefits of the café licence for a total period of less than one year in the whole interwar period.

The petitions of other licence holders seeking a transfer show once more the variety of strategies pursued by indigenous claimants. In their correspondence with colonial officials, claimants stressed the difficulty of uprooting or abandoning their families to move to distant regions. The veteran Bachir Belkacem unsuccessfully requested a transfer of his café licence from the southern town of Ghardaïa to his home region of Bou-Saada (some 400 kilometres away) on the basis of the financial and emotional distress that it would cause his family of nine children.[130] Another veteran denounced the huge costs entailed in making what he claimed was a 912 kilometre journey to the location of his new café, asserting transport alone for the nine members of his family would come to 1350 francs.[131] Many claimants emphasized the challenges of adapting to new climates. The veteran Abdelkader Ben Mostefa Ben Mohamed abandoned his café in the mountainous region of Djelfa in the hope of securing a transfer to 'a warmer region',[132] while his former comrade-in-arms Amar ben Saïd Rabai fled the 'desert', declaring 'it is impossible for me to live in the South, for me and for my family'.[133] The veteran Bouzid Embarek combined both concern for his family and

[125] Note from the Director of Indigenous Affairs and Military Personnel to the Secretary General of the Government, 6 June 1939, ANOM/GGA/3H/20.

[126] President of the LACMO to the Governor General, 17 February 1939, President of the LACMO to the Governor General, 29 March 1939 and President of the LACMO to the Governor General, 8 May 1939, ANOM/GGA/3H/20.

[127] Secretary General of the Interfédération Nord-Africaine to the Governor General, 25 November 1937, ANOM/GGA/3H/20.

[128] Deputy Enjalbert to the Governor General, 7 March 1940, ANOM/GGA/3H/20.

[129] Note from the General Security Director to the Director of Indigenous Affairs and Military Personnel, 23 May 1940, ANOM/GGA/3H/20.

[130] Application by Bachir ben Belkacem for a café maure, 31 December 1937, ANOM/GGA/3H/20.

[131] Said Mahia to the Minister of Pensions, 29 August 1939, ANOM/GGA/3H/20.

[132] Abdelkader Ben Mostefa Ben Mohamed to the Administrator of the Commune Mixte pf Djelfa, 19 September 1939, ANOM/GGA/3H/20.

[133] Rabai Amar ben Said to the Governor General, 21 December 1937, ANOM/GGA/3H/20.

complaints about the climate in his application for a transfer from the southern town of Touggourt: 'the Saharan climate is totally unbearable and I do not even earn enough money to support my family'.[134] Given that transfers required a freeing up of the already extremely limited places available in larger cities, they were rarely granted, leaving veterans either forced to travel great distances or renounce their licence and go to the end of the waiting list.

The evident injustice of a system that made claimants so dependent on administrators gave rise to a fascinating blend of the language of almost servile supplication and that of exasperation in their correspondence with the authorities. In 1939, a letter sent by the veteran Saïd Mahia addressed the minister of pensions in fawning terms before launching a stinging attack on the administration in Algeria. He began the letter by declaring that he 'bowed before' the minister and closed by assuring him that he was 'your child, mutilated in the war of 1914–1918'. The body of the letter, however, railed against an unfair system of patronage that reflected the wider injustice of the colonial regime where 'the law of Algeria, the big eats the small', reigned supreme.[135] As was the case for claimants in the pension system, potential licence holders and their intermediaries had to walk a tightrope between ingratiating themselves with the colonial official whose near absolute power was crucial for a successful resolution to their case and angrily raising their grievances in an effort to battle the apathy of many officials.

The application of the reserved jobs scheme in interwar Algeria is symbolic of the potential pitfalls that accompanied any attempt to extend the politics of post-war provision from the metropole into the colonies. A combination of administrative inadequacy/indifference, the scarcity of financial resources, and the desire of many colonial officials to maintain networks of political patronage that underpinned the colonial system served to undermine even the most limited attempt to grant a right of priority of employment to indigenous veterans. The internal debates within the colonial regime around the distribution of jobs highlighted the enduring tension between the dual mission of post-war provision in the empire: the rewarding of past loyalty and the ensuring of future loyalty. While this principle, which qualified the right to compensation of the indigenous on the grounds of political expediency, was universally shared across the administration, its implications for policy were contested. For many local officials, the continued

[134] Bouzid Embarek to the Governor General, 24 January 1938, ANOM/GGA/3H/20.
[135] Said Mahia to the Minister for Pensions, 29 August 1939, ANOM/GGA/3H/20.

security of the regime was dependent on low-level patronage that would require diluting the rights of veterans in favour of the rights of indigenous elites. For the military in Algeria and for many officials in Paris, guaranteeing the rights of veterans was key to securing recruits for the future defence of the empire. In both cases, the right of the veterans themselves was only a secondary consideration.

Yet, indigenous claimants were not simply pawns in the politicking of colonial officials. Some indigenous claimants managed to secure important interventions by influential third parties. Individual claimants, veterans' associations, and even politicians contested the tendency of certain local officials to disregard the 'moral economy of sacrifice', favouring over veterans those with an inferior moral right to a reserved job. Significantly, individual veterans themselves displayed an impressive wiliness when it came to 'playing the system'. Many claimants accepted offers of positions they knew they could never take up, hoping to either sublet them illegally or use them as a bargaining chip to gain a better deal from the colonial authorities. The scheme's application in Algeria dealt indigenous veterans a very bad hand, but veterans tried to play it as best they could. The results, which were slow to come, if they came at all, were often disappointing. Nevertheless, the story of the *emplois réservés* scheme in interwar Algeria is as much about the persistence of certain indigenous veterans in attempting to vindicate their rights as it is about the parsimonious and politically biased colonial state's efforts to undermine these rights.

Conclusion

More than any other element of the post-Great War settlement in Algeria, the system of provision for indigenous veterans and other rights-holders had a dramatic and daily impact on the lives of a large cross-section of the indigenous community. While by no means divorced from important political debates around citizenship and subjecthood, the regulation, administration, and extension of pensions and reserved jobs to indigenous rights-holders represented a tangible and potentially transformative legacy of the war that would shape the interaction between state and subject in many complex and contradictory ways. The rich sources this interaction left behind bear testament to a 'world of contact' that extended beyond political elites, where illiterate veterans, widows, and orphans, through the mediation of public writers and other intermediaries, corresponded with colonial officials. Both the forms that shaped this correspondence and the results it secured point once more to a 'world of contact' characterized as much, if not more, by its imbalanced power dynamics and its commitment to European hegemony as by its facilitation of transcommunal solidarity and dialogue.

Many indigenous rights-holders and their intermediaries proved aware of their power within this world and where its limitations lay. They showed at least a basic understanding of their right to compensation and the fact that legibility was a precondition for the vindication of this right. Achieving legibility was a complex and costly process that was not without its pitfalls, but one that many claimants pursued to an ultimately successful end within the pensions system. This example highlights how even in that most repressive of modern polities, the colonial state, legibility was not simply imposed top down through coercion but the state also incentivized a bottom-up drive for standardization through the concept of eligibility. Charging indigenous rights-holders with the responsibility for their own legibility may have constituted a serious financial burden but it also offered them a chance to shape their own interaction with the state by withholding or even falsifying information. Certain claimants, and the intermediaries assisting them, proved adept at manipulating gaps in the state's knowledge to their own benefit while for others, these same gaps would delay or even invalidate their claims in intrinsically unjust ways. The story of the system of pension provision, and in particular its poorer cousin, the *emplois réservés* scheme, expose an underresourced, ill-informed, and often indifferent colonial state that exercised limited control over its indigenous subjects.

If colonial officials exercised little control over indigenous subjects' lives outside this system, once these subjects embarked on the long process of securing some form of compensation for their contribution to the war, the goodwill of colonial officials became an essential commodity. In the pensions system, the sympathy of a colonial official had an important bearing on the speed at which an application was resolved. In the case of the reserved jobs, the discretion of colonial and/or military officials ruled over every stage of the scheme from the assessment of eligibility to the allocation of jobs and the granting of transfers. Indigenous claimants and their intermediaries acknowledged this, adopting a supplicatory form of language that stressed their dependence on the generosity of the colonial official to save them from poverty. This was particularly true of female claimants, who played on gender stereotypes in an effort to optimize their compensation. Their correspondence reflected an understanding of the colonial political system grounded both in traditional forms of provision and in the arbitrary rule of local officials.

Nevertheless, indigenous claimants also understood the essential rights-based nature of post-war provision. The notion that the 'moral economy of sacrifice' had engendered a right to compensation, which so permeated political discourse, also filtered down into the language of indigenous claimants. The extent to which their conception of their moral right to compensation corresponded directly with the legal right extended by the colonial state varied widely. When claimants felt that their moral entitlement was not being met, whether this was through insufficient pensions or the inadequate provision of reserved jobs/café licences, they would often evoke the language of rights. Not only did the legal framework that shaped provision blend elements of equality with significant measures of discrimination, but also the inconsistent and often incompetent application of the law left indigenous rights-holders at a distinct disadvantage compared to citizen claimants. Although individual figures within the colonial regime acted, on occasion, in favour of both indigenous claimants and wider principles of rights-based provision, policies on provision remained driven by political interests, above all the desire to maintain the integrity of the structure of the colonial regime. The right to compensation was secondary to the necessity to shore up loyalty to an increasingly contested colonial regime.

The story of the interaction between indigenous claimants and the system of post-war provision in interwar Algeria offers insight into the intricate web of contacts that shaped the daily life of the colony. At the heart of this web lay the common notion that the Great War had transformed the relationship between the state and the subject who served it. The exact nature of this transformation and the rights, moral, legal, and financial, to which it gave rise were often unclear to colonial administrators, indigenous rights-holders, and their various intermediaries. This lack of clarity opened a space of conflict, of disappointment, and of opportunity to the various stakeholders involved in post-war provision. From this space emerged an indigenous rights-holder who was simultaneously a client, collaborator, and contester of the colonial state.

Conclusion

In his seminal book on Algeria's Great War, Gilbert Meynier begins his discussion of the conflict's political legacies in the colony with a quote from the letter of an indigenous *tirailleur* written in October 1914: 'Once we have spilled our blood for France, we will, once more, be treated in our country like the lowest of the pagans because we can never count on the recognition of those for whom we allow ourselves to be killed'.[1] While this soldier's pessimism may seem prescient in its anticipation of the lack of a fundamental change to the colonial regime in the years that followed the war, it was not shared by most political actors in the colony. For them, Algeria's participation in the war represented an opportunity to rebalance the colonial system in their favour. Like their equivalents in the other belligerent countries, the inhabitants of Algeria, from the highest ranks of the political elite down to the lowliest indigenous veteran, sought to use the legitimacy conferred by participation in the war to impose their vision of a just post-war society. As this book has shown, their efforts were hampered by both the constraints and the complexities of political action in the colonial context.

At various points throughout the interwar period, actors from all ethno-religious and ideological backgrounds believed that the evocation of their individual and/or communal contribution to the Great War was the best means of pursuing their personal and collective interests. Over the course of the two decades between the wars, as the public sphere gradually opened up to the claims of actors who lay outside the traditional frameworks of political action, a shared language of politics emerged in interwar Algeria. Broad concepts such as the 'moral economy of sacrifice' and 'mutual obligation' were mobilized in defence of a whole range of claims, giving rise to a common linguistic framework in which both the great debates and the everyday encounters that defined life in the colony would be expressed. The same tropes employed in the pension request of an illiterate indigenous war

[1] Meynier, *L'Algérie Révélée*, 689.

widow could also be found in the speeches of the governor general. A trade union activist might have recourse to the same points of reference as the leader of the Algerian branch of a metropolitan extreme-right movement. The Great War had become if not *the*, then one of the 'languages of contact' in political debate in colonial Algeria. Of course, a shared language rarely, if ever, translated into a shared understanding of the legacies of the war or a shared vision for Algeria's future. Just like the broader concept of the 'world of contact', this 'language of contact' was constrained by and permeated with the racially informed and legally established discriminations that defined colonial rule. It did, however, mean that political debate in the colony would be conducted in a language that was both widely intelligible and broadly perceived as legitimate.

The versatility of the Great War as a rhetorical strategy reflected the plurality and complexity that had marked Algerian participation in the conflict itself. Wartime precedents could be found to legitimize almost any claim in the interwar period. Actors drew from a common pool of reference points but picked and chose those that best suited their own programmes. Where for the supporters of indigenous reform, the service of indigenous troops despite their lack of citizenship marked them out as especially worthy, their opponents mobilized the particular conditions that regulated this service to diminish its value. Similarly, while the conservative in the Algiers of 1920 saw the wartime military hierarchy as a model for post-war society, his socialist compatriot defended the reconstruction of society on the basis of the 'equality of sacrifice' that had reigned in the trenches. This adaptability meant that the war became a fiercely contested source of legitimacy, as rival groups sought to establish a monopoly over the symbolic and political capital conferred by participation in the conflict.

The strategic choice to use the language of the Great War proved better suited to certain causes and collectives than others. Veterans, whether acting as individuals or groups, had a particularly convincing claim to legitimacy stemming from their service in the war. Their evocation of the war proved difficult to dismiss. In contrast, arguments grounded in participation in the Great War proved challenging for the indigenous intellectual elite, whose perceived shirking of their wartime duties was a constant line of attack for their opponents. In other cases, the Great War proved an appropriate framing strategy for some elements of a movement's programme but not for others. For example, reference to the 'fraternity of arms' was a particularly effective means for the extreme right to articulate its policy on the 'indigenous question' but was singularly ineffective in doing so when it came to the 'Jewish question'. Here again, the multi-layered experience of the war strengthened one line of argument advanced by a political movement while simultaneously bolstering opposition to another. In the constant struggle over the Great War as a source of legitimacy, there were occasionally outright winners and losers. Groups could successfully assert an almost total monopoly over the evocation of the Great War in certain debates while others might stage a tactical retreat, choosing to frame their claims in an alternative language. More often than not, however, political rivals took advantage of the variety of meanings that could be assigned to the war to cloak their own vision for Algeria's future in the legitimacy of their wartime participation.

Although the potential polysemy of the Great War as a rhetorical strategy held true in all former belligerent societies, the multiple meanings that could be ascribed to the war took on a particular significance in the context of a colonial society. When the whole power structure of the colonial system depended on maintaining the boundaries of 'difference' that defined the triangular relationship between colonial citizen, colonial subject, and colonial administrator, the use of a language that could potentially shift these boundaries would prove problematic. In the wake of the war, the need for some form of reordering of Algerian society to recognize the colony's participation in the conflict was acknowledged by administrators and their interlocutors, both indigenous and European. The shape that this reordering should take was, however, bitterly contested. The fact that many of the debates around prospective reform—colonial, political, economic, or social—were framed in the language of the Great War had important, and often unforeseen, consequences. As actors mobilized their wartime service to recalibrate the triangular relationship between citizen, subject, and administrator, the 'conflicting impulses' that had shaped colonial participation in the war altered and contradicted their original claims in significant and complex ways.[2] It is these unintended consequences of the evocation of the Great War that make the kind of discourse analysis pursued in this book so interesting for scholars of colonial history. By applying concepts from the field of First World War studies to post-war societies beyond the boundaries of Europe, this book has stripped back the language of political actors in Algeria, revealing the tensions and contradictions that underpinned political life in the colony. In response to contemporary debates in the field of colonial history, it has offered an alternative methodology grounded in

[2] Fogarty, *Race and War*, 293.

the analysis of political discourse that is designed to complement the social history methodology currently pursued by many scholars in the all-important task of disentangling the concept of the 'world of contact'. In doing so, it exposed two disjunctures at the heart of the political language articulated around the Great War: the discrepancy between official discourse and the reality of policy as applied on the ground and the gap between the desired outcomes and the end results of the evocation of the Great War.

For the colonial authorities themselves, the commemorative discourse around the Great War was a means of cultivating unity between the colony's different populations. The notion that the inhabitants of Algeria, from all ethno-religious, social, and ideological backgrounds, had answered the call of the *Patrie* was proffered as evidence of the popular legitimacy of the colonial regime. It also was mobilized to defuse communal tensions, as the authorities asserted that each element of the colony's population had complied with the 'moral economy of wartime sacrifice'. The omnipresence of the Great War served to ensure that much of the political debate in the colony was conducted in a language that prioritized loyalty to and defence of the French state as the primary source of legitimacy. The limited appeal of Wilsonian rhetoric in the colony testifies to the success of this strategy. However, the colonial authorities' constant trumpeting of the value of the wartime service of its citizens and its subjects in Algeria emboldened those who had served in the war and their allies to challenge the status quo. At the most basic level, the colonial state's concession of a very limited form of equality in pension rights to indigenous veterans simultaneously empowered them financially and politically while also leading them to question why a broader form of equality could not be instituted. Whether acting as individuals or as collectives, indigenous veterans would use the state's somewhat grudging acknowledgement of their moral right to compensation to push for economic, social, and political rights that the state had not originally envisioned granting to them. In this, they were joined by their political allies in the movements for indigenous reform, who persistently mobilized the communal contribution to advance their claims for citizenship rights. This clashed directly with the colonial state's promise to reward the service of those inhabitants of Algeria who were already citizens. Their desire to maintain, and even possibly expand, European hegemony in the colony would also be cloaked in the legitimacy garnered from their participation in the war. Any attempt to meet what the state itself had posited as its 'mutual obligation' to Algeria's different communities would struggle to reconcile these directly contradictory visions. Thus, while the state's evocation of the war did foster the creation of a common political language that recognized French sovereignty, it could not resolve, and perhaps even exacerbated, the essential tensions that would eventually lead many to question the desirability of French rule in the colony.

The state was not the only actor in colonial Algeria to struggle with the unintended consequences of the evocation of the Great War. In the immediate aftermath of the Armistice, the left's mobilization of the 'equality of sacrifice' in defence of their vision of a new, moral post-war order successfully rallied workers of all ethnic backgrounds to the cause of labour. However, their use of an egalitarian language grounded in the Great War sat uneasily with the largely unstated commitment of the movement's European leadership to continued European hegemony. The suggestion that the left's dedication to equality extended beyond the urban European proletariat to the mass of the indigenous population was an important factor in conservatives' successful mobilization of civil society against the labour movement. It also hinted at the wider divisions, strategic and ideological, that would plague the Algerian left for the rest of the colonial period. While the evocation of the war served to briefly mask these divisions, it could not efface them. Indeed, its success in bringing thousands of workers, indigenous and European, onto the streets of the colony's major cities and towns served, in the end, to radicalize Algerian society and, thus, hasten the defeat and disintegration of the left.

The extreme right's mobilization of the 'fraternity of the trenches' proved only marginally less problematic than the left's evocation of the 'equality of sacrifice'. Although mainstream conservatives successfully evoked the 'fraternity of the trenches' against the left in the immediate post-war moment, their rivals on the extreme right would struggle to use the same rhetorical strategy to reframe European hegemony throughout the rest of the interwar period. For the extreme right in Algeria, the Great War was always tainted with the 'original sin' of the Jewish communal contribution. The Jewish community and its allies would constantly point to the participation of Algeria's Jews in the defence of the *Patrie* to refute the charges of treachery made by the anti-Semitic extreme right. Their spirited defence of the Jewish community's wartime service proved relatively successful, leading the extreme right to increasingly shift towards an alternative language grounded in the celebration of the settler. The 'fraternity of the trenches' did, however, continue to frame the extreme right's appeals to the indigenous community. Initially, some anti-communists and veterans among the indigenous community flirted with the extreme right and its desire to return to the glorious days of unity that had marked the war. Nevertheless, as it became increasingly evident that the celebration of the wartime *Union Sacrée* between the races implied little to no concrete change to the existing colonial system, any traction the extreme right had gained among the indigenous dissipated. Once more, a vague commitment to fraternity would not satisfy those seeking concrete steps towards equality.

Evoking the war was not without its perils for the defenders of indigenous reform. We have seen how the specificities of indigenous service and the personal war records of certain of its leaders were mobilized against the pro-reform camp in the immediate aftermath of the war. In the Blum-Viollette debate, the problematic nature of the evocation of the Great War was linked to the specific provisions of the reform project. The exclusion of most indigenous veterans from the reform provided the project's opponents with a powerful argument to counter claims that Blum-Viollette represented the state's fulfilment of its 'mutual obligation' to those who had defended it. It reinforced the long-standing claim that the advocates of political reform were seeking to reap the rewards of the sacrifices of others. Even those who most firmly advocated equality could be accused of failing to respect the 'moral economy of wartime sacrifice' at the expense of the indigenous troops.

No movement struggled more with the unforeseen consequences of evoking the Great War than the *Amicale des Mutilés et des Anciens Combattants du Département d'Alger*. Its demands that the French state respect the 'primacy of the veteran' and its constant evocation of the 'equality of sacrifice' had the unintended result of providing indigenous veterans with a platform, a language, and an incontestable form of legitimacy that they would mobilize in defence of a wide-reaching programme of radical reform. The attempts of the European leadership of the *Amicale* and other cross-community veterans' organizations to subsume indigenous complaints into their wider language of claims-making increasingly faltered with the growing politicization of the indigenous masses. Efforts to secure the support of indigenous veterans by endorsing a restricted form of equality through what I have called the policy of 'segregated primacy' met with limited success. Many indigenous veterans opted to throw their lot in with the emergent indigenous veterans' movements, for whom the evocation of the war was the means by which a new, reconfigured imperial citizenship could be achieved. An organization like the *Amicale*, which had served as a bulwark of the established colonial order during the strikes of 1920, had inadvertently fostered the development of groups that sought to radically reimagine this same order. The evocation of the Great War proved to be a double-edged sword for the *Amicale*. The use of a language grounded in the Great War may have allowed the *Amicale* and its leaders to secure positions of influence and power within Algerian society but it also provided indigenous veterans with the means and the justification to challenge European hegemony, both within the veterans' movement and in colonial society at large.

The evocation of the war was never the sole preserve of political actors seeking to legitimize a collective project. The story of indigenous rights-holders and their pursuit of compensation for their wartime service underlines the extent to which the language of the war had become central to the renegotiation of the relationship between colonial state and colonial subject. Their struggle to claim their just reward, whether this was through the assertion of legal rights, the supplication of colonial administrators, or a combination of both, shows the real effects of the gap between the rhetoric of remembrance and recognition and the reality of post-war provision. Indigenous rights-holders combined older forms of claims-making with arguments grounded in post-war notions of the 'moral economy of sacrifice' and 'mutual obligation' in an effort to hold the colonial state to its word. The combination of parsimony and political patronage that defined post-war provision in Algeria meant that many would go unsatisfied. And yet, their correspondence with the agents of the colonial state bear testament to a whole facet of the 'world of contact', which has hitherto gone unstudied, where often marginal indigenous actors used their contribution to the Great War to secure financial and social capital from an otherwise indifferent, if not hostile, colonial state.

The ambiguous position of the indigenous rights-holder is illustrative of a much wider feature of political action in the colony in this period. By anchoring the rights, both existing and prospective, of the indigenous in their wartime service, political actors had accepted, whether openly or tacitly, that these rights were conditional on loyalty to the French state. This dynamic manifested itself in different forms across political life in the colony, encompassing the post-war left, the extreme right, the veterans' movements, and the veterans themselves. However, what many indigenous actors failed to realize was that as long as these rights were conditional, they could never be equal to those extended to the Europeans. The nascent nationalist movement, largely confined to metropolitan France until the mid- to late 1930s, was alone in realizing that the problem was not that the colonial state was unwilling to create a just post-war order but rather that it was incapable of doing so. Its commitment to upholding the logic of European supremacy would always trump its stated desire to build a post-war Algeria that respected the wartime moral code.

For the nationalists, the contradictions at the heart of the French imperial state's commemorative discourse became just one element in a wider narrative of French hypocrisy and betrayal. When the whole colonial project was condemned as rotten, the colonial state's failure to fulfil its wartime promises was seen as symptomatic of a relationship defined not by reciprocity but rather by domination and coercion. Although the nationalists attacked the French authorities' restrictions of the rights of Algerians by evoking the Great War, it never became a central rhetorical strategy for Messali Hadj and his comrades. The nationalist project, premised on the rejection and destruction of French sovereignty in Algeria, was disinclined to employ a language that celebrated and valorized the defence of this same sovereignty. Instead, it developed an alternative language grounded in the rhetoric of proletarian revolution, national liberation, and the defence of Arabo-Islamic identity. This was less a 'language of contact' than it was a 'language of conflict'; its central goal was not to reshape French colonial rule in Algeria but rather to bring it to an end.

For actors in colonial Algeria, the Great War became the touchstone in debates that sought to delineate the rights and responsibilities of different individuals and collectives within the colony. The concepts of 'moral economy of sacrifice' and 'mutual obligation' underpinned the broad visions of reform—economic, social, and political—articulated by rival political actors in the colony. While these visions may have differed significantly and were, indeed, often vigorously opposed to one another, they were all united by one common thread: a desire for a reconfiguration of the imperial polity. It is no coincidence, then, that actors as diverse as the European supporters of Algerian autonomy in the immediate post-war period and the Islamic reformists of the *Association des 'Ulama Musulmans Algériens* turned to the Great War to frame their calls for reform. The evocation of the Great War was the perfect means of cloaking projects that sought to alter the triangular relationship between citizen, subject, and administrator in the legitimacy of republican patriotism. In this regard, the Algerian nationalist movement, so often the central focus of historians of this period, stood outside the mainstream. The nationalists' binary vision of colonial society, which only became dominant in the years after the Second World War, was marginal in the colony for most of this period, at least until the late 1930s. Instead, political actors in Algeria, like their equivalents across the empire, proposed a whole range of alternative imperial futures. The language of the Great War was key to the articulation, dissemination, and legitimization of these rival visions for Algeria within a reformed empire.

The fact that these proposals were met with the indifference or hostility of colonial administrators and, thus, went unrealized, does not mean that they hold no interest for the historian. Rather, this book has shown, in line with much of the most recent historiography in the fields of Algerian and French colonial history, that these stillborn projects for a reshaped imperial polity hold the key to understanding how citizens and subjects in the colonies saw their place within the evolving imperial project. The strategies pursued by political actors in colonial Algeria, as recounted in this book, demonstrate that the constraints on political action in the colonies were not always evident to actors on the ground, and even when they were, they were not necessarily understood as unsurmountable. While the coercive power of the colonial state and its unyielding commitment to European hegemony should never be underestimated, many of the politically engaged inhabitants of the colonial world in this period, citizens and subjects, did not have a static understanding of the colonial system. Rather, they believed in the possibility of carving out a new, more powerful place for themselves in the imperial polity. The Great War provided them with both the hope that their visions might be realized and the language through which they could push for this realization.

Indeed, it was the desire to reimagine the relationship between post-imperial France and independent Algeria that motivated presidents Hollande and Bouteflika to turn once more to the long dormant common language of the Great War in the summer of 2014. Although this new iteration of the 'language of contact' unquestionably recognized distinct Algerian and French sovereignties, its challenge to long-standing national narratives on both sides of the Mediterranean proved contentious. The outrage it provoked was less a condemnation of the political instrumentalization of the dead than it was a rejection of a return to a language premised on a sanitised vision of a shared past, present, and future for Algeria and France. A century on from the Great War and a half-century after Algerian independence, the potential potency of the evocation of Algeria's wartime contribution as a language, shared between Algerian and French elites, is once more a recognized, if controversial, feature of Franco-Algerian relations. By turning to the Great War to redefine the relationship between the former colonial power and the former colony, Hollande and Bouteflika are just the latest in a long line of actors in the entangled Franco-Algerian space to seek to cloak their political programmes in the legitimacy of the wartime sacrifice. And by vigorously opposing them, nationalists in Algeria and the extreme right in France are, to a certain extent, reprising the roles played by their political ancestors. The debates of July 2014 bear testament, yet again, to both the versatility and the adaptability of the Great War as a rhetorical strategy. However, before they rush to embrace this rediscovered shared language, political elites in Algeria and France would do well to bear in mind the unintended consequences that have often followed previous attempts to reconfigure Franco-Algerian relations through the evocation of the Great War.

Bibliography

Unpublished Primary Sources

Algeria

Archives de la Wilaya d'Alger (AWA)
Série 1Z – Associations
Archives de la Wilaya d'Oran (AWO)
I/14/4063: Anciens Combattants

France

Archives de l'Armée de Terre, le Service Historique de la Défense, Château de Vincennes (SHD)
GR/9N/122: Organisation des troupes nord-africaines, 1920–1940
Sous-série GR/13/YF 'Pensions des troupes coloniales et des troupes indigènes 1850–1950'
Archives du Consistoire Central (ACC)
Dossier Antisémitisme-Algérie (as yet unclassed)
Archives Nationales d'Outre-Mer, Aix-en-Provence (ANOM)
Fonds du Gouvernement Général (GGA)
2CAB: Cabinet du Gouverneur Général Jules Carde
3CAB: Cabinet du Gouverneur Général Georges Le Beau
Série H: Affaires Musulmanes
Sous-Série 3H: Questions militaires
Sous-Série 9H: Surveillance politique des indigènes
Sous-Série 11H: Rapports politiques périodiques Algérie
Fonds de la Préfecture d'Alger (91)
Série F: Police et maintien de l'ordre
Sous-Série 1F: Direction de la Police Générale
Sous-Série 1K: Cabinet du préfet d'Alger
Série I: Administration des Indigènes
Sous-Série 2I: Administration des indigènes du territoire civil
Sous-Série 4I: Service des liaisons nord-africaines (1936/62)
Fonds de la Préfecture d'Oran (92)
Cabinet Série Continue
Fonds de la Préfecture de Constantine (93)
Série Continue
Série B: Préfecture: Cabinet
Sous-Série B/3: Affaires Indigènes

Fonds Ministériels (FM)
Série 81/F: Ministère d'Etat chargé des affaires algériennes
Série SLOTFOM: Service de liaison avec les originaires des territoires français d'outre-mer
Fonds Privés
Sous-Série 100/APOM: Comité central français pour l'Outre-Mer
Sous Série 119/APOM: Amitiés Africaines

Printed Primary Sources

Periodicals and Newspapers

Bulletin de la Fédération des Sociétés Juives d'Algérie
Bulletin de l'Amicale des Mutilés du Département d'Alger
Bulletin de liaison du Mouvement Croix de Feu en Algérie
Bulletin Officiel du Gouvernement Général de l'Algérie
Demain: Journal Socialiste et de Défense Syndicaliste
El Ouma
El Watan
Jeune Afrique
L'Afrique Latine
L'Akhbar
L'Algérie Mutilée
Le Cri des Mutilés
La Défense
La Dépêche Algérienne
Le droit de vivre
Le Droit du Peuple Nord-Africain (SFIO)
L'Echo d'Alger
L'Echo d'Oran
L'Eclair Algérien
L'Entente Franco-Musulmane
L'Evolution Nord-Africaine
La Flamme
L'Ikdam
L'Ikdam Nord-Africain
La Justice
La Lutte Sociale
Le Matin
Le Monde
Le Mutilé de l'Algérie
L'Oranie Populaire
Le Paria
Le Petit Oranais
Le Pionnier
La Revue Indigène

Le Soir: Journal Quotidien d'Oran
La Tranchée
La Tribune
La Vérité
La Voix des Colons
La Voix des Humbles
Oran-Matin

Published Works

Barrès, Maurice. *Les Diverses Familles Spirituelles de la France*. Paris: Editeurs Emile-Paul Frères, 1917.

Bencherif, Mohamed. *Ahmed Ben Mostapha, goumier*. Paris: Edilivre, 2014; 1st Edition 1920.

Boukabaya, Rabah (Lt. El Hadj Abdellah). *L'Islam dans l'Armée Française*. Istanbul: 1915.

Bulletin des Lois de la République Française: Lois et Décrets d'intérêt Général. Partie Principale, 11th Volume, No. 264.

Bulletin Officiel du Gouvernement Général de l'Algérie (1924), No. 2652.

Clemenceau, Georges. 'Intervention de M. Georges Clemenceau, président du Conseil des ministres, ministre de la guerre pour une déclaration du Gouvernement, à l'occasion de son investiture'. *Annales de la Chambre des Députés*, 20 November 1917.

Dareste de La Chevanne, Pierre-Rodolphe. *Traité de droit colonial*, Tome I. Cannes: 1932.

Délégations Financières. Algiers: Gouvernement Général, 1924.

'Emplois Civils Réservés aux Indigènes de l'Afrique du Nord'. *Bulletin officiel du Ministère de la Guerre, Edition Méthodique*. Paris: Charles-Lavauzelle, 1931.

'Emplois Réservés aux Indigènes d'Algérie'. *Bulletin officiel du Ministère de la Guerre, Edition Méthodique*. Paris: Charles-Lavauzelle, 1917.

Inauguration au Cimetière Israélite de Saint-Eugène à Alger du Monument aux Morts de la Grande Guerre (1914–1918). Algiers: Association Consistoriale Israélite d'Alger, 13 November 1927.

Interfédération Nord-Africaine des Victimes de la Guerre et Anciens Combattants, Le XVI Congrès Interfédéral d'Alger, 16 et 17 avril 1938. Algiers: Imprimerie Imbert, 1938.

Journal Officiel de la République Française: Décrets et Lois.

Khaled, L'Émir. *La Situation des Musulmans d'Algérie: Conférences faites à Paris les 12 et 19 juillet 1924 devant plus de 12000 auditeurs*. Algiers: Éditions du 'Trait-d'union' Victor Spielmann, 1924.

La Rocque, Colonel de. *Service Public*. Paris: Éditions Bernard Grasset, 1934.

Le Livre d'Or du Judaïsme Algérien. Algiers: Publications du Comité D'Etudes Sociales, September 1919.

Legrand, Albert. *La législation sur les emplois réservés*. Paris: Librairie Générale de Droit et de Jurisprudence, 1941.

Les Israélites dans l'Armée Française, 1914–1918. Angers: Commission historique de recherche de documents sur les Israélites de France pendant la guerre, 1920.

Mangin, Charles. *La Force noire*, 3rd Edition. Paris: Hachette, 1911.

Valentino, Charles-Louis. *La Loi Lugol sur les Pensions Militaires aux Infirmes, Veuves, Orphelins et Ascendants (Loi du 31 mars 1919)*. Paris: Edition de la Revue Interalliée, 1920.

Valentino, Charles-Louis. *Les Pensions aux indigènes des colonies et à leur ayants cause: textes et commentaires*. Paris: Berger-Levrault, 1925.

Secondary Sources

Abitbol, Michel. *Les Juifs d'Afrique du Nord sous Vichy*. Paris: Editions Maisonneuve, 1983.

Adams, R.J.Q. and Poirier, Philip. *The Conscription Controversy in Great Britain, 1900–18*. Basingstoke: Macmillan, 1987.

Ageron, Charles-Robert. 'Enquête sur les origines du nationalisme algérien. L'émir Khaled, petit-fils d'Abd El-Kader, fut-il le premier nationaliste algérien?' *Revue de l'Occident musulman et la Méditerranée* 2, No. 1 (1966): 9–49.

Ageron, Charles-Robert. *Histoire de l'Algérie Contemporaine Vol. 2 1871–1954: De l'insurrection de 1871 au déclenchement de la guerre de liberation*. Paris: Presses Universitaires de France, 1979.

Ageron, Charles-Robert. *'L'Algérie algérienne' de Napoléon III à De Gaulle*. Paris: Éditions Sindbad, 1980.

Ageron, Charles-Robert. 'L'Etoile nord-africaine et le modèle communiste. Eléments d'une enquête comparative'. *Les Cahiers de la Tunisie* 117–18 (1981): 199–236.

Ageron, Charles-Robert. 'La pétition de l'Emir Khaled au Président Wilson (mai 1919)', in Genèse de l'Algérie algérienne (Algiers: Editions Bouchène, 2005): 165–78.

Ageron, Charles-Robert. 'Les Communistes français devant la question algérienne de 1921 à 1924'. *Mouvement Social* 78 (January–March 1972): 7–37.

Ageron, Charles-Robert. 'Une émeute anti-juive à Constantine (août 1934)'. *Revue de l'Occident musulman et de la Méditerranée* 13–14 (1973): 23–40.

Ageron, Charles-Robert. 'Une politique algérienne libérale sous la troisième République (1912–1919): Étude historique de la loi du 4 février 1919'. *Revue d'histoire moderne et contemporaine* 6, No. 2 (April–June 1959): 121–51.

Aissaoui, Rabah. 'Between Two Worlds: Emir Khaled and the Young Algerians at the Beginning of the Twentieth Century in Algeria', in Algeria Revisited: History, Culture and Identity, edited by Rabah Aissaoui and Claire Eldridge, 56–78. London: Bloomsbury, 2017.

Aissaoui, Rabah. *Immigration and National identity: North African Political Movements in Colonial and Postcolonial France*. London: Tauris Academic Studies, 2009.

Alcalde, Angel. *War Veterans and Fascism in Interwar Europe*. Cambridge: Cambridge University Press, 2017.

Aldrich, Robert and Hilliard, Christopher. 'The French and British Empires', in A Companion to World War I, edited by John Horne, 524–39. London: Wiley-Blackwell, 2010.

Amara, Nourredine. 'Les nationalités d'Amina Hanim. Une pétition d'hérédité à la France (1896–1830)', in La nationalité dans le monde arabe: Négocier les appartenances et le droit, edited by M'hamed Oualdi, 49–72. Aix-en-Provence: Presses Universitaires de Provence, 2015.

André-Bercovici, Samuel. 'Les anciens combattants dans l'Algérie coloniale: Les associations d'anciens combattants et l'Algérie française'. Master 2 Thesis, Université Paris 1- Panthéon-Sorbonne, 2014.

Audoin-Rouzeau, Stéphane and Becker, Annette. *14–18: retrouver la Guerre*. Paris: Gallimard, 2000.

Bakhtin, Mikhail. *The Dialogic Imagination: Four Essays*, edited by Michael Holquist; translated by Caryl Emerson and Michael Holquist. Austin, TX: University of Texas Press, 2008.

Barry, Gearóid, Dal Lago, Enrico, and Healy, Róisín, eds. *Small Nations and Colonial Peripheries in World War I*. Leiden: Brill, 2016.

Bekraoui, Mohammed. *Les Marocains dans la Grande* Guerre, *1914–1918*. Rabat: Publications de la Commission Marocaine d'Histoire Militaire, 2009.

Bette, Peggy. 'Veuves françaises de la Première guerre mondiale: statuts, itinéraires, combats'. PhD diss., Université Lumière Lyon, 2012.

Berque, Jacques. *Le Maghreb entre deux guerres*. Paris: Éditions La Seuil, 1962.

Blanchard, Emmanuel and Thénault, Sylvie. 'Quel "monde du contact"? Pour une histoire sociale de l'Algérie pendant la période coloniale'. *Le Mouvement Social* 236, No. 3 (2011): 3–7.

Blanchard, Pascal. 'La vocation fasciste de l'Algérie coloniale dans les années 1930', in De L'Indochine à l'Algérie: la jeunesse en mouvements des deux côtés du miroir colonial 1940–1962, edited by Nicolas Bancel, Daniel Denis, and Youssef Fates, 177–94. Paris: La Découverte, 2003.

Böhler, Jochen, Borodziej, Włodzimierz, and Puttkamer, Joachim von. 'Introduction', in Legacies of Violence: Eastern Europe's First World War, 1–6. Munich: Oldenbourg Verlag, 2014.

Bouchène, Abderrahmane, Pyroulou, Jean-Pierre Siari Tengour, Ouanassa, and Thénault, Sylvie. 'Pour une histoire partagée et critique à la période colonial', in Histoire de l'Algérie à la période coloniale, 7–16. Paris: La Découverte, 2012.

Boum, Aomar. 'Partners against Anti-Semitism: Muslims and Jews respond to Nazism in French North African colonies, 1936–1940', *Journal of North African Studies* 19, No. 4 (2014): 554–70.

Carlier, Omar. 'Le café maure. Sociabilité masculine et effervescence citoyenne (Algérie 17e–18e)'. *Annales. Economies, sociétés, civilisations* 4 (1990): 975–1004.

Carlier, Omar. *Entre Nation et Jihad: Histoire sociale des radicalismes algériens*. Paris: Presses de la Fondation Nationale des Sciences Politiques, 1995.

Choukroun, Jacques. 'L'Internationale Communiste, le PC français et l'Algérie (1920–1925)'. *Cahiers d'histoire de l'Institut Maurice Thorez* 25–6 (1978): 133–59.

Christelow, Allan. *Muslim Law Courts and the French Colonial State in Algeria*. Princeton, NJ: Princeton University Press, 1985.

Cody, Francis. *The Light of Knowledge: Literacy Activism and the Politics of Writing in South India*. London: Cornell University Press, 2013.

Cohen, David. 'Les Circonstances de la Fondation du Comité Algérien d'Etudes Sociales ou la prise de conscience d'une élite intellectuelle juive face au phénomène antisémite en Algérie (1915–1921)'. *Revue des études Juives* 161, No. 1–2 (January–June 2002): 179–225.

Cohen, Deborah. *The War Come Home: Disabled Veterans in Britain and Germany, 1914–1939*. Berkeley, CA: University of California Press, 2001.

Cole, Joshua. 'Constantine before the Riots of August 1934: Civil Status, Anti-Semitism, and the Politics of Assimilation in Interwar French Algeria'. *Journal of North African Studies* 17, No. 5 (December 2012): 839–61.

Collins, Kirstin A. '"Petitions without Number": Widows' Petitions and the Early Nineteenth-Century Origins of Public Marriage-Based Entitlements'. *Law and History Review* 31, No. 1 (2013): 1–60.

Collot, Claude and Henry, Jean-Robert. *Le mouvement national algérien, Textes 1912–1954*. Paris: L'Harmattan, 1978.

Cooper, Frederick. *Citizenship between Empire and Nation: Remaking France and French Africa, 1945–1960*. Princeton, NJ: Princeton University Press, 2014.

Cooper, Frederick. 'Conflict and Connection: Rethinking Colonial African History'. *American Historical Review* 99, No. 5 (December 1994): 1516–45.

Cooper, Frederick and Stoler, Ann Laura. 'Between Metropole and Colony: Rethinking a Research Agenda', in Tensions of Empire: Colonial Cultures in a Bourgeois World, edited by Frederick Cooper and Ann Laura Stoler, 1–56. Berkeley, CA: University of California Press, 1997.

Cross, Gary S. 'The Quest for Leisure: Reassessing the Eight-Hour Day in France'. *Journal of Social History* 18, No. 2 (Winter 1984): 195–216.

Darmon, Pierre. L'Algérie des passions, 1870–1939. Paris: Editions Perrin, 2012; 1st Edition 2009.

Darwin, John. 'A Third British Empire? The Dominion Idea in Imperial Politics', in The Oxford History of the British Empire, Vol. IV, The Twentieth Century, edited by Judith Brown and W.R. Louis, 64–87. Oxford: Oxford University Press, 1999.

Das, Santanu. 'Introduction', in Race, Empire and First World War Writing, 1–32. Cambridge: Cambridge University Press, 2011.

DeGeorges, Thomas. 'A Bitter Homecoming: Tunisian Veterans of the First and Second World Wars'. PhD diss., Harvard University, 2006.

Dermenjian, Geneviève. *La Crise anti-juive oranaise (1895–1905), l'antisémitisme dans l'Algérie colonial*. Paris: L'Harmattan, 1986.

Deroo, Eric. 'Dying: The Call of the Empire (1913–1918)', in Colonial Culture in France since the Revolution, edited by Pascal Blanchard, Sandrine Lemaire, Nicolas Bancel, and Dominic Thomas, 132–9. Bloomington, IN: Indiana University Press, 2014.

Drew, Allison. *We Are No Longer in France: Communists in Colonial Algeria*. Manchester: University of Manchester Press, 2014.

Echenberg, Myron. *Colonial Conscripts: The Tirailleurs Sénégalais in French West Africa, 1857–1960*. London: James Currey, 1991.

Fedorowich, Kent. *Unfit for Heroes: Reconstruction and Soldier Settlement in the Empire between the Wars*. Manchester: Manchester University Press, 1995.

Fogarty, Richard S. *Race and War in France: Colonial Subjects in the French Army, 1914–1918*. Baltimore, MD: Johns Hopkins University Press, 2008.

Fogarty, Richard S. 'The French Empire', in Empires at War: 1911–1923, edited by Robert Gerwarth and Erez Manela, 109–29. Oxford: Oxford University Press, 2014.

Fogarty, Richard S. and Killingray, David. 'Demobilization in British and French Africa at the End of the First World War'. *Journal of Contemporary History* 50, No. 1 (2015): 100–23.

Frémeaux, Jacques. *Les Colonies dans la Grande Guerre: Combats et Epreuves des Peuples d'Outre-Mer*. Paris: SOTECA, 14–18 Editions, 2006.

Frevel, Ute. *A Nation in Barracks: Modern Germany, Military Conscription and Civil Society*. Oxford: Berg, 2004.

Fromage, Julien. 'L'expérience des "Jeunes Algériens" et l'émergence du militantisme moderne en Algérie (1880–1919)', in Histoire de l'Algérie à la période colonial, edited by Jean-Pierre Pyroulou, Abderrahmane Bouchène, Ouanassa Siari Tengour, and Sylvie Thénault, 238–44. Paris, La Découverte, 2012.

Gallois, William. *A History of Violence in the Early Algerian Colony*. Basingstoke: Palgrave Macmillan, 2013.

Ganachari, Aravind. 'First World War: Purchasing Indian Loyalties: Imperial Policy of Recruitment and 'Rewards'. *Economic and Political Weekly* 40, No. 8 (February 2005): 779–88.

Gerwarth, Robert, and Horne, John. 'Vectors of Violence: Paramilitarism in Europe after the Great War, 1917–1923'. *Journal of Modern History* 83, No. 3 (September 2011): 489–512.

Gerwarth, Robert and Manela, Erez. 'Introduction', In Empires at War, 1911–1923, 1–16. Oxford: Oxford University Press, 2014.

Gorman, Daniel. 'Fractured Empire: Ideas of Imperial Citizenship in the British Empire after the First World War'. *Comparitiv* 26, No. 6 (2016): 15–34.

Guillon, Armand. 'Une œuvre du Maréchal Franchet d'Espèrey: les Amitiés Africaines'. *Cahiers Charles de Foucauld* 41 (1956): 95–103.

Hassett, Dónal. 'Contested Commemoration: The Great War, Memory and Politics in Contemporary Algeria'. *International Journal of Francophone Studies* 21, Nos 3–4 (October 2018): 209–31.

Hassett, Dónal. 'Proud Colons, Proud Frenchmen: Settler Colonialism and the Extreme Right in Interwar Algeria'. *Settler Colonial Studies* 17, No. 1 (2017): 1–19.

Hassett, Dónal. '*Pupilles de l'Empire*: Debating the Provision for Child Victims of the Great War in the French Empire'. *French Historical Studies* 39, No. 2 (April 2016): 315–45.

Hassett, Dónal. 'Reinventing Empire in the Wake of the Great War: Imperial Citizenship and the "Wilsonian Moment" in Colonial Algeria'. *Comparitiv* 26, No. 6 (2016): 37–54.

Henry, Jean-Robert. 'Le centenaire de l'Algérie, triomphe éphémère de la pensée algérianiste', in Histoire de l'Algérie à la période colonial, edited by Abderrahmane Bouchène, Jean-Pierre Peyroulou, Ounassa Siari Tengour, and Sylvie Thénault, 369–75. Paris: La Découverte, 2012.

Horne, John. 'Defending Victory: Paramilitary Politics in France, 1918–1926: A Counter-Example', In *War in Peace: Paramilitary Violence in Europe after the Great War*, edited by Robert Gerwarth and John Horne, 216–35. Oxford: Oxford University Press, 2012.

Horne, John. 'Immigrant Workers during World War I'. *French Historical Studies* 14, No. 1 (Spring 1985): 57–88.

Horne, John. 'Introduction: Mobilising for "Total War", 1914–1918', in State, Society and Mobilization in Europe during the First World War, 1–17. Cambridge: Cambridge University Press, 1997.

Horne, John. *Labour at War: France and Britain, 1914–1918*. Oxford: Clarendon Press, 1991.

Horne, John. 'L'impôt du sang: Republican rhetoric and industrial warfare in France, 1914–1918'. *Social History* 14, No. 2 (1989): 201–23.

Horne, John. 'Social Identity in War: France, 1914–1918', in *Men, Women and War*, edited by T.G. Fraser and Keith Jeffrey, 119–36. Dublin: Lilliput Press, 1993.

Horne, John. 'The Living', in *The Cambridge History of the First World War, Vol. 3: Civil Society*, edited by Jay Winter, 592–617. Cambridge: Cambridge University Press, 2014.

Horne, John. 'The State and the Challenge of Labour in France 1917–1920,' in *Challenges of Labour: Central and Western Europe 1917–1920*, edited by Chris Wrigley, 239–261. London: Routledge, 1993.

Hureau, Joëlle. *La mémoire des pieds-noirs de 1830 à nos jours*. Paris: Perrin, 2001.

Jansen, Jan C. *Erobern und Erinnern: Symbolpolitik, öffentlicher Raum und französischer Kolonialismus in Algerien*. Munich: Oldenbourg, 2013.

Jansen, Jan C. 'Une autre "Union Sacrée"? Commémorer la Grande Guerre dans l'Algérie colonisée (1918–1939)', translated by Augustin Jommier. Revue d'histoire moderne et contemporaine 61–2, No. 2 (2014): 32–60.

Jarboe, Andrew Tait and Fogarty, Richard S. 'Introduction: An Imperial Turn in First World War Studies', in Empires in World War I: Shifting Frontiers and Imperial Dynamics in a Global Conflict, 1–22. London: I.B. Tauris, 2014.

Jeffrey, Keith. *Ireland and the Great War*. Cambridge: Cambridge University Press, 2000.

Johnson Jr., G. Wesley. *The Emergence of Black Politics in Senegal: The Struggle for Power in the Four Communes 1900–1920*. Stanford, CA: Stanford University Press, 1971.

Julien, Charles-André. *Histoire de l'Algérie Contemporaine: La Conquête et les débuts de la colonisation (1827–1871)*. Paris: Presses Universitaires de France, 1964.

Julien, Charles-André. *L'Afrique du Nord en marche- Algérie, Tunisie, Maroc, 1880–1952*. Paris: Julliard, 1953.

Kaddache, Mahfoud. *Histoire du nationalisme algérien, Tome I 1919–1939*. Algiers: EDIF, 2003; 1st Edition 2000.

Kaddache, Mahfoud. *La vie politique à Alger de 1919 à 1939*. Algiers: SNED, 1970.

Kaddache, Mahfoud, ed. *L'Emir Khaled: Documents et témoignages pour servir à l'étude du nationalisme algérien*. Algiers: Office des Publications Universitaires, 1987.

Kaddache, Mahfoud and Guenaneche, Mohamed, eds. *L'Étoile Nord-Africaine 1926–1937: Documents et témoignages pour server à l'étude du Nationalisme Algérien*. Algiers: Office des Publications Universitaires, 1984.

Kalman, Samuel. 'Avec une brutalité toute particulière: Fascist Sympathies, Racial Violence, and the Municipal Police and Gendarmerie in Oran, 1936–37', in The French Right between the Wars: Political and Intellectual Movements from Conservatism to Fascism, edited by Samuel Kalman and Seán Kennedy, 48–64. Oxford: Bergham, 2014.

Kalman, Samuel. 'Criminalizing Dissent: Policing Banditry in the Constantinois, 1914–18', in Algeria Revisited, edited by Rabah Aissaoui and Claire Eldridge, 20–38. London: Bloomsbury, 2017.

Kalman, Samuel. *French Colonial Fascism, The Extreme-Right in Algeria, 1919–1939*. New York: Palgrave Macmillan, 2013.

Katz, Ethan B. 'Jews and Muslims in the Shadow of Marianne: Conflicting Identities and Republican Culture in France (1914–1975)'. PhD Diss., University of Madison-Wisconsin, 2009.

Killingray, David. 'The Idea of a British Imperial African Army'. *Journal of African History* 20, No. 3 (1979): 421–36.

Koller, Christian. 'Representing Otherness: African, Indian and European Soldier's Letters and Memoirs', in Race, Empire and First World War Writing, edited by Santanu Das (Cambridge: Cambridge University Press, 2011): 127–42.

Koller, Christian. 'The Recruitment of Colonial Troops in Africa and Asia and their Deployment in Europe during the First World War'. *Immigrants and Minorities* 26, Nos 1–2 (March 2008): 111–33.

Korieh, Chima J. '"May It Please Your Honour": Letters of Petition as Historical Evidence in an African Colonial Context'. *History in Africa* 37 (2010): 83–106.

Koulakssis, Ahmed and Meynier, Gilbert. *L'Emir Khaled: premier za'îm?* Paris: L'Harmattan, 1987.

Koulakssis, Ahmed and Meynier, Gilbert. 'Sur le mouvement ouvrier et les communistes d'Algérie au lendemain de la Première Guerre mondiale'. *Le Mouvement social* 130 (January–March 1985): 3–32.

Kriegel, Annie. *La grève des cheminots: 1920*. Paris: Armand Colin, 1988.

Lacheraf, Mostefa. *L'Algérie: nation et société*. Paris: Maspero, 1965.

Landau, Philippe. 'La communauté juive de France et la Grande Guerre'. *Annales de démographie historique* 103 (2002): 91–106.

Landau, Philippe. *Les Juifs de France et la Grande guerre: Un patriotisme républicain*. Paris: CNRS Editions, 2008.

Lawrence, Benjamin N. 'Petitioners, 'Bush Lawyers', and Letter Writers: Court Access in British-Occupied Lomé, 1914–1920', in Intermediaries, Interpreters and Clerks: African Employees in the Making of Colonial Africa, edited by Benjamin N. Lawrence, Emily Lynn Osborn, and Richard L. Roberts, 94–114. Madison, WI: University of Wisconsin Press, 2006.

Le Van Ho, Mireille. *Des Vietnamiens dans la Grande Guerre: 50000 recrues dans les usines françaises*. Paris: Vendémiaire, 2014.

Liebau, Heike, Bromber, Katrin, Lange, Katharina, Hamzah, Dyala, and Ahuja, Ravi, eds. *The World in World Wars: Experiences and Perspectives from Africa and Asia*. Boston, MA: Brill, 2010.

Lunn, Joe. *Memoirs of the Maelstrom: A Senegalese Oral History of the First World War*. Oxford: James Currey, 1999.

Machefer, Philippe. *Ligues et fascisme en France 1919–1939*. Paris: Presses Universitaires de France, 1974.

MacMaster, Neil. *Colonial Migrants and Racism: Algerians in France, 1900–62*. London: Macmillan, 1997.

Maghraoui, Driss. 'Moroccan Colonial Soldiers: Between Selective Memory and Collective Memory'. *Arab Studies Quarterly* 2, No. 2 (Spring 1998): 21–41.

Maghraoui, Driss. 'The 'Grande Guerre Sainte': Moroccan Colonial Troops and Workers in the First World War'. *Journal of North African Studies* 9, No. 1 (Spring 2004): 1–21.

Magraw, Roger. 'Paris 1917–1920: Labour Protest and Popular Politics', in Challenges of Labour: Central and Western Europe, 1917–1920, edited by Chris Wrigley, 125–48. London: Routledge, 1993.

Mamdani, Mahmood. *Citizen and Subject: Contemporary Africa and the Legacy of Late Colonialism*. Princeton, NJ: Princeton University Press, 1996.

Manela, Erez. *The Wilsonian Moment: Self-Determination and the International Origins of Anticolonial Nationalism*. Oxford: Oxford University Press, 2007.

Mann, Gregory. *Native Sons: West African Veterans and France in the Twentieth Century*. London: Duke University Press, 2006.

Mann, Michelle. 'The Young Algerians and the Question of the Muslim Draft, 1900–14', in *Algeria Revisited: History, Culture and Identity*, edited by Rabah Aissaoui and Claire Eldridge, 39–55. London: Bloomsbury, 2017.

Marynower, Claire. 'Être socialiste dans l'Algérie coloniale: Pratiques, cultures et identités d'un milieu partisan dans le département d'Oran, 1919–1939'. PhD diss., IEP Paris, 2013.

McDougall, James. *A History of Algeria*. Cambridge: Cambridge University Press, 2017.

McDougall, James. *History and the Culture of Nationalism in Algeria*. Cambridge: Cambridge University Press, 2006.

McDougall, James. 'Savage Wars? Codes of Violence in Algeria, 1830s–1990s'. *Third World Quarterly* 26, No. 1 (2005): 117–31.

Merad, Ali. *Le réformisme musulman en Algérie de 1925 à 1940: Essai d'histoire religieuse et sociale*. The Hague: Mouton & Co., 1967.

Meynier, Gilbert. *L'Algérie Révélée: La guerre de 1914–1918 et le premier quart du XXe siècle*. Geneva: Librairie Droz, 1981.

Meynier, Gilbert. 'L'Emir Khaled, "premier nationaliste algérien"?' In Histoire de l'Algérie à la période coloniale: 1830–1962, edited by Jean-Pierre Pyroulou, Abderrahmane Bouchène, Ouanassa Siari Tengour, and Sylvie Thénault, 439–42. Paris, La Découverte, 2012.

Michel, Marc. *Les Africains et la Grande Guerre: l'appel à l'Afrique (1914–1918).* Paris: Karthala, 2003.

Millington, Chris. *From Victory to Vichy: Veterans in Interwar France.* Manchester: Manchester University Press, 2012.

Morrow, John H. *The Great War: An Imperial History.* Oxford: Routledge, 2004.

Mortimer, Edward. *The Rise of the French Communist Party, 1920–1947.* London: Faber and Faber, 1984.

Moyd, Michelle R. *Violent Intermediaries: Africans Soldiers, Conquest and Everyday Colonialism in German East Africa.* Athens, OH: Ohio University Press, 2014.

Nasson, Bill. *Springboks on the Somme: South Africa in the Great War, 1914–1918.* Johannesburg: Penguin, 2007.

Nouschi, André. 'La dépossession foncière et la paupérisation de la paysannerie algérienne', in Histoire de l'Algérie à la période coloniale: 1830–1962, edited by Jean-Pierre Pyroulou, Abderrahmane Bouchène, Ouanassa Siari Tengour, and Sylvie Thénault, 189–94. Paris, La Découverte, 2012.

Omissi, David, ed. *Indian Voices of the Great War, 1914–1918.* Basingstoke: Macmillan, 1994.

Passmore, Kevin. 'L'historiographie du "fascisme" en France'. *French Historical Studies* 37, No. 3 (2014): 469–99.

Planche, Jean-Louis. 'Grèves en Méditerranée Maghrébine'. *Cahiers du GREMAMO* 4 (1987): 67–72.

Prost, Antoine. *Les anciens combattants et la société française 1914–1939 Volume 1. Histoire, Volume 2. Sociologie. Volume 3. Mentalités et Idéologies.* Paris: Presses de Sciences Po, 1977.

Purseigle, Pierre. *Mobilisation, sacrifice et citoyenneté: Angleterre-France 1900–1918.* Paris: Les Belles Lettres, 2013.

Raman, Bhavani. *Document Raj, Writing and Scribes in Early Colonial South India.* Chicago, IL: University of Chicago Press, 2012.

Recham, Belkacem. *Les musulmans algériens dans l'armée française 1919–1945.* Paris: L'Harmattan, 1996.

Robert, Jean-Louis. *Les ouvriers, la patrie et la révolution: Paris 1914–1919.* Paris: Annales Littéraires de l'Université de Besançon, 1995.

Robert, Jean-Louis. 'The Image of the Profiteer', in Capital Cities at War: London, Paris, Berlin 1914–1919, edited by Jay Winter and Jean-Louis Robert, 104–32. Cambridge: Cambridge University Pres, 1997.

Roberts, Sophie B. 'Anti-Semitism and Municipal Government in Interwar French Colonial Algeria'. *Journal of North African Studies* 17, No. 5 (December 2012): 821–37.

Roy, Kaushik. *The Army in British India: From Colonial Warfare to Total War: 1857–1947.* London: Bloomsbury, 2013.

Saïd, Edward. '"Always on Top" Review of the Book *Civilising Subjects: Metropole and Colony in the English Imagination 1830–67. London Review of Books* 25, No. 6 (March 2003): 3–6.

Sahli, Mohamed. *Décoloniser l'histoire: Introduction à l'histoire du Maghreb.* Paris: Maspero, 1965.

Sanos, Sandrine. *The Aesthetics of Hate: Far-Right Intellectuals, Anti-Semitism and Gender in 1930s France*. Stanford, CA: Stanford University Press, 2013.

Schor, Ralph. L'Antisémitisme en France dans l'entre-deux-guerres. Brussels: Editions Complexe, 2005; 1st Edition 1992.

Scott, James C. *Seeing like a State: How Certain Schemes to Improve the Human Condition Have Failed*. New Haven, CT: Yale University Press, 1998.

Scott, James C. *Weapons of the Weak: Everyday Forms of Peasant Resistance*. New Haven, CT: Yale University Press, 1985.

Sessions, Jennifer, E. *By Sword and Plow: France and the Conquest of Algeria*. London: Cornell University Press, 2011.

Siari Tengour, Ouanassa. 'La révolte dans l'Aurès', in *Histoire de l'Algérie à la période coloniale*, edited by Jean-Pierre Pyroulou, Abderrahmane Bouchène, Ouanassa Siari Tengour, and Sylvie Thénault, 255–60. Paris: La Découverte, 2012.

Sivan, Emmanuel. *Communisme et nationalisme en Algérie 1920–1962*. Paris: Presse de la Fondation Nationale des Sciences Politiques, 1976.

Smith, Leonard V. *Between Mutiny and Obedience: The Case of the French Fifth Infantry Division during World War I*. Princeton, NJ: Princeton University Press, 1994.

Smith, Richard. *Jamaican Volunteers in the First World War: Race, Masculinity and the Development of National Consciousness*. Manchester: Manchester University Press, 2004.

Soucy, Robert. *French Fascism: The Second Wave, 1933–1939*. New Haven, CT: Yale University Press, 1995.

Stoler, Ann Laura. *Along the Archival Grain: Epistemic Anxieties and Colonial Common Sense*. Princeton, NJ: Princeton University Press, 2009.

Stoler, Ann Laura. 'Colonial Archives and the Arts of Governance'. *Archival Science* 2, No. 1 (2002): 87–109.

Stora, Benjamin. *Algeria 1830–2000: A Short History*. Ithaca, NY: Cornell University Press, 2001.

Stora, Benjamin. *Dictionnaire Biographique de Militants Nationalistes Algériens*. Paris: L'Harmattan, 1985.

Stora, Benjamin. *Histoire de l'Algérie Coloniale (1830–1954)*. Paris: La Découverte, 2004.

Stora, Benjamin. *Messali Hadj, 1898–1974*. Paris: Hachette Littératures, 2004.

Stora, Benjamin. *Nationalistes algériens et révolutionnaires français au temps du Front Populaire*. Paris: L'Harmattan, 1987.

Stovall, Tyler. 'Love, Labor, and Race: Colonial Men and White Women in France during the Great War'. In French Civilization and Its Discontents: Nationalism, Colonialism, Race, edited by Tyler Stovall and Georges Van den Abeele, 297–321. Lanham, MD: Lexington Books, 2003.

Stovall, Tyler. 'The Color Line behind the Lines: Racial Violence and the Great War during the Great War'. *American Historical Review* 103, No. 3 (June 1998): 737–69.

Strachan, Hew. *The First World War in Africa*. Oxford: Oxford University Press, 2004.

Tai-Yong, Tan. 'An Imperial Home-Front: Punjab and the First World War'. *Journal of Military History* 64, No. 2 (April 2000): 371–410.

Thomas, Martin. *The French Empire between the Wars: Imperialism, Politics and Society* (Manchester: Manchester University Press, 2005).

Thompson, E.P. 'The Moral Economy of the English Crowd in the Eighteenth Century'. *Past and Present* 50 (February 1971): 76–136.

Valensky, Chantal. *Le Soldat occulté: Les Malgaches de l'Armée française, 1884–1920*. Paris: L'Harmattan, 2000.

Vermeren, Hugo. 'Les migrations françaises et européennes vers l'Algérie au début de la IIIe République', in *Histoire de l'Algérie à la période coloniale*, edited by Jean-Pierre Pyroulou, Abderrahmane Bouchène, Ouanassa Siari Tengour, and Sylvie Thénault, 194–200. Paris: La Découverte, 2012.

Waites, Bernard. 'The Government of the Home-Front and the "Moral Economy" of the Working Class', in Home Fires and Foreign Fields: British Social and Military Experience in the First World War, edited by Peter Liddle, 175–93. London: Brassey's, 1985.

Wansbrough, John. 'The Decolonization of North African History'. *Journal of African History* 9, No. 4 (1968): 643–50.

Weil, Patrick. *How to Be French: Nationality in the Making since 1789*, translated by Catherine Porter. London: Duke University Press, 2008; first published in French 2002.

Wilder, Gary. *The French Imperial Nation-State: Negritude and Colonial Humanism between the Two World Wars*. Chicago, IL: University of Chicago Press, 2005.

Winock, Michel. *La France et les Juifs: de 1789 à nos jours*. Paris: Seuil, 2004.

Zemon Davis, Natalie. *Fiction in the Archives: Pardon Tales and their Tellers in Sixteenth-Century France*. Cambridge: Polity Press, 1987.

Zessin, Phillip. 'Presse et journalistes "indigènes" en Algérie coloniale (année 1890–années 1950)'. *Le Mouvement Social* 236, No. 3 (2011): 35–46.

Ziemann, Benjamin. *Contested Commemorations: Republican War Veterans and Weimar Political Culture*. Cambridge: Cambridge University Press, 2013.

Index

Note: Figures are indicated by an italic "*f*" following the page number.